Hegel and the Problem of Beginning

Hegel and the Problem of Beginning

Scepticism and Presuppositionlessness

Robb Dunphy

ROWMAN & LITTLEFIELD
Lanham • Boulder • New York • London

Published by Rowman & Littlefield
An imprint of The Rowman & Littlefield Publishing Group, Inc.
4501 Forbes Boulevard, Suite 200, Lanham, Maryland 20706
www.rowman.com

86-90 Paul Street, London EC2A 4NE

Copyright © 2023 by The Rowman & Littlefield Publishing Group, Inc.

All rights reserved. No part of this book may be reproduced in any form or by any electronic or mechanical means, including information storage and retrieval systems, without written permission from the publisher, except by a reviewer who may quote passages in a review.

British Library Cataloguing in Publication Information Available

Library of Congress Cataloging-in-Publication Data Available

ISBN 978-1-5381-4755-9 (cloth)
ISBN 978-1-5381-4757-3 (paper)
ISBN 978-1-5381-4756-6 (electronic)

Contents

Acknowledgements	vii
Abbreviations	ix
Introduction: "With What Must the Beginning of the Science be Made?"	1
1 Hegel and Pyrrhonian Scepticism	27
2 A Short History of the Problem of Beginning	67
3 The Problem of Beginning	109
4 Mediation I – Phenomenology	149
5 Mediation II – Completed Scepticism	175
Bibliography	201
Index	209
About the Author	213

Acknowledgements

I have been working on issues related to the beginning of Hegel's *Logic* for some time now. Accordingly, much of the material collected in this book has been presented in various forms at conferences over the past few years, and I am grateful to audiences at the Universities of Sussex, Brighton, Winchester, Oxford, Southern Denmark, São Paulo, University College Dublin, and others for their feedback and insight.

The arguments of significant parts of this book, especially chapters 3 and 4, were first developed as parts of a doctoral thesis that I wrote at the University of Sussex under the supervision of Tanja Staehler. I owe Tanja a great deal of thanks for her support, encouragement, and critical feedback as these ideas came together. I am similarly grateful to Katerina Deligiorgi and Stephen Houlgate, who examined that thesis and provided a great deal of helpful responses in person and in writing. Additional thanks are also due to Stephen since it was he who first introduced me to Hegel's philosophy when I was a student at the University of Warwick. The influence of his work on Hegel's *Logic* and its beginning should be evident throughout this book.

The majority of the final version of this book was written in 2020–2021, while I was the recipient of a postdoctoral research fellowship from the Irish Research Council (IRC) and hosted by Brian O'Connor at University College Dublin. To the IRC, and to Brian, I am very grateful.

Earlier versions of some of the material that appears in this book have previously been published in article form. Some of the material appearing in chapter 3 was originally published as "Hegel and the Problem of Beginning" in the *Hegel Bulletin*. I am grateful to the Hegel Society of Great Britain for granting permission to reuse this material here. Some of the material appearing in chapter 4 was originally published as "On the Incompatibility of Hegel's *Phenomenology* with the Beginning of his *Logic*", in the *Review of*

Metaphysics. I am likewise grateful for the permission to reuse that material here. Sincere thanks are also due to Natalie Mandziuk, Linda Kessler and Yu Ozaki at Rowman and Littlefield for their patience, support, and feedback during the completion of this book.

Sincere thanks are also due to my brothers, Alex and James, and to my partner, Inken, for all of their love and support. Lastly, I dedicate this book to my parents, Jane and Shaun Dunphy, without whom this book would never even have had a beginning, let alone been completed.

Abbreviations

HEGEL

Translations from Hegel refer firstly to the English translation and then to the 1986 *Werke in Zwanzig Bänden*, eds. E Moldenhauer and K. Michel (Frankfurt am Main: Suhrkamp). The exception to this is the *Lectures on Logic*, where the German text to which I refer is the 2001 edition of *Vorlesungen über die Logik Berlin 1831, Nachgeschrieben von Karl Hegel*, eds. U. Rameil and H. Lucas (Hamburg: Felix Meiner Verlag). Although I have usually consulted the English translations, the quotations from Hegel in this book follow the German texts and are my own translations, for the most part.

D	*The Difference Between Fichte's and Schelling's System of Philosophy* trans. H. Harris and W. Cerf (Albany, NY: State University of New York Press, 1977)
EG	*Philosophy of Mind* trans. M. Inwood (Oxford: Oxford University Press, 2007)
EL	*Encyclopaedia of the Philosophical Sciences in Basic Outline, Part I: Science of Logic* trans. K. Brinkmann and D. Dahlstrom (Cambridge: Cambridge University Press, 2010)
GW	*Faith and Knowledge* trans. H. Harris and W. Cerf (Albany, NY: State University of New York Press, 1977)
PhG	*Phenomenology of Spirit* trans. T. Pinkard (Cambridge: Cambridge University Press, 2018)
VGP	*Hegel's Lectures on the History of Philosophy* trans. E. Haldane and F. Simson (Delhi: Lector House, 2020)
VL	*Lectures on Logic* trans. C. Butler (Indianapolis, IN: Indiana University Press, 2008)

VSP   "On the Relationship of Scepticism to Philosophy, Exposition of its Different Modifications and Comparison of its Latest Form with the Ancient One" trans. H. Harris in G. di Giovanni and H. Harris (eds.) *Between Kant and Hegel: Texts in the Development of Post-Kantian Idealism* (Indianapolis, IN: Hackett Publishing Company, 2000)

WL   *Science of Logic* trans. G. di Giovanni (Cambridge: Cambridge University Press, 2010)

KANT

KPV   *Critique of Practical Reason* trans. A. Heath (Cambridge: Cambridge University Press, 2015)

KRV   *Critique of Pure Reason* trans. P. Guyer and A. Wood (Cambridge: Cambridge University Press, 1998)

KU   *Critique of the Power of Judgement*

P   *Prolegomena to Any Future Metaphysics* trans. G. Hatfield (Cambridge: Cambridge University Press, 2004)

SEXTUS EMPIRICUS

Translations from Sextus have occasionally been slightly altered.

AE   *Against the Ethicists* trans. R. Bett (Oxford: Oxford University Press, 2007)

AL   *Against the Logicians* trans. R. Bett (Cambridge: Cambridge University Press, 2005)

AP   *Against the Physicists* trans. R. Bett (Cambridge: Cambridge University Press, 2012)

M   *Against Those in the Disciplines* trans. R. Bett (Oxford: Oxford University Press, 2018)

PH   *Outlines of Scepticism* trans. J. Annas and J. Barnes (Cambridge: Cambridge University Press, 2000)

Introduction

"With What Must the Beginning of the Science be Made?"

0.0 INTRODUCTION

This book is intended to serve three principal purposes. First and foremost, I provide here an interpretation of the problem with which Hegel opens his *Science of Logic*, the centrepiece of his philosophical system, and supplement this with a critical analysis and evaluation of his proposed solution(s) to that problem. The problem in question I shall refer to as the "problem of beginning", and I take it to be concerned with the following challenge: if one is to elaborate a scientifically rigorous, a priori account of the fundamental conceptual structure of thought (a science of logic), one must begin this elaboration somewhere, but it can look as though any such beginning will be open to sceptical objections concerning arbitrariness which threaten to undermine the scientific status of the account of thought that one develops on its basis. How it is that Hegel understands and attempts to overcome this challenge at the start of his *Logic* is at the heart of this book.[1]

Secondly, because I take Hegel's approach both to the problem of beginning and its solution to be importantly informed by his engagement with the Pyrrhonian Sceptical tradition, this book is also intended as a contribution to the growing body of literature which attempts to explain the importance of Pyrrhonian material for understanding Hegel.[2] I believe that the significance

---

1. Solving this problem is by no means the *only* thing that one must do if one wants to develop such a science of logic, but I have found Hegel's treatment of this particular task sufficiently rich to dedicate this work to its study. It is my hope that the conclusions I draw will prove helpful in considering and evaluating other significant aspects of Hegel's systematic philosophical endeavour.

2. Throughout this book I shall capitalise "Sceptic" and "Sceptical" when referring to the position of the Pyrrhonian Sceptics.

of Hegel's engagement with Pyrrhonism as it applies specifically to the beginning of his *Logic* has thus far gone underappreciated. Lastly, this book is also intended to function as a critical guide which can accompany a reading of Hegel's essay, "With what must the beginning of the science be made?", with which he opens the first book of his *Logic*. It might be pointed out that it is only a relatively brief essay, and that it might, therefore, be unnecessary to dedicate a monograph to its exposition, but Hegel's writing is dense, and the background against which he is writing is not always made apparent to the reader. It therefore takes some unpacking, which I attempt to carry out here. Additionally, I think that the matter of the beginning is of some importance for Hegel's logical project, as I shall indicate in what follows. I am therefore of the opinion that it is worth focusing a good amount of critical attention on the essay in question.

In this introduction I briefly elaborate on each of these three goals in turn in order to frame the project of this book.

0.1 HEGEL'S *LOGIC* AND ITS BEGINNING

As its title suggests, the central topic of this book is a problem Hegel discusses at the beginning of his *Science of Logic*. This problem is the problem of with what one ought to begin a scientific treatment of logic, or of the fundamental structures of thinking. Hegel's answer to this problem is well-known: he famously begins his *Logic* with an examination of the concept of '*Being, pure being,*—without any further determination' (*WL* 59/5:82). Understanding and evaluating Hegel's argument for the claim that this concept is a legitimate starting point, indeed, the only legitimate starting point, for such an investigation is the principal goal of this work.[3] And it is worth noting that, in comparison with the analysis of the first few steps of Hegel's argument which *follow* from the concept of pure being, the specific argument he provides for beginning with this concept has achieved rather less attention

---

3. It is perhaps worth pointing out that I am concerned here only with Hegel's case for beginning logic with the concept of pure being and *not* with the topic, often and not unreasonably discussed in terms of "the beginning of Hegel's *Logic*", of the first few steps of the body of the *Logic*, from pure being through the concepts of pure nothing and becoming, to the concept of determinate being (*Dasein*). A great deal of ink has been spilled on this latter topic, but I take it that the matter at hand here has a certain priority over it. If Hegel does not make a good case for beginning a science of logic with the concept of pure being, then validity of his account of being, nothing, becoming, and determinacy which follows from this beginning is equally compromised. For some examples of significant treatments of the first few moves of Hegel's *Logic*, see Henrich 1971: 73–94, Willett 1990, Houlgate 2006: 263–303, Koch 2014: 61–82, Nuzzo 2018: 120–25, and Pippin 2019: 183–95. This material also receives attention in various broader commentaries on the *Logic*. See, for example, Carlson 2007: 9–53. Rosen 2014: 101–22, Stekeler-Weithofer 2019: 289–376.

in the literature on the *Science of Logic*.⁴ I intend to go some way towards compensating for this lack of attention in what follows.

In order to see what is at stake in the discussion of this problem, however, some comments should be made about the *Science of Logic* as a whole. These remarks apply to both the greater *Science of Logic* and Hegel's shorter presentation of the same material in his *Encyclopaedia Logic*. I shall first sketch the contents of the work and then briefly introduce the sense in which it is supposed to constitute a *scientific* treatment of that content, to the extent that is necessary in order to see why the beginning of the science merits particular attention.⁵ Several of the remarks I make address topics that are matters of controversy in the world of Hegel scholarship, but I will undertake no detailed defence of the positions I take on those topics here. These remarks are intended only to frame the project of this book within the context of Hegel's *Logic* as I understand the work. This should be helpful, especially for readers less well-acquainted with the work, but I am also confident that the majority of the arguments and interpretative claims of this book do not require the reader to agree with every element of the following sketch. Where this is not the case, those elements receive further discussion in the chapters that follow this introduction, but detailed engagement with controversies concerning Hegel's *Logic* not immediately relevant to its beginning can safely be put aside for treatment elsewhere.

As I have already indicated, the *Logic* is, first and foremost, a treatment of thought: in it Hegel attempts to set out in a rigorous manner the fundamental categories or "thought determinations" (*Denkbestimmungen*) with which thinking takes place.⁶ This means that, although in logic these categories are treated for their own sake, they are what is required for the thinking of anything at all, and thus crucial for any philosophical investigation of natural or "spiritual" (*geistig*) matters which might follow.⁷ The content of at least the first two books of the *Logic*—the Doctrine of Being and the Doctrine of Essence—is therefore commonly taken to constitute Hegel's attempt at an improved version of Kant's metaphysical deduction of the categories in the *Critique of Pure Reason*. There Kant sought to derive, a priori, the fundamental qualitative, quantitative, relational, and modal concepts required for the

---

4. Some important contributions are Maker 1993: 81–91, Wolff 2013: 86–87 (which draws on Wolff 1996), Rosen 2014: 82–86, Hentrup 2019, Stekeler-Weithofer 2019: 239–57, Vieweg 2020: 3–8, Krijnen 2021: 58–59, and Stang 2021: 115–21.
5. For a good example of a more detailed overview of Hegel's logical project, see Wolff 2013.
6. In what follows "concepts", "categories", and "thought determinations" will be used interchangeably.
7. The other two parts of Hegel's philosophical system are a philosophy of nature and a philosophy of spirit (*Geist*), where the latter includes not only philosophical treatment of the mind as it is ordinarily understood in English, but also of ethics, social and political philosophy, as well as treatments of art, religion, and philosophy itself.

thinking of any object as such. And the first two books of Hegel's *Logic* do include treatments of qualitative, quantitative, relational, and modal categories but in far greater number and in far greater detail than Kant's deduction in his first *Critique*.[8] Thus Hegel's account includes treatments of the categories of unity, plurality, reality, limitation, substance, causality, reciprocity, possibility, existence, necessity, but also many others besides, including, for example, the finite, the infinite, quantum, degree, measure, essence, seeming (*Schein*), identity, difference, ground, appearance, relation, and actuality.

This account is not merely an attempt to provide an exposition of the fundamental categories of thought, however. In deriving these categories from one another, Hegel seeks to display, systematically, the relations between them, and, in so doing, criticise any account of the categories which grasps them in isolation from one another and supposes that they can be adequately understood independently of the overarching structure in which they are connected to or imply one another. Thus, Hegel's treatment of a given category tends to include a moment where that category is understood in isolation, before its rational examination shows that it implies, or "goes over" into further, related categories. The suggestion is that an attempt to understand a concept in isolation, or as "finite" as Hegel likes to say, will result only in an artificial abstraction rather than a genuine grasp of the category in question. Hegel's derivation of the fundamental categories of thought is therefore also just as much a critique of inadequate accounts of that same content.[9]

The derivation of the categories which constitutes the first two books of the *Logic* culminates in the derivation of what Hegel calls "the Concept".[10] This concept, Hegel says, 'is the foundation of the determinate concepts' which have been examined thus far in the work (*WL* 19/5:30), or 'the ground and the *totality* of the previous determinations' (*WL* 545/6:295). What Hegel refers to as the Concept is the fundamental structure of thought which determines how the various categories relate to one another and, in doing so, determines the content of those categories as 'moment[s] of the form as a totality' (*WL* 19/5:29–30). The Concept is, as Karin de Boer puts it, 'the principle of self-determination constitutive of thought as such' (de Boer 2010: 50–51). The final book of Hegel's *Logic*—the Doctrine of the Concept—explores, still in

---

8. Of course, Kant's position is that 'a complete system of transcendental philosophy' would address numerous other pure categories which could be derived from the twelve that he sets out in the *Critique* (*KRV* A81/B107-A83/B109). I take it that Hegel's aim, in deriving the categories of logic from one another as he does, is in part motivated by the desire to make good on this task which Kant sketches but does not accomplish.

9. This critical aspect of the content of the first two books of Hegel's *Logic* is especially forcefully presented by Bowman (2013: 33–37).

10. I try to avoid unnecessary capitalisation when translating from Hegel's German, but I make an exception for "the Concept" in order to distinguish it from the various other concepts treated in the *Logic*.

the domain of thought alone rather than by appealing to actually existing objects, increasingly adequate forms in which the structure of the Concept might be realised: in the forms of judgement, of inference, of mechanical, chemical, or teleological systems; in the concepts of life, of cognition and action; and, ultimately, in the form of what Hegel calls "the absolute idea". Hegel's *Logic* concludes with two important claims: (i) that 'logic, in the absolute idea, has returned to the simple unity that is its beginning; the pure immediacy of being' (*WL* 752/6:572), so that Hegel's account of logic has a circular structure and thus forms a systematically organised, self-sufficient whole, or totality; and (ii) that, on the basis of the satisfactory completion of the expression of thought in the absolute idea, 'the idea *freely releases* itself' as nature (*WL* 753/6:573). While the exact nature of this move itself is subject to ongoing discussion,[11] it at least clear that, for the philosophical investigator, it has the consequence that an investigation of *realphilosophische* topics, of natural and spiritual matters, can be carried out with the conceptual resources developed in the *Logic* in hand.

Before moving to say something about the sense in which Hegel's treatment of logic is meant to be a scientific one, there is one more aspect of the content of the work which I cannot avoid mentioning, although I will address it as briefly as I possibly can: Hegel's account of logic is, explicitly, not *only* a logic, which is to say, an account of the fundamental structure of thought, but also a metaphysics, or an account of the fundamental structure of being. Hegel is quite explicit about this, referring to his project as 'the logical science which makes up metaphysics proper' (*WL* 9/5:16) and claims that '*Logic* . . . coincides with *metaphysics*, the science of *things* captured in *thoughts*, which have counted as expressing the *essentialities of things*' (*EL* §24).[12]

In holding that his treatment of fundamental categories is of metaphysical significance, Hegel is not unusual.[13] Aristotle is, in his *Categories*, 'engaged in a search for fundamental concepts', as Kant puts it (*KRV* A81/B107). Yet it is not uncommon to read Aristotle as claiming also that his ten categories are the highest or most general kinds of entity, and his discussion of the categories in his *Metaphysics* at times seems to confirm such a reading.[14] Kant himself, of course, could not be more explicit in claiming that his table of

---

11. See Houlgate 2005: 106–10, Berger 2019, and Pippin 2019: 319–22 for some discussion.
12. This is not to say that Hegel's logic exhausts his metaphysics but only that it expresses the fundamentals of that metaphysics. His philosophies of nature and of spirit are works of metaphysics too, but there, the method, I think, is primarily that of bringing the concepts treated in his *Logic* into contact with the results of the natural and human sciences in order to categorise and understand natural and spiritual things.
13. See Haaparanta and Koskinen 2012, for example, for an excellent collection of essays treating the role of the categories in logic and in metaphysics from Aristotle through the history of Western philosophy up to and including contemporary work in metaphysics.
14. See Aristotle 1984 :1028a9–1032a5, for example.

twelve categories has as its subject matter the pure concepts of human understanding, yet these obviously also have a metaphysical significance in that they amount to an account of the fundamental ways in which it is possible for something to be an object. Kant's categories are therefore also an account of the more general kinds which structure the world, albeit with the critical proviso that the categories structure the *phenomenal* world and constrain objects insofar as they are appearances, not things in themselves (Hegel, of course, is among those who reject this restriction). The demand for a metaphysical treatment of the categories is also far from unusual in contemporary philosophy. As a recent commentator has put it in a manner that Hegel would no doubt approve of:

> The plethora of metaphysical theories and concepts that has come to prominence in recent analytical metaphysics invites more than the standard piecemeal treatment of problem after problem characteristic of earlier analytical philosophy. It invites systematization, as practised by all the great metaphysicians . . . it becomes more important to formulate anew and set in connection with one another the system of *categories* which inform such a metaphysics (Simons 2013: 726).

It is important to acknowledge the fact that Hegel's *Logic* is also such a metaphysics here, since some of the work that I carry out in this book, especially in Sections 2.1–2.4, involves situating the beginning of Hegel's *Logic* in the history of Western metaphysics, and especially the attempt to identify and set out fundamental principles within that tradition. The claim that logic coincides with metaphysics, however precisely it should be understood, is also clearly essential to the nature of the *idealism* that characterises Hegel's philosophy, and which is significant for a specific argument I make in Section 4.2.3. For the most part, however, little of the substance of this book turns on the fact that Hegel understands logic to coincide with metaphysics. Where it does, I shall indicate this explicitly, but most of the time, no harm would be done if the reader were to proceed as if Hegel's *Logic* were merely an attempt to present a scientific treatment of the fundamental conceptual scheme essential to thought and no more than that (although it is clear that this is not the case!). I think that it is therefore unnecessary to address here the plethora of interpretative controversies which exist concerning the claim that Hegel understands his *Logic* to be a metaphysics.[15]

---

15. For some time now work has been produced, particularly in English, which unhelpfully distinguishes between so-called "anti-" or "non-metaphysical" and "metaphysical" interpretations of Hegel's *Logic*. This can give the misleading impression that a lot of serious cases are being made for thinking that Hegel's *Logic* makes no metaphysically significant claims, whereas really the vast majority of genuine disagreements occurring under these labels concern either what it is that Hegel considers unsatisfactory about earlier, especially pre-Kantian metaphysics, or specific claims about the character or the content of the metaphysics that Hegel is presenting in his *Logic*, but not whether

It is perhaps worth pointing out, however, that the significance of the beginning of Hegel's *Logic*, which I am investigating here, is primarily methodological rather than metaphysical. The fact that Hegel begins his science of logic with the concept of pure being, I will argue, has significant implications for the legitimation of his system of logico-metaphysical categories, but the concept of pure being alone tells us next to nothing about Hegel's metaphysical commitments, since, as 'pure indeterminacy and emptiness' (*WL* 59/5:82), it is the most inadequate possible concept for saying anything about the way that the world is and is quickly supplanted by more determinate, adequate concepts as the *Science of Logic* progresses.

That concludes the extremely brief sketch of the content of Hegel's *Logic*. The important matter to address now is the fact that Hegel understands his treatment of that content to amount to a scientific one. It would be possible to say a great deal about this topic, and I will engage with it further in the chapters that follow, but an abridged discussion will suffice here. In a recent piece, Michael Wolff has suggested, reasonably, in my view, that an adequate account of the scientific method of Hegel's logical project must pay attention to the beginning of the science, to the dialectical progression of Hegel's derivation of the categories, and to the end of the logical project.[16] Unsurprisingly, it is the issue of the beginning of the science that will take priority here, but a more general sketch is required to introduce its significance.

---

he is doing metaphysics at all. To provide a prominent example, Pippin's influential work on Hegel has often been held up as a exemplary case of the "non-metaphysical Hegel", yet the primary purpose of his most recent book is precisely to explain how, in Hegel's view, 'logic properly understood can be understood as a new metaphysics' (Pippin 2019: 37). Applying the label "non-metaphysical" to such work is inappropriate and obstructs the prosecuting of genuine interpretative disagreements.

The situation seems to be improving, however, in that more and more work is appearing which deals with genuinely significant controversies that exist concerning Hegel's metaphysics, examples of which include questions about the argument by which Hegel seeks to establish his idealism (by way of the criticisms of versions of realism his *Phenomenology of Spirit*? By the attempt to identify a thinking that takes nothing for granted with the concept of being? By appeal to the way in which the investigations of his *Realphilosophie* confirm or verify the contents of his *Logic*?), disagreements about the character and methodology of his conception of metaphysics (does the metaphysics that Hegel sets out in his *Logic* retain, for all of his differences from Kant, an ultimately Kantian focus on what it is for objects to be thinkable by an apperceptive subject, or does Hegel think that his criticisms of Kant entitle him to speculatively set out the fundamental structure of reality in a manner closer to that of pre-Kantian rationalists but without their naiveté or dogmatism?) as well as various disagreements about exactly which first-order metaphysical positions he commits to in his *Logic* (does Hegel defend or reject a metaphysical monism, or perhaps a metaphysical foundationalism? Is there or is there not an ineliminably theological character to Hegel's metaphysics?). These are all worthwhile topics which are the subject of ongoing debates in contemporary literature on the topic of Hegel and metaphysics. This is not to say that one cannot find *any* readers of Hegel who understand him as entirely without metaphysical commitments, but such accounts seem to be very much in the minority and do not strike me as plausible.

16. See Wolff 2014: 86. The focus of Wolff's paper is the second of the three aspects of Hegel's method.

It seems to me that the criteria with which Hegel is operating in characterising his treatment of logic (and metaphysics) as a scientific one are best understood in the context of the German rationalist tradition running from Christian Wolff and his followers, through Kant, Reinhold, and Fichte to Hegel himself. I will expand on this claim in Sections 2.3–2.4, but for now, it should be sufficient merely to indicate that certain key criteria belonging to the conception of what constitutes a scientific treatment of logic or of metaphysics are fairly continuous throughout that tradition. These include the claim that the investigation in question be understood as proceeding in an empirically unaided fashion, so that the knowledge developed is a priori knowledge of the subject matter, and that this knowledge be ultimately grounded on and derived from a foundational principle. Also crucial among these criteria are the demand that the treatment in question proceed by strict demonstration and that it results in a systematic and complete treatment of its subject matter.

Such a characterisation is clearly present in Wolff's insistence that a systematic understanding proceed from propositions known to be true and prove, by way of the application of the appropriate principles, others to be true, thus developing a system of interconnected true propositions, in the fashion of a geometer (Wolff 2019: §2, §6). Of course, this idea receives one of its most powerful expressions in Spinoza's *Ethics*, but it is Descartes who is probably most responsible developing the idea that the elaboration of metaphysics approximate this kind of model. In *The Search for Truth*, for example, he has his spokesman, Eudoxus, argue:

> [A]ll truths follow logically from one another, and are mutually interconnected. The whole secret is to begin with the first and simplest truths, and then to proceed gradually and as it were step by step to the most remote and complex truths. (Descartes 1985: II, 419–20)

This is what Kant endorses as the "dogmatic procedure" when he claims that 'science must always be dogmatic, i.e., it must prove its conclusions strictly *a priori* from secure principles' (*KRV* Bxxxv). Kant goes on to insist that any future systematic metaphysics should conform to such a model, and later idealists like Reinhold and Fichte follow him here, I think.

Hegel accordingly insists of his treatment of logic that it must amount to a demonstration of the necessity of its content (*EL* §1), or a 'systematic derivation' or '*proof*' of its results (*EL* 5/8:11).[17] Since the content of logic is first and foremost the basic categories or determinations of thought, this demand for proof amounts, in Hegel's eyes, to the demand that each thought determination considered emerge from or proceed necessarily from the preceding ones that

---

17. See also *EL* §42A.

have been considered, in a manner that he compares to the making of mathematical inferences (although he admits that elements of his presentation do not live up to this ideal) (*WL* 19-20/5:30–31). And this is how the *Logic* proceeds: it starts, as I have already mentioned, with the concept of "pure being", from which is derived the concept of "nothing", and then "becoming", and then "determinate being" (*Dasein*), and so on through the various qualitative, quantitative, relational, and modal concepts until "the Concept" is derived as the organising principle of the system of the various concepts examined thus far. And the subsequent examination, in the Doctrine of the Concept, of the forms of the realisation of the Concept, continues in this step-by-step, demonstrative vein.

The method of this demonstration, however, differs somewhat from the traditional geometrical model of Wolffian and earlier rationalists, which began by stipulating fundamental principles and axioms, before then deriving further content from these by way of rules of inference which are quite indifferent to the content to which they are applied. As Hegel's analogy to the making of mathematical inferences indicates, it is not the idea that later material be derived strictly from or be shown to be entailed by earlier material that he objects to in traditional geometrical presentations of logic and metaphysics. In fact, the primary criticisms Hegel makes of the geometrical model seem to be those which, in his opinion, constitute problems for the claim that such a method enables one to elaborate a genuine proof, or to have established that one step of one's treatment follows necessarily from another. He sees such problems occurring, for example, in the attempt to establish the relationship between the method and the content of what is considered when the two are conceived of as distinct from one another (*WL* 32/5:47–48), or in establishing the axioms or lemmas of such a demonstration (*WL* 23/5:35).[18] Accordingly, Hegel insists the method of logic must be determined by the content of what is thought rather than by the application of an externally provided set of rules: 'It is the content itself, *the dialectic that it has within itself*, which moves it forward' (*WL* 33/5:50). Instead of the steps of a mathematical or geometrical proof then, which require the mathematician to apply to the content of what is considered the agreed-upon rules of inference, Hegel's claim is that, in the explication of a particular logical category, it

> dissolves itself [and] has its own negation as a result . . . in that the result, the negation, is a *determinate* negation, it has a *content*. It is a new concept, but a higher, richer one than the preceding one . . . in this way above all the system of concepts has to be formed, and must complete itself in an unstoppable, pure process that takes in nothing external (*WL* 33/5:49).

---

18. See Bowman 2013: 167–200 for a thorough discussion of Hegel's critique and transformation of the geometrical model of metaphysical demonstration.

The nature of dialectical demonstration is not the subject matter of this book, but it is important to notice here that Hegel's insistence on a method of strict demonstration, its various idiosyncrasies notwithstanding, gives rise to the question of the beginning of that demonstration, just as any such demand for demonstration must.

To see that the demand for a step-by-step, demonstrative proof of the results of Hegel's science of logic point us to the matter of the beginning of that science, it is not really necessary to address in detail the exact manner in which Hegel understands this method of demonstration to proceed necessarily from determination to determination, nor how this method differs from the method of Fichte, or from that of earlier rationalist forebears, nor even to address the contentious topic of Hegel's attitude towards the notion of a fundamental first principle. All that is necessary is to note that Hegel is committed to the claims (a) that a properly scientific treatment of logic must proceed by way of strict derivation, and (b) that this derivation begins from his account of the concept of pure being. The obvious question that arises in the face of these two claims is the following: why should one accept that the concept of pure being is the legitimate starting point for a demonstrative science of logic?

Hegel's claim is that the results of his science of logic have been *proved* to be the true fundamental determinations of thought (and indeed, of being), but if it should turn out that there is no good reason to agree with him that such a proof should begin from the concept of pure being, if the beginning is merely *arbitrary*, then it would seem that this claim to have provided a proof is undermined since it would be equally legitimate to begin with some other concept and derive an alternative system of logic from there with perhaps just as good a claim to capturing the true structure of thought. Such concerns appear to threaten not only the beginning of Hegel's logic but also the entire systematic, demonstrative science since it is derived from this concept.[19]

Clearly it will not do, as Hegel acknowledges, 'to make or accept *presuppositions* or *assurances*' about the contents of what is supposed to be a science of logic. Yet, as he goes on to say, 'The difficulty of making a *beginning*, however, occurs at once, since a beginning, as *something immediate*, makes a presupposition, or rather, is itself such a thing' (*EL* §1). As Hegel is perfectly aware, *sceptical* challenges tend to arise in the vicinity of what gets put forward as the beginning of a derivation, the results of which are held up

---

[19]. I have introduced here two of the three elements that Wolff took to be essential to an examination of Hegel's claim to have provided a logical science: the legitimacy of its beginning and the rigour of its model of demonstration. What is at stake in the case of the third element, concerning the end of the *Logic*, is less clear and less important to the argument of this book. I take it that Wolff has in mind Hegel's claim, mentioned above, that the end of the *Logic* in some sense coincides with its beginning in a manner that lends a systematic unity to its treatment of thought. I discuss this briefly in Section 3.4.1.

as having been proved to be true, precisely because such a beginning tends to look as if it has this arbitrary character, or as if it has been merely presupposed. The sceptical challenge of how to legitimise the beginning of a science of logic is what I will refer to as "the problem of beginning".

The occurrence of this problem explains why it is necessary for Hegel to make a case for beginning the *Science of Logic* with the concept of pure being, and he makes this case, I think, by inserting an essay after the introduction to that work entitled "With what must the beginning of the science be made?" In that essay, he attempts to answer the sceptical objections that tend to be levelled at the beginning of such a project. Before introducing the essay and saying more about Hegel's specific formulation of the problem of beginning, however, I will provide some introductory remarks on the topic of his engagement with Pyrrhonian Scepticism, since I take it to be of central importance when it comes to discussing the beginning of Hegel's *Logic*.

0.2 HEGEL AND PYRRHONIAN SCEPTICISM

As I indicated in the introduction, this book is intended as a contribution to the now-sizeable body of literature which engages with the influence of Pyrrhonian Scepticism on Hegel's philosophy. Since at least as early as Michael Forster's major 1989 work, *Hegel and Skepticism*, the significance of Pyrrhonism for Hegel has become ever more widely acknowledged.[20] Following suit, I will have quite a bit to say about the Pyrrhonian Scepticism of Sextus Empiricus and its influence on Hegel in this book. In this introduction, however, my goal is only to provide some context for the claims I make about Hegel and Pyrrhonism in the chapters that follow by briefly introducing the significant episodes of Hegel's engagement with Pyrrhonian materials over the course of his philosophical career, and indicating, although not in an exhaustive manner, the focus of recent scholarship on this topic. My contention is that, for all the excellent work that has been done on this topic, the significance of Hegel's engagement with Pyrrhonism for understanding the beginning of his *Logic* has not yet received the attention it requires.

The topic of scepticism was widely discussed in the philosophical context of Germany during Hegel's formative years, thanks in large part to Schulze

---

20. There are, of course, still earlier significant works on Hegel and Scepticism (Röttges 1987 is a good example), but Forster's book seems to me to have provoked the most widespread attention to the topic. Forster was attempting, in that work, to remedy what he saw as a widespread 'failure to pay sufficient attention to Hegel's critical interpretation of the sceptical tradition' (Forster 1989: 3). It seems to me that he largely succeeded, in that the importance of Pyrrhonism to Hegel's philosophy is now well known. In fact, it seems that rather less has been written about Hegel's attitude to typically modern sceptical problems, but see Testa 2013, for a start.

and Maimon's sceptical arguments against Kant's and Reinhold's systematic works.[21] Klaus Vieweg, in his 1999 *Philosophie des Remis*, for example, offers a valuable study of the young Hegel's developing engagement with sceptical philosophy and of the significance of sceptical thought in the German philosophy of the period, stretching from Hegel's time as a student in Tübingen up to and including his early works in Jena.[22] A great deal of work on Hegel and scepticism focuses on his early period in Jena, since there, in 1802, he published an essay entitled "On the Relationship of Scepticism to Philosophy, Exposition of its Different Modifications and Comparison of its Latest Form with the Ancient One". This essay begins as a (very) critical review of Schulze's then recently published *Critique of Theoretical Philosophy*, but Hegel takes the opportunity to reflect in a more general manner on ancient and modern scepticisms and on the relationship between scepticism and speculative philosophy as he understands it. Although this is still an immature work, certain claims Hegel makes here about scepticism and philosophical reasoning reoccur in the context of his mature, systematic philosophy, so it is quite reasonable that work on Hegel and scepticism tends to pay close attention to it. Thus it receives extended treatment, for example, not only by Vieweg, but also in significant studies by Forster, by Trisokkas, and by several others.[23]

After "On the Relationship of Scepticism to Philosophy", the text that has received the most attention by scholars considering Hegel's engagement with Pyrrhonism is probably his 1807 *Phenomenology of Spirit*: Hegel's famous introduction to his system, the method of which he describes as a 'self-completing scepticism' (*PhG* §78/3:72), and the introduction to which centres on Hegel's engagement with the classical Pyrrhonian problem of the criterion. Hegel's engagement with Pyrrhonism in the *Phenomenology* accordingly receives extended attention from Forster, Westphal,[24] and numerous other accounts of the *Phenomenology*.[25]

---

21. For a good overview of the substance of Schulze's and Maimon's criticisms, see Beiser 1987: 266–323. A recent defence of Schulze's sceptical rejection of the type of systematic metaphysical projects typical of German Idealist philosophers is offered by Berry (2020). For a response, see Dunphy (forthcoming).

22. Vieweg 2007 extends this project to include an important discussion of the notion of immediacy in the early 1800s and then to questions of aesthetics and religiosity. Franks 2005 includes good discussions of the significance of Pyrrhonian Scepticism in the context of post-Kantian philosophy more generally.

23. See Vieweg 1999: 207–20, Forster 1989: Chs. 1–2, and Trisokkas 2012: Ch. 2. For further material on this essay, see Harris 2000: 256–65, Bristow 2007: 133–40, Franks 2008: 52–62, Heidemann 2011: 81–84, Hentrup 2018: 105–19, or Brandão 2020.

24. See Forster 1989 and Westphal 1989. See also Westphal's later work on Hegel, for example, Westphal 2017: Chs. 8 and 10.

25. See, for example, Düsing 1973, Heidemann 2011: 84–92, Staehler 2017: 21–29, or Hentrup 2018.

I will give a brief account of the significance of the treatment of scepticism in these two texts and of Hegel's explicit treatment of Pyrrhonian Scepticism in his *Lectures on the History of Philosophy* in Sections 1.2–1.2.2.[26] The argument of the *Phenomenology* and its relationship to the beginning of Hegel's *Logic* is the major focus of chapter 4 of this book.

In comparison with "On the Relationship of Scepticism to Philosophy" and the *Phenomenology*, Hegel's engagement with Pyrrhonism in his *Science of Logic* and his *Encyclopaedia Logic* has received rather less attention.[27] An exception is an important study by Ioannis Trisokkas, the major goal of which is to defend the claim that Hegel refutes Pyrrhonian Scepticism early in the third book of the *Logic*, the Doctrine of the Concept.[28] I believe, however, that *this* book is the first study to make an extended case for the importance of Hegel's engagement with Pyrrhonism for the *beginning* of his *Logic*. A little more explicitly, my contention here is that Hegel's engagement with Pyrrhonism is crucial both to his understanding of the problem of how to begin a science of logic and to its solution.[29] The principal elements of this book which contribute to making this case are as follows. In Sections 1.1–1.1.4, I provide a discussion of what I take to be the relevant essentials of Pyrrhonism as it is presented by Sextus Empiricus, culminating in a discussion of the kind of problem the Pyrrhonist poses by way of the Agrippan modes. I call such problems "Agrippan problems" and characterise them, following Sextus' account of the Two Modes, in terms of a dilemma between an arbitrary claim and an unsatisfactory regress of supporting claims. I go on, in Sections 1.2–1.2.2, to provide a more detailed overview of Hegel's engagement with Sextus, where I show that he is sensitive to the nature of Agrippan problems,

---

26. See Dudley 2003, for a good discussion of Hegel's lectures on Academic and Pyrrhonian Scepticism.

27. There is also more to say about the importance of Pyrrhonism in the context of Hegel's treatment of epistemological and practical topics in his *Philosophy of Spirit*, and in other Hegelian contexts besides, but it is not necessary to address these topics in this book. See the papers in Fulda and Horstmann 1996 and in Kozatsas et al. 2017, as well Heidemann 2007, for more wide-ranging treatments of Hegel's engagement with Pyrrhonism.

28. Trisokkas 2012. See also Röttges 1987, Chs.3 and 5, or Scarfe 2003, for the claim that Hegel's engagement with scepticism informs the character of the idealist position which he develops in the Doctrine of the Concept.

29. I am aware of one other piece which makes a similar claim. Hentrup (2019:151) suggests, as I do here, that we should understand Hegel's problem of beginning as modelled on Sextus' presentation of the two modes of Agrippa. Hentrup and I seem to have arrived at this conclusion independently of one another. I take it that this speaks in favour of its interpretative plausibility. I say more about Hentrup's account of the beginning of the *Logic* in Section 3.4.1. Stekeler-Weithofer (2019: 244) also suggests that the problem of beginning 'leads to the structure of the trilemma of Agrippa', but this claim is not made in the context of an examination of Hegel's engagement with Pyrrhonism, while Röttges (1987: 134) relates the problem to the Agrippan modes, but in the context of a discussion of Hegel's more general response to Pyrrhonian Scepticism rather than an analysis of a specific problem of beginning, such as the one provided here.

and that he understands them to have the same fundamental form, based on the Two Modes, as the one I have described in the first part of the chapter.

In Sections 2.3–2.4, I make a brief case for the importance of Agrippan problems as they occur in the history of the development of the problem of beginning among pre-Hegelian German Idealists. Then, in Section 3.2, I argue that Hegel's problem of beginning is itself a distinctive Agrippan problem and that its presentation reflects Sextus' account of the two Agrippan modes in his *Outlines of Pyrrhonism*. I also provide, in Section 3.3.1, an account of the form of Hegel's solution to this problem. Unpacking versions of this solution take up most of the remainder of the book, but I argue that Hegel's attitude toward Pyrrhonian Scepticism, and specifically his attempt to incorporate the Pyrrhonian tendency to construct oppositions between arguments, judgements, or concepts within his account of speculative reasoning, is essential to the nature of any version of that solution.

Finally, I also note, in Section 3.3.2, that in the *Encyclopaedia Logic*, Hegel entertains the possibility of a sceptical project which might be presupposed by the beginning of a science of logic. Hegel's discussion of this possibility is only brief, as he quickly rejects the idea. Still, in the final chapter of this book, I attempt to do three things: firstly, in Section 5.1, I argue that, in light of the form of the solution that he develops to the problem of beginning, Hegel should not have been so quick to reject the sceptical project in question. Secondly, in Section 5.2, I argue that the evidence suggests that Hegel is thinking of a specifically Pyrrhonian Scepticism when he makes these remarks. Finally, in Sections 5.2.1–5.2.2, I attempt to rehabilitate this idea on Hegel's behalf in order to explore its consequences for the validity of Hegel's solution to the problem of beginning.

Before continuing, I should like to make one more prefatory remark on the topic of the influence of Pyrrhonian Scepticism on Hegel's thought: it is not my intention to exaggerate the significance of this influence in this book. Hegel is a great reader of the history of philosophy, and while there is no doubt that his reading of Pyrrhonian texts played an important role in his philosophical development in various ways, in emphasising this influence as I do here, I am not suggesting that an understanding of Pyrrhonism is somehow *more* important for a reading of Hegel than an understanding of Aristotle, say, or of Neoplatonist philosophers. Questions having to do with the comparative importance of historical influences on a thinker can be difficult to adjudicate even when it comes to considering quite specific doctrines or ideas, and I am not sure how helpful it is at all to pursue them at a more general level. Accordingly, my claim in what follows is only this: that Hegel's engagement with Pyrrhonism is decisive when it comes *specifically* to thinking about the beginning of the *Science of Logic*, and that therefore an emphasis on this influence is useful when it comes to making sense of this specific topic in Hegel's works.

I turn now to the third major purpose of this book: to provide a helpful but critical commentary on Hegel's essay "With what must the beginning of the science be made?" To that end, I shall now provide a brief précis of the essay in question, explaining which sections of this book accompany which of its significant parts.

0.3 A PRÉCIS OF "WITH WHAT MUST THE BEGINNING OF THE SCIENCE BE MADE?"

I provide here an overview of the contents of "With what must the beginning of the science be made?" Hegel positions this essay at the start of the first book of his *Science of Logic*, the Doctrine of Being, after the prefaces and introduction to the *Logic* as a whole but before launching into the examination of the fundamental categories of thought (and of being) which begins with the examination of the concepts of "pure being", "nothing" and "becoming".[30] As I suggested earlier, I think that Hegel includes this essay in his *Logic* in order to discuss and attempt to solve the sceptical problem which occurs when one attempts to set out a systematic, scientific treatment of logic: whatever is selected as the beginning of such a project, if it is merely arbitrary, seems to threaten the scientific status of the results that one derives from that beginning.

The most important conclusion that Hegel draws in "With what must the beginning of the science be made?" is that a science of logic of the kind he is attempting ought to begin with the exposition and analysis of the concept of "pure being". And sure enough, it is with this concept that the text of the *Logic* proper begins, after Hegel draws the essay to a close. What follows thereafter—the account of the first concepts Hegel treats in the *Logic*: pure being, pure nothing, and becoming—has received a great deal of intense scrutiny from Hegel's own time up to the present day, and in fact, it is the relationship between these basic concepts that is often discussed under the title of "the beginning of Hegel's *Logic*". It is not my intention to discuss this material here, however.[31] The relationship between the project of this book

---

30. There are two versions of this essay, corresponding to the two editions of the first book of Hegel's *Logic* in 1812 and 1832. The two are not identical. The earlier version begins with a discussion of the relation the beginning of the logic bears to the outcome of Hegel's *Phenomenology of Spirit* before explicitly discussing the problem of beginning, while the later version begins with the problem and then discusses the relation to the *Phenomenology*, for example. Such a difference in the ordering of the material, however, does not strike me as philosophically significant. The précis provided here of the essay follows the presentation of the 1832 edition.

31. And indeed, in the preface to the second edition of the *Logic*, Hegel himself appears to warn against spending too much time considering whether the account of the transition from pure being to nothing to becoming is valid, especially if it comes at the cost of 'the going further, the study, and the production of the entire development' of the logical project (*WL* 21/5:33). The precise extent to which Hegel here is seeking to dissuade readers from critically scrutinising the first few moves of his *Logic*

and that material should be clear: Hegel's discussion of the concepts of pure being, pure nothing, and becoming presupposes and relies upon the results of his discussion of why a science of logic ought to begin with the concept of pure being in the first place. It is the latter that is under investigation here.

Elements of the material that Hegel treats in "With what must the beginning of the science be made?" reoccur in the preliminaries to his *Encyclopaedia Logic*. This is not terribly surprising, since that text addresses the same material as the greater *Science of Logic*, albeit in a compressed manner. Importantly for the argument of this book, however, elements of the treatment of the topic of the beginning in the *Encyclopaedia Logic* differ interestingly from those in the greater *Logic*. I will indicate in this précis of "With what must the beginning of the science be made?" those places where I think that important parallel material is to be found in the preliminaries to the *Encyclopaedia Logic*.

What follows is only a sketch of the contents of Hegel's essay. The claims I make below receive more detailed treatment and justification in the main body of this work. The account here is intended firstly to introduce Hegel's essay and secondly to direct the reader considering its various parts to their discussion in the relevant sections of this book.

0.3.1 The Statement of the Problem of Beginning

Hegel begins the essay with his statement of the problem at the heart of this study. As I indicated earlier, I refer to it as "the problem of beginning":

> The beginning of philosophy must be either *something mediated* or *something immediate*, and it is easy to show that it can be neither the one nor the other; so that either way of beginning finds its rebuttal (*WL* 45/5:65).

This problem concerns Hegel's attempt to provide an a priori derivation of the fundamental categorial structure of thought. More specifically, it concerns the attempt to provide such a derivation in such a way that the opening of his account is not undermined by its vulnerability to sceptical objection. The

---

is not completely clear; he obviously thinks that the validity of the transitions between these concepts is crucial since he holds that a science of logic must exhibit 'the development of thought in its necessity' (*WL* 18/5:30), and he certainly seems to believe that his account is valid, if possibly flawed in its presentation. Additionally, the targets he has in mind when making this complaint seem to be those who approach the material in question on the basis of 'presuppositions and prejudices' (*WL* 21/5:33). A charitable, rigorous interrogation of the first concepts of his *Logic*, we might therefore conclude, is not what Hegel is attempting to dissuade readers from carrying out. In any case, these remarks of Hegel's explicitly concern the material which is presented *after* the presentation and solution of the problem of beginning, not the treatment of that problem and its solution themselves, so there is no suggestion that the topic of "With what must the beginning of the science be made?" should not be studied in detail. As Hegel deemed it necessary to include a distinct essay specifically dedicated to this problem, I do not think that one need worry that I am paying too much attention to something unimportant in the context of Hegel's *Logic* in this book.

problem with which Hegel is grappling here could be alternately phrased in the following manner: with which concept can the derivation of the fundamental categories of thought begin so that the argument is not immediately rebutted by a sceptical interlocutor who suggests that we have at least as good a reason to begin elsewhere? The problem therefore concerns Hegel's attempt to secure the beginning of his logical project against objection on grounds of arbitrariness. As I have already suggested, this concern about arbitrariness threatens to extend to the logical and metaphysical conclusions at which Hegel arrives on the basis of that beginning. Certainly, solving the problem of beginning will not secure Hegel's results from all possible objections (each "dialectical" step of Hegel's derivation from concept to concept must also prove to be valid, for example), but it is a necessary condition for doing so.

Parallel Encyclopaedia Material: Hegel discusses the key elements of the problem of beginning in the introduction to the *Encyclopaedia Logic* as well, perhaps most significantly in §§1 and 10.

In This Book: Taking Hegel's statement of the problem above in isolation, it is not clear exactly what it is about beginning with something "immediate" or "mediated" that might open his logical project to a rebuttal, but I provide a detailed explanation of the nature of this problem in Section 3.2, the key element of which is that beginning with something mediated here means beginning with something that presupposes some other material which supports it and demonstrates its validity, while beginning with something immediate means beginning with something that presupposes nothing at all. Both of these options, in Hegel's view, will be rebutted by a sceptic. The first option involves merely taking for granted the presuppositions the beginning relies upon for its validity, so the sceptic is entitled to object that these presuppositions offer no real support at all, or that the beginning could just as easily be exchanged for an opposing beginning which presupposes something else. The second option, in presupposing nothing at all, is indistinguishable from something wholly arbitrary, so the sceptic is entitled to put forward an alternative beginning, equally groundlessly, with just as much legitimacy. Other sections of this book especially relevant to the problem of beginning itself include 1.1.3, 1.2.2, 2.3, 2.4, 3.1, and 5.1.

0.3.2 A Brief Historical Sketch

Hegel places, between his statement of the problem of beginning and his discussion of its solution, a very brief sketch of how the issue of beginning has been approached in the history of philosophy. We can divide his account into four parts:

(1) A treatment of the idea of the "objective beginning" or of the "subjective beginning" of a system of philosophy, not in the sense of where one

ought to begin a philosophical inquiry but instead in the sense of indicating 'the beginning of *all things*' (*WL* 45/5:65) or a metaphysical principle. Here "beginning" in the sense of "principle" means something like "fundamental ground", whether taken to be "objective" in its character—taking water, like Thales, to be the fundamental ground of everything, for example—or "subjective" in its character, if one suppose everything to depend ultimately on thought, or on the "I", for example.

(2) An account of what I will refer to as a "methodological beginning", where this names precisely what the previous treatments did not: a concern for where one ought to begin the task of evaluating the legitimacy of philosophical claims. The primary goal here, as Hegel characterises it, is to identify a 'subjective criterion' against dogmatism, in order to avoid endorsing philosophical claims, metaphysical, logical, or otherwise, on fundamentally arbitrary grounds (*WL* 45/5:65). This kind of arbitrariness, Hegel thinks, clearly vitiates the metaphysical systems he has in mind in when discussing the objective and subjective beginnings mentioned earlier, since, in their enthusiasm for identifying 'the *absolute ground* of everything', the question of where one ought to begin the presentation of the systems if the case for them is to be properly justified is left 'disregarded and indifferent' by their proponents (*WL* 45/5:65).

(3) A treatment of the matter of beginning which insists that "beginning" understood as a fundamental metaphysical principle should coincide with the "beginning" understood in terms of the subjective activity of thinking. Here the concern for the proper justification of any philosophical claims from (2) is to some extent combined with a concern for the identification of a fundamental metaphysical principle from (1), and that principle itself is now taken to be both "subjective" and "objective" in character. Hegel presumably has in mind various post-Kantian idealists, perhaps principally Reinhold, Fichte, and Schelling, for whom, as he puts it, 'the *subjective* activity is also grasped as an essential moment of objective truth' (*WL* 46/5:66). According to those who endorse this idea, Hegel claims, 'the *principle* should also be the beginning, and what is the *Prius* for thought should also be the *first* in the *course* of thinking' (*WL* 46/5:66). In other words, for those committed to such an approach, the fundamental logical or metaphysical principle from which it is to be shown that everything derives ought to be established at the beginning of the investigation. It is with the emergence of this kind of approach, Hegel suggests, that the seriousness of the problem of beginning is recognised, since it is not clear how one should go about arguing that a candidate first principle can be known to be the right one.

(4) Hegel's own approach to the problem of beginning, which seems to share with (3) the demand that a systematic, scientific metaphysics be shown to be grounded on a fundamental principle, as well as an appreciation of the

difficulty of establishing the legitimacy of what comes first in the order of thinking, but does *not* share with it the assumption that what comes first in the order of thinking must be identical with the fundamental principle of the system in question. Instead, as I have already suggested in Section 0.1, Hegel thinks that the fundamental principle can be derived as one of the *results* of his logical project. This is to say, of course, that a great deal, including the derivation of the categories, and proof that they are ultimately grounded in the structure of the Concept, depends on the legitimacy of beginning a science of logic, as Hegel does, with the concept of pure being.

Parallel Encyclopaedia Material: There is no section of the *Encyclopaedia* which directly corresponds to Hegel's sketch of the history of the problem of beginning.[32]

In This Book: I expand upon Hegel's historical sketch in Sections 2.1–2.3 and upon his own approach to the relationship between first principles and the matter of beginning in Section 2.4.

0.3.3 The Presentation of a Solution to the Problem of Beginning

After the brief, historical interlude, Hegel turns back to the problem of beginning and attempts to provide a solution. He presents the solution over the next four pages of the essay and describes it as a 'simple exposition of what initially belongs . . . to the logical beginning' (*WL* 48/5:69). Although the concept which Hegel takes to emerge as the solution the problem of beginning, the concept of '*pure being*' (*WL* 48/5:69), may itself be simple, I think that he overstates the simplicity of his argument here. As I will reconstruct it, the argument involves four important steps:

Firstly, Hegel challenges the assumption that the "or" in his statement of the problem of beginning must be understood exclusively, suggesting instead of the alternatives of beginning with something mediated *or* something immediate that it might instead be the case that 'both of these determinations show themselves to be *unseparated* and *inseparable* and opposition between them to be a nullity' (*WL* 46/5:66). The suggestion here is that it might also be possible to begin a science of logic with a thought that is both mediated *and* immediate.

Secondly, Hegel suggests that the beginning of a science of logic might be mediated if it were to presuppose the outcome of an earlier investigation. The

---

32. One should not make the mistake of thinking that the historical sketch in question coincides with Hegel's longer treatment of dogmatic metaphysics, empiricism, Kant's critical philosophy, and Jacobian appeals to immediate knowledge in the preliminaries to the *Encyclopaedia Logic*. The sketch under investigation here is concerned specifically with the question of beginning, while the "three positions of thought towards objectivity" examined in the preliminaries of the *Encyclopaedia* are concerned with accounts of philosophical cognition more generally.

candidate he has in mind is the critical investigation of natural consciousness which he carried out in his earlier *Phenomenology of Spirit*, the work which was supposed to serve as an introduction to his systematic philosophy. "Natural consciousness" here indicates a position opposed to the governing approach of Hegel's science of logic in that it rejects the idea of an a priori investigation of thought in favour of an approach whereby instead one must begin with 'empirical, *sensuous* consciousness' (*WL* 47/5:67). He suggests here that the final outcome of his critical investigation of that position is the concept of '*pure being*' (*WL* 47/5:68).

Thirdly, Hegel suggests that the beginning of a science of logic might be immediate if it were to presuppose nothing at all, or if it were to be nothing more the simple result of a resolve to think, but without thinking anything specific. Hegel suggests that this radically minimal or simple thought would have 'no content' and would again amount to the concept of pure being (*WL* 48/5:69).

Finally, I take Hegel to be suggesting that, understood properly, the coincidence of what is thought in second and third steps, in the sense that both amount to thinking the concept of "pure being", confirms the suggestion he made in first step: that it is possible to begin a science of logic with a thought that is both mediated and immediate. Additionally, he must be claiming that, understood as both mediated and immediate in this fashion, the concept of pure being is not vulnerable to either kind of sceptical objection expressed in the problem of beginning in the way that any other starting point for a science of logic would be. Making sense of this final step of Hegel's argument also requires us to address a well-known puzzle facing readers of the beginning of Hegel's *Logic*: his solution of the problem of beginning seems to demand at the same time both that the beginning of a science of logic presuppose the results of *Phenomenology of Spirit* and that it presupposes nothing at all.

Parallel Encyclopaedia Material: It seems to me that Hegel provides an alternative statement of the solution to the problem of beginning in his *Encyclopaedia Logic* §78. This version is importantly different from the solution presented in "With what must the beginning of the science be made?" The significant differences are, firstly, that the appeal to the examination of natural consciousness carried out in Hegel's *Phenomenology of Spirit* is replaced by an appeal to a different project which might be thought to play the same role: a 'negative science' of 'completed scepticism' (*EL* §78A) and, secondly, that even this alternative suggestion appears then to be discarded in favour of 'the resolve *to think purely*' (*EL* §78A).

In This Book: I address the general form of Hegel's solution to the problem of beginning and the differences between the two versions of the solution that Hegel presents in Sections 3.3.1–3.3.2. Evaluating the version of the solution from the greater *Science of Logic*, which relies upon the argument of his

Phenomenology of Spirit, is the principal task of chapter 4 of this book, while doing the same for the alternative version suggested in §78 of the *Encyclopaedia Logic* is the focus of chapter 5.

What follows in the remainder of "With what must the beginning of the science be made?" is a series of remarks and arguments which serve two principal goals. Firstly, Hegel anticipates and criticises potential misunderstandings and objections or alternative suggestions concerning the beginning of logic. Secondly, he attempts to clarify the relationship between the topic of the essay—the need to begin with pure being—and the project of the *Logic* as a whole. These two topics are not clearly distinguished in the text, but I think that it is preferable to treat them separately here.

0.3.4 Additional Remarks on the Beginning of the Science of Logic

The objections and alternatives to his procedure which Hegel considers here are not exhaustive, but they are significant. The first of these is motivated by the suggestion, a version of which Hegel himself endorses, that 'absolute truth must be a result' (*WL* 48/5:69). If this is the case, which is to say, one arrives at a result of which one can be sure only as the outcome of a process of reasoning, then this might be thought to cast a certain amount of doubt on wherever it is that one must begin that process of reasoning, insofar as it falls short of absolute truth. The suggestion, therefore, is that 'philosophy can begin only with something which is *hypothetically* and *problematically* true' (*WL* 48/5:69).[33]

Another objection that Hegel considers is that if, as he has argued, it is crucial that a science of logic begin without presuppositions and without content, then perhaps even the concept of pure being presupposes too much or is too substantial. Instead, the objection goes, would it not be better to begin with the idea of 'pure beginning' itself? (*WL* 51/5:73).[34]

The final alternative that Hegel discusses is the Fichtean claim that all philosophy ought to begin from the "I" because of 'the demand that the first truth be something familiar, and even more, an *immediate certainty*' (*WL* 53/5:76). Hegel rejects all three of these objections and alternatives as he discusses them.

---

33. Hegel cites Reinhold as the primary proponent of this view. This claim does not belong to Reinhold's earlier defence of the infallibility of beginning with his "principle of consciousness". Reinhold comes to defend the idea of a hypothetical beginning only after becoming convinced of the insufficiency of his earlier approach, and that of the early Fichte, which he also briefly endorsed. Bondeli 1995 traces this development in Reinhold's attitude towards the topic of the beginning in detail.

34. Hegel also very briefly considers the possibility of beginning with the subject matter of logic itself, in an effort to avoid so much abstractness (*WL* 53/5:75), but he quickly concludes that, at the beginning, the subject matter of logic must precisely be 'empty being'. See Stang 2021: 118–20, for a sympathetic treatment of this idea.

Parallel Encyclopaedia Material: Hegel discusses the notion of beginning logic with a hypothesis in *EL* §10A. He does not discuss the possibility of beginning with the idea of "pure beginning" in the *Encyclopaedia*, and only briefly discusses the Fichtean strategy of beginning with the "I", in *EL* §60Z2.

In This Book: I offer some discussion of the suggestion that a science of logic might begin with a hypothesis in Section 3.4.1 and some discussion of the suggestion that logic might beginning by considering the notion of a "pure beginning" in Section 3.4.2. Hegel's critical attitude towards Fichte's suggested beginning is discussed in Section 2.3.4.

0.3.5 The Relationship of the Beginning to the Project of the *Logic*

The claims that Hegel makes in this context about the progression of the argument of his science of logic itself are, he points out more than once, made only in an anticipatory and clarificatory manner. He is perhaps uniquely wary of giving the impression that any of the claims that he defends in his *Logic* are expressions of assumptions or intuitions which he already happened to hold, since he holds that logic as a science cannot rely upon any assumed laws, axioms, intuitions, or presuppositions concerning either method or content from elsewhere. Rather, he believes, all such things 'make up part of its content and they first have to be established within it' (*WL* 23/5:35).[35] These preliminary claims in "With what must the beginning of the science be made?", therefore, involve sketches of significant positions which Hegel defends in the *Logic* but do not receive a proper defence in the context of that preliminary essay. I am accordingly unable to provide as detailed a discussion of this material as of the other elements of "With what must the beginning of the science be made?" in this work, since that task would require its transformation from an examination of Hegel's problem of beginning to an examination of Hegel's *Logic* as a whole. Still, I will provide what analysis I take to be necessary for the clarification of Hegel's approach to the beginning of the *Logic*. The significant claims that Hegel makes in this preliminary context are as follows:

Firstly, Hegel endorses a version of the claim mentioned in the previous section of this introduction, that 'absolute truth must be a result' (*WL* 48/5:69). In the context of the problem of beginning the significance of this

---

35. This is a significant claim, and it has struck many readers as implausible. I shall say only this here: this work concerns Hegel's justification for beginning a science of logic with the concept of pure being. This is a concept which, Hegel argues, is radically indeterminate, or which has no real content. If his defence of this opening move is thought to be convincing, then it seems to me that one should allow Hegel the claim that his *Logic* at least *begins* without dogmatically relying upon axioms, assumptions, laws, and the like. The significant question then becomes whether his account is able to generate the principles, method, and content that he claims that it does without illicitly introducing prior assumptions later on in the argument. Answering this question falls beyond the limits of this work.

claim is that, although the beginning of a science of logic must not be vulnerable to sceptical objection, nor be understood merely as a hypothesis, it also falls significantly short of the truth, where by the latter is meant a fully adequate account of the nature of thought. Hegel's attempt to provide this adequate account develops over the course of the *Logic*, culminating in the material on the Concept, and, ultimately, the absolute idea. This confirms that he takes truth to be a result since clearly a process of reasoning is required to get from the exposition of the concept of pure being to that of the Concept itself.

The second significant claim that Hegel makes in a preliminary fashion in this context is that the Concept, which he designates as the absolute truth, is the ground or foundation of thought, so that derivation of the categories of thought which Hegel elaborates, beginning with the concept of pure being, is ultimately grounded upon the foundation of the account of the Concept in which it results. Accompanying this is Hegel's claim that, for the argument of the *Logic*, which begins from the concept of pure being, 'progression is a *retreat* into the *ground*' (*WL* 49/5:70).

The third significant claim Hegel makes here is that the science of logic 'is in itself a circular course in which the first becomes also the last, and the last also the first' (*WL* 49/5:70). The motif of a science which forms a circle appears frequently in Hegel's accounts of the various parts of his systematic philosophy, and of his system taken as whole.

Parallel Encyclopaedia Material: The three significant claims mentioned here also occur in various places in the *Encyclopaedia Logic*. For the claim that the Concept must be a result, see *EL* §§159A, 159Z, for example. For the claim that the Concept is the absolute foundation or ground of the various concepts treated in the *Logic*, see *EL* §§159A, 160Z, for example. For the claim that the logical science takes the form of a circle, see *EL* §§15, 17, for example.

In This Book: I provide a brief discussion of Hegel's claim that the Concept which is the absolute truth of thought is a result which is also a foundation and that, therefore, the progression of the argument of the *Logic* is a "retreat into the ground" of thought, in Section 2.4. I discuss the importance of the circular structure of Hegel's logical science as it pertains to the matter of the beginning in Section 3.4.1.

That concludes this brief précis of the contents of "With what must the beginning of the science be made?"

0.4 CONCLUSION

In this introduction I have set out the three main goals of this work: to examine and evaluate Hegel's problem of beginning and his solution(s) to that problem, to make a case for the significance of Hegel's engagement with Pyrrhonism for understanding the beginning of his *Logic*, and to provide a critical commentary on his essay "With what must the beginning of the science be made?"

The remainder of the work proceeds as follows: in chapter 1, I introduce what I take to be the relevant essentials of Pyrrhonian Scepticism and supplement this with an overview of Hegel's interpretation of Pyrrhonism in his key works on the topic. In chapter 2, I expand on the historical sketch Hegel provides in "With what must the beginning of the science be made?" in order to situate Hegel's work on the problem of beginning in the context of his relation to his significant forebears, particularly in the rationalist and the idealist traditions in Germany.

In chapter 3, I provide a detailed analysis firstly of Hegel's account of the problem of beginning, and then of the form of its solution. I argue that Hegel's expression of the problem of beginning, with its dilemma between equally unsatisfactory alternatives of beginning with something mediated or with something immediate, owes its format to Sextus' presentation of the two Agrippan modes in his *Outlines of Pyrrhonism*. I also differentiate two versions of Hegel's solution to the problem of beginning, both of which share the same form in that they conceive of the concept of pure being as importantly combining elements of mediation and immediacy. The first of these, presented in "With what must the beginning of the science be made?" identifies the element of mediation in Hegel's solution with the argument of his *Phenomenology of Spirit*. The second, presented in his *Encyclopaedia Logic*, identifies the element of mediation with a "negative science" of "completed scepticism". Finally, in that chapter, I provide some criticisms of alternative interpretations of the beginning of Hegel's *Logic* and attempt to anticipate some objections that might be made to the account I offer here.

In chapter 4, I evaluate the first of Hegel's two solutions to his problem of beginning. I consider the relationship between the beginning of the *Logic* and the *Phenomenology of Spirit* and argue that the interpretation of this relationship that makes best sense of Hegel's remarks concerning the problem of beginning is the one supported by William Maker, most notably in his 1994 work, *Philosophy Without Foundations*. I then offer a series of arguments which purport to show that, despite the strengths of this interpretation, the results of the argument of the *Phenomenology* are incompatible with the beginning of Hegel's *Logic*. I conclude, accordingly, that Hegel's first solution to the problem of beginning fails. In chapter 5, I evaluate the second of Hegel's two solutions to the problem of beginning. This requires some reconstructive work, since Hegel unfortunately dismisses this solution immediately after suggesting it, but I will argue that this solution turns out not to be vulnerable to any of the objections which caused problems for the first. I will conclude that this version of Hegel's solution to the problem of beginning makes a good case for establishing the legitimacy of the beginning of his science of logic (and, accordingly, that Hegel was wrong to dismiss it). If this is right, then a good case has been made for beginning a science of logic with the concept of pure being, as Hegel does. Since making this case is, as I understand it, the primary goal of the essay, "With what must the beginning of the science be made?", this book accordingly concludes with a tentative endorsement of a *version* of the solution to the problem of beginning that Hegel develops there. It is important not to overstate what has been achieved if this solution is successful, however. *All* that a successful solution to the problem of beginning guarantees is the legitimacy of beginning logic with pure being. It does not amount to a more general Hegelian refutation of scepticism, nor to an argument in favour of Hegel's developed idealist metaphysical position, nor for the validity of any of the conceptual transitions which make up most of the body of Hegel's *Logic*, nor, for that matter, for the validity of the specifically "dialectical" method of demonstration which characterises those transitions. From the perspective of the conclusion of this work, such topics remain quite open. They can only be decided by a careful reading of the remainder of the *Science of Logic*.

Chapter One

Hegel and Pyrrhonian Scepticism

1.0 INTRODUCTION

Since one of the central contentions of this book is that an understanding of Hegel's engagement with Pyrrhonian Scepticism is important when it comes to understanding both his statement of the problem of beginning and its solution, this chapter is intended to provide some useful context for the reading of "With what must the beginning of the science be made?" that I develop in the subsequent chapters by setting out what I take to be the key elements of that engagement.

In the first part of the chapter, I offer a brief statement of the relevant essentials of Pyrrhonian Scepticism itself, primarily with reference to its presentation in the surviving works of Sextus Empiricus. I should note that while this brief account reflects what I take to be a reasonably accurate interpretation of Sextus' presentation of Pyrrhonism, I do not undertake here a lengthy defence of my interpretation against those contemporary scholars of Pyrrhonism who might disagree with its various elements. I think that doing so would detract from its principal purpose, which is to introduce the nature of *Hegel's* engagement with Pyrrhonism, particularly as it applies to the beginning of his *Logic*. The account I provide here is therefore weighted towards those elements of Sextus' Pyrrhonism which are most relevant to Hegel's engagement with Sceptical thought, while other elements of Sextus' account, even arguably central ones, are passed over in silence. A lengthier defence of my understanding of Sextus on his own terms will be accomplished in other, more appropriate contexts.[1]

---

1. I have begun to defend such an interpretation in Dunphy 2022.

In the second part of this chapter, I discuss Hegel's engagement with Pyrrhonian Scepticism, from his reasonably concentrated work on the topic in his earlier essay "On the Relationship Between Scepticism and Philosophy" and his *Lectures on the History of Philosophy* to the more infrequent discussions of ancient scepticism which occur in the *Phenomenology of Spirit*, the *Science of Logic*, and in the *Encyclopaedia Logic*. In doing so, I characterise what seem to me to be the key aspects of Hegel's understanding of Pyrrhonian Scepticism. I suggest that, in considering these elements, we can distinguish between Pyrrhonism as a specific shape of historically appearing spirit, with various theoretical and practical commitments, and Pyrrhonism more narrowly as a set of argumentative procedures. Historical Pyrrhonism, as Hegel understands it, I think, combines these two elements, but while various aspects of historical Pyrrhonism just seem to belong to the development of Western philosophy as Hegel understands it, without standing out as being especially significant in the context of this book, both the strengths and the limitations Hegel perceives in Sceptical argumentation are crucial, I think, for understanding his work on the problem of beginning in his *Logic*.

1.1 SEXTUS' ACCOUNT OF PYRRHONISM

The primary sources for any account of Pyrrhonian Scepticism are the surviving works of Sextus Empiricus.[2] This material receives the majority of the focus of contemporary scholars of Pyrrhonism, just as it received Hegel's focus in his work on the topic.[3] Remaining to us are the three books that make up Sextus' *Outlines of Pyrrhonism*, five books of a probable ten "Sceptical Treatises" and six books which provide sceptical criticism of various other academic disciplines: *Against the Learned*.[4] Since the remaining five books of the "Sceptical Treatises" consist of sceptical criticisms of prominent positions defended by philosophers on matters of logic, natural science, and ethics, thereby overlapping with the subject matter of books II and III of the *Outlines*, it is often thought that they were preceded by a lengthy discussion of Pyrrhonian philosophy itself. As it is, however, only book I of the *Outlines* remains to us as a 'general account' of 'the distinctive character of

---

2. Another major source for discussions of Pyrrhonism is Diogenes Laërtius' *Lives of the Eminent Philosophers*, which Hegel also makes use of. See Diogenes Laërtius 2018: IX, 61–108.
3. Hegel also relies heavily on Sextus in his lectures on ancient Greek philosophy more generally. He writes that Sextus is 'the most prolific source for the history of ancient philosophy' (*VGP* 95/18:191).
4. Hegel follows the (probably) mistaken academic consensus of his time and supposes that *Against the Logicians*, *Against the Physicists*, and *Against the Ethicists* are books VII–XI of *Against the Learned* rather than the remainder of a separate work (See *VGP* 465/19:367).

Scepticism' (*PH* I:5). It is primarily to this text, therefore, that I appeal in what follows.

1.1.1 The Sceptic's Way of Life

In the first book of his *Outlines of Pyrrhonism*, Sextus sets out and defends the essentials of what he calls the Sceptical "way of life" (*agōgē*). This way of life, he says, amounts to an 'account showing how it is possible to live correctly (where 'correctly'... extends to the ability to suspend judgement)' (*PH* I:17). It is striking that the only idiosyncratically Sceptical aspect of this way of life that Sextus mentions in the precise context of this remark is the attitude of suspension of judgement (*epochē*). This serves to emphasise the central importance of this attitude for Sextus' account of the nature of Pyrrhonism.

The basic nature of the importance of suspension of judgement for the Sceptic can be expressed straightforwardly. The Sceptical way of life is presented as a response to the predicament of disturbance (*tarachē*) in the face of a conflict (*anōmalia*) of appearances or thoughts which prevents one from reasonably holding a belief about whatever matter is at hand (*PH* I:12, 26). The primary component of this response is a commitment to a distinctive form of inquiry (*zētēsis*). Sextus says, accordingly, that 'the Sceptical way of life, then, is also called zetetic, from its activity in inquiring and investigating' (*PH* I:7).[5] This form of inquiry, in turn, is one that has suspension of judgement as its goal, since the Sceptic holds, surprisingly, that suspension of judgement is the key to relieving the state of disturbance and living instead in a state of undisturbedness (*ataraxia*) (*PH* I:25–31).[6]

The primary component of the Sceptical way of life, then, is the activity of inquiry. The discussion of the nature and methods of this activity takes up the majority of book I of Sextus' *Outlines*, while books II and III, as well as the remaining books of the "Sceptical Treatises" and the six books of *Against the Learned*, would seem to amount to examples of the activity being put into practice by way of inquiries into matters of logic, natural science, ethics, and various other academic disciplines, with the works of various non-Sceptical philosophers ("Dogmatists") functioning as interlocutors and disputants in that inquiry.[7] Despite this, Sceptical inquiry and its methods are not the only focus of book I of the *Outlines*. Sextus also discusses, however briefly, a form

---

5. The Sceptic is, of course, quite literally an investigator (*skeptikos*).
6. See also *PH* I:232, where Sextus agrees with the Academic sceptic Arcesilaus when 'he says that the goal is suspension of judgement, which, we said, is accompanied by undisturbedness'.
7. The vast majority of Sextus' surviving work, in fact, is weighted towards investigations in the epistemology of metaphysical, natural scientific, and ethical claims (as well as those made in the disciplines considered in *Against the Learned*) rather than in extolling in detail the virtues of a particular "Sceptical" way of life.

of disturbance which inquiry is unable to relieve: 'We do not, however, take Sceptics to be undisturbed in every way—we say that they are disturbed by things which are forced upon them; for we agree that at times they shiver and are thirsty and have other feelings of this kind' (*PH* I:29).

The inquiry that Sextus presents concerns matters of belief, suspension of judgement, and disbelief, but the passage just cited could suggest that the Sceptical way of life does not consist only in a zetetically focused ethics of belief. Besides an ethics of belief which aims at 'undisturbedness in matters of belief', Sextus also appears to be recommending an ethics of 'moderation in matters of feeling forced upon us' (*PH* I:30). This is enough to show that Sextus' claim is not that the Sceptical way of life entails complete and utter undisturbedness, but undisturbedness only in matters of belief. It would be possible to say much more about what is involved in Sextus' recommendation of moderation in matters of feeling, but since I do not think that this topic is important to the argument of this book, I will not do so here.[8] Instead, I will proceed to a more detailed discussion of the character of Sceptical inquiry.

1.1.2 Sceptical Inquiry

It is important to say more about the nature of Sceptical inquiry here, not just because it is clearly essential to Sextus' presentation of Pyrrhonism, but also because it will feature significantly in the discussion of the solution to Hegel's problem of beginning I provide in Sections 5.2.1–5.2.2. The clearest characterisation of the nature of Sceptical inquiry is that provided by Sextus as an answer to the question, "What is Scepticism?"

---

8. This topic can lead to thorny matters regarding the interpretation of Sextus. Sextus' claim is that moderation in matters of feeling consists in avoiding compounding the disturbance caused by the feeling by believing that the fact of having such a feeling 'is bad by nature' (*PH* I:30). The course of moderation, he therefore recommends, includes abandoning beliefs about what is good or bad. This might look as though it is simply a reiteration of his general point that striving to hold beliefs is the source of disturbance, but the context of this remark complicates matters. In *PH* I:27–8 (and again *PH* III:235–38 and *AE*:110–67), Sextus appears to give an alternative diagnosis of what is disturbing about holding specifically *evaluative* beliefs which appeal not to the problem posed by conflicting appearances and thoughts but rather to the consequences which follow from holding this specific kind of belief. He suggests that they will result in disturbance because people striving after what they take to be goodwill understand themselves to be 'persecuted by natural evils' while those who believe themselves to be in possession of something good will live 'in fear of change' (*PH* I:27). It is not clear how this concern about the troubling consequences of evaluative beliefs relates to Sextus' position on the relationship between disturbance and belief in general. For the unusual claim that specifically evaluative beliefs are at the root of all doxastic disturbance, according to Sextus, see Machuca 2019b: 202–10. I have attempted to provide some criticism of this view in Dunphy 2022: 468–71. See also Vogt 2011: 37–38, for the suggestion that Sextus' expression of more eudaemonistic concerns are a concession to the interests of his Dogmatic interlocutors and should not be allocated too much weight in the interpretation of his Scepticism.

Scepticism is the ability to set out oppositions among things which appear and are thought of in any way at all, an ability by which, because of the equipollence in the opposed objects and arguments, we come first to suspension of judgement and afterwards to undisturbedness (*PH* I:8).

This rather concise account requires some elaboration. Sextus seems to suggest that Sceptics (or "proto-Sceptics", where this indicates those philosophers who would become Sceptics, during the period before they presumably recognised the "correctness" of the Sceptical way of life) approached philosophy with the same intentions as any other philosopher:

Talented people, struck by the conflict in things and puzzled as to which of them they ought rather to assent to, came to inquire into what in things is true and what false, thinking that by deciding these issues they would become undisturbed. (*PH* I:12)

A lot of the time, then, one does not need a Sceptic with their practised ability to construct an opposition between how things appear or how they are thought of. A tower can appear round from a distance and square from up close. One can think about the composition of the tower, noticing that it is made of stones, and then think in turn about the composition of those stones. Ultimately, one might come to think that matter might be infinitely divisible, or one might come to think that it must ultimately be composed of indivisible parts. In both cases, of appearance and of thought, one encounters oppositions quite naturally. The appearance of a round tower is opposed to the appearance of the square one, the thought of infinite divisibility is opposed to that of indivisible parts. Sextus characterises such situations in terms of disturbance—one is disturbed by the fact that one does not know which of the opposed positions one ought to believe.[9]

What is more, each of the opposed positions can appear convincing. A tower looking round can seem like all the evidence one needs to suppose that it is round, and the same goes for a tower looking square. Apparently strong arguments can be adduced both for and against the infinite divisibility of

---

9. See Perin 2010: 33–58 for a defence of the view that Sextus understands the Sceptic as primarily motivated by the demands of reason, and thus concerned with what they rationally *ought* to believe. Such an interpretation is not universally accepted. Against interpreters like Perin are views which suppose that the Sceptic's philosophical inquiry and its characteristic result in suspension of judgement are best understood as merely causal, psychological processes or habits, rather than an attempt by the Sceptic to believe, suspend judgement, or disbelieve according to the demands of reason. For a good overview of the various positions in this debate, see Eichorn 2020: 188–97. I am of the opinion that the more "rational" interpretations of Pyrrhonian Scepticism, like that developed by Perin, make best sense of Sextus' text, but I cannot defend this view here. Hegel, I think, considers Pyrrhonism from a perspective concerned with the demands of reason, so this kind of interpretation is a better fit for the project of this book, even if some readers should arrive at the conclusion that Hegel has therefore not properly appreciated the Pyrrhonian position (see Berry 2020, for an example of this kind of view).

matter. As Katja Vogt has put it, the philosopher's mind is 'upset—it is pulled in different directions because conflicting views or appearances induce her to assent' (Vogt 2011: 39). Little wonder, then, that Sextus describes such a situation as a disturbing one: one is concerned with what one ought to believe, but does not know, and is pulled in different directions, each representing the danger that one might end up believing incorrectly.[10]

The proto-Sceptics, according to Sextus, began philosophical inquiry like anyone else, 'in order to decide among appearances [and thoughts] and to apprehend which are true and which are false so as to become undisturbed' (*PH* I:26). This seems reasonable enough. The thing to do in the face of these disturbing oppositions is to sort the matter out or solve the problem: figure out which position is true and which is false, and believe the true. That, one would think, ought to relieve the disturbance in question. Yet this is clearly not the model of inquiry which the Sceptics ended up with. As Sextus puts it, '[w]hen people are inquiring into any subject, the likely result is either a discovery, or a denial of discovery and a confession of inapprehensibility, or else a continuation of the inquiry' (*PH* I:1). Those who, after inquiring into some subject, *think* that they have discovered the truth, Sextus calls "Dogmatists". Those who claim that it will be impossible ever to discover the truth about the matter at hand, he calls "Academics".[11] This claim involves, of course, some sort of discovery. It amounts to saying that it is true that one will never discover the truth about the matter at hand. This "Academic" position is also a species of Dogmatism then. '[T]he Sceptics', Sextus adds, 'are still inquiring' (*PH* I:3).

As well as reiterating the centrality of inquiry to the Sceptical life, these passages contribute to conveying something of the puzzling nature of Sceptical inquiry. Combined with the answer to the question "What is Scepticism?", cited earlier, these passages from the opening of Sextus' *Outlines* suggest that Sceptical inquiry, rather than resulting in the discovery of the truth, tends to result in suspension of judgement about the matter being investigated and in the continuation of the inquiry. And yet it is precisely this, Sextus claims, that results in the relief of disturbance in the Sceptic: the proto-Sceptics, inquiring into whichever opposition in thought or appearance happened to have struck them, with the hope of discovering the truth, instead 'came upon equipollent

---

10. Vogt, in her (2011), thinks that the Sceptic is concerned with avoiding false beliefs. I have elsewhere suggested that the Sceptic is primarily concerned with avoiding unjustified beliefs (Dunphy 2022: 457–61, 477–83).

11. As has been remarked often enough, using this term to indicate this position is rather misleading, especially if it is taken to imply that *all* of the philosophers of the more sceptical phases of Academy tend towards this kind of position, or if it is taken to imply that inapprehensibility will be the result of *all* inquiry. Sextus makes neither claim, but a discussion of the specifics of the positions of various Academic sceptics and the adequacies and inadequacies of Sextus' appreciation of those positions cannot be achieved here.

dispute, and being unable to decide this they suspended judgement. And when they suspended judgement undisturbedness in matters of opinion followed fortuitously' (*PH* I:26). Instead of being able to decide which of the opposing positions in question is true and which false, the inquirers found that there were equally strong arguments in favour of each and suspended judgement accordingly. Since they found that this relieved the disturbance they felt in the face of the conflict, they adopted a model of inquiry which has the construction of equally strong opposing arguments as its defining feature, with the result that the position of the Pyrrhonian Sceptic is one of 'suspension of judgement about everything' (*PH* I:31).

The obvious question to ask at this point is the following: why should suspension of judgement relieve the disturbance that the Sceptic felt in the face of the conflicting thoughts and appearances? It certainly has not relieved the conflict, after all. I think that the answer to this question comes from remembering that it is not merely that conflicting appearances and thoughts are disturbing in and of themselves to the philosopher, Sceptic or otherwise, but that they are disturbing given that the philosopher is concerned with believing what they ought to, given the evidence.[12] It is because of this rational commitment on behalf of the philosopher that conflicting appearances, which both pull one's mind in incompatible directions and function as an obstacle to knowing what one ought to believe, are disturbing. If they simply didn't care about the correctness or rationality of their beliefs, there would presumably be no reason to be disturbed by conflicting appearances and thoughts, and no need for philosophical inquiry.[13]

The Sceptic's apparently peculiar claim that undisturbedness follows from suspension of judgement therefore follows, I think, from two things. The first is that the Sceptic is concerned with believing, disbelieving, and suspending as they ought to, or as it is rational to do so. And in the case of opposing claims with equipollent arguments in their favour, as Sextus says, 'it is right to suspend judgement' (*PH* II:96).[14] In cases where the opposing arguments are genuinely equipollent, the appropriate, rational response is to suspend judgement. So long as one does this, then, in such cases, one need no longer

---

12. As Sextus portrays them, the Sceptic's suspension of judgement is always on the basis of evidence and argument, or reasons (See, e.g., *PH* I:8, III:49, 135). The accounts of the various Sceptical modes (*PH* I:35–186), too, are, in general, accounts of arguments intended to show that there is equally strong evidence for and against a candidate belief).

13. This account follows the more "rational" interpretations of Sceptical inquiry that I mentioned above, although I have not defended their correctness. For a very different account which denies that the Sceptic is operating with any rational norms, see Williams 2010.

14. Here I am again following Perin 2010: 33–58. Perin has suggested that the norm according to which the Sceptic organises their doxastic attitudes is that of truth (Perin 2015). I have elsewhere argued that it makes better sense to suppose that the norm in question is that of justification (Dunphy 2022), but it is not necessary to rehearse this disagreement here.

struggle with the disturbing thought that one might believe irrationally. The second thing is that the Sceptic tends to find that *all* of their philosophical inquiries, prosecuted carefully, tend to end up with equipollent, opposing arguments. This leads them to the principle, 'opposed to every argument there is an equal argument' (*PH* 1:12, 202). Sextus is careful to avoid slipping into a Dogmatic position here, however: the Sceptic is not entitled to declare this slogan as if it is a truth they have discovered about the nature of the world. Instead, Sextus insists that it is merely to be understood as the Sceptic's report on the results of every inquiry they have engaged in so far: 'To every argument I have scrutinised which purports to establish something in a dogmatic fashion, there appears to me to be another opposed argument . . . equal to it in convincingness or unconvincingness' (*PH* 1:203).

This goes some way towards explaining the Sceptic's commitment to ongoing inquiry. Since it is always possible that further evidence or a new argument in favour of one position over another might turn up or be put forward, the Sceptic cannot view their inquiries as definitively concluded with their suspension of judgement. And should it turn out in the future that one side of the opposition in question is clearly stronger, the Sceptic would presumably accept that the appropriate thing to do in such a case is to believe the claim that the arguments in question support. According to Sextus, at least, this has not yet happened to the Pyrrhonian Sceptics, so their principle concerning equipollent opposing arguments remains intact.

This account of Sceptical inquiry also explains what it is that the Sceptic finds so unsatisfactory about Dogmatic philosophies of various stripes. The chief sin of the Dogmatist, Sextus often points out, is "rashness". The Dogmatists' claims to have discovered the truth about the matter of various inquiries are always, in the eyes of the Sceptics, the result of an over-hasty positive estimation of the strength of the arguments in favour of one position and a lack of the appropriate, careful appreciation of the strength of the arguments that can be made against their favoured position. Dogmatic claims to the truth should, therefore, not be treated as genuinely resolving the disturbance the philosopher feels in the face of challenges to the task of believing as they ought to. This, in turn, explains why the construction of equipollent arguments has such a central place in Sceptical inquiry: the larger part of that inquiry seems to be taken up in showing that various Dogmatic philosophers have been rash in supposing some argument to have established the truth of a particular claim by showing that there are, in fact, equally strong opposing arguments to be found for each Dogmatic candidate.[15]

---

15. As Palmer (2000: 369) has emphasised, the Sceptics are therefore occupied with curing the Dogmatists of their rashness, like philosophical physicians. I do not think that this philanthropic end is all there is to Sceptical inquiry, however. The Sceptics are also concerned with making sure that they themselves believe, suspend judgement, or disbelieve as they should.

As Sextus presents them, the Sceptics have been extraordinarily successful in carrying out their inquiries according to the model set out in *PH* I:8, since they have come, as I have indicated, to suspend judgement about "everything".[16] On the strength of their (so far) successful principle concerning equipollent arguments, the Sceptics have 'come to hold no beliefs' (*PH* I:12).[17] The most important remaining question at this point is that of how it is that the Sceptics are supposedly able to construct equipollent opposing arguments so reliably and so thoroughly. The answer is that they make extensive use of various "modes"—forms of argument which make up problems for the justification of any claim to or supposed discovery of the truth. These, too, will prove to be crucial for Hegel's understanding of Pyrrhonism, so a dedicated discussion of the most important of these is now required.

1.1.3 Agrippan Problems

Sextus is explicit in saying that these modes are the means by which the Sceptics carry out their inquiries and arrive at suspension of judgement (*PH* I:35). He sets out several collections of Sceptical modes, assembled during different periods in the development of Pyrrhonian Scepticism. The most important for my purposes here are the Agrippan modes.[18] It is these modes

---

16. See Smith 2022: 78–83, for a good recent discussion of the Sceptic's claim to "suspend judgement about everything", with an emphasis on the *completion* of the Sceptic's inquiries.

17. Precisely how one understands these claims to the effect that the Sceptics suspend judgement about everything and hold no beliefs depends on the position one takes on a debate that has received extensive treatment in the literature on Pyrrhonism—that of the so-called "scope" of the Sceptics' beliefs. It is not necessary to address this debate here (a helpful overview is provided in Morison 2019: §3.4), since this discussion is intended to lay the ground for an examination of Hegel's engagement with Pyrrhonism, and Hegel clearly takes Sextus plainly at his word here and adopts the most radical interpretation: that the Sceptic genuinely has no beliefs of any kind at all (see Forster 1989: 13-24, for discussion). A different point is made in this context by Ribeiro. He supposes that the Sceptic's claim to have no beliefs represents a goal to which the Sceptics aspired, but would never completely reach (Ribeiro 2002: 325-330), by appeal to the fact that the Sextus says that the Sceptical phrase "to every argument an equal argument is opposed" can also function as an exhortation to other Sceptics: 'To every argument . . . let us oppose an argument' (*PH* I:204). I cannot fully address this suggestion here, but I note that the Sceptics' use of such an exhortation is at least compatible with the idea that they have genuinely reached a point at which they have suspended judgement about everything, yet continue to inquire and to encounter sometimes apparently compelling new Dogmatic arguments, and thus still need to be careful not to slip into Dogmatist rashness. I shall suggest that Hegel thinks it is plausible that the Sceptics would come to believe nothing at all below.

18. Hegel holds the Agrippan modes in high esteem, as I shall detail in Section 1.2.1. Sextus himself does not explicitly claim that the Agrippan modes are the most fundamental, saying merely that the different sets of modes can be used by the Sceptics 'to refute the rashness of the Dogmatists in a more varied way' (*PH* I:177). Nevertheless, when he discusses the Ten Modes and the Eight Modes, both of which are attributed to Aenesidemus, one detects the possibility that the Sceptic exercising these modes can always fall back on the Agrippan modes. Sextus points out that the Five (Agrippan) Modes 'will also suffice' against Dogmatic causal explanations which are the object of the Eight Modes (*PH* I:185). And when he discusses the fifth of the Ten Modes, which are, in general, concerned with problems posed by matters of apparent relativity among objects and the humans making judgements about them, he suggests that attempts to argue in favour of one appearance over another

and the problems which they combine to form which are the main focus of this section.[19]

Sextus attributes two sets of modes to 'the more recent Sceptics' (*PH* I:164). These are the Five Modes (*PH* I:164–77) and the Two Modes (*PH* I:178–79). In his account of Pyrrhonian Scepticism, Diogenes Laërtius attributes the Five Modes to a Sceptic called Agrippa.[20] Accordingly, it is common to refer to these as the "Agrippan modes". Since it is not unusual firstly to hold that the Two Modes amount to a compact restatement of the problem expressed by way of the Five Modes,[21] and secondly to attribute the Two to the same author as that of the Five,[22] once can also refer to the Two Modes as "Agrippan modes". Ultimately, the attribution of these modes to Agrippa is not terribly important, since none of his works survive and we know nothing about him beyond his brief mention in Diogenes' account of the Pyrrhonian tradition, but it provides a useful label with which to group together the Sceptical material under examination here.

In what follows, I shall suggest that the famous trilemma embedded in the Five Modes and its more compact expression as a dilemma in the Two Modes provide us with the basic form of philosophical problems which can be called "Agrippan problems". These include the "epistemic regress problem", the "problem of the criterion", and others besides, although it is not my intention to provide an exhaustive list. I suggest that, at their simplest, these problems confront us with a dilemma between the equally unsatisfactory alternatives of the arbitrariness of a claim put forward without any support and the arbitrariness of a claim put forward on the basis of fundamentally inadequate support. In Section 3.2, I will argue that Hegel's problem of beginning is an Agrippan problem.

As I indicated in the previous section, the Sceptical modes are intended to bring about a suspension of judgement concerning the subject matter of an inquiry. They achieve this by the generation of equipollent oppositions, whereby both some claim that p and some opposing claim that $\neg p$ are

---

will be answered by an appeal to the Agrippan modes (*PH* I:122–23), a strategy which it seems could be generalised for all of the Ten Modes.

19. I have provided a more detailed discussion of the Agrippan modes in Dunphy 2020b, which also very loosely connects them to Hegel's problem of beginning.

20. See Diogenes Laërtius 2018: IX: 89.

21. See, for example, Barnes 1990: 117, Hankinson 1995: 189, Bett 2019: 108–9, and, significantly, *VSP* 335/2:244.

22. See, for example, Barnes 1990: 117, n.3, or Brennan and Lee 2014: 269. See Janáček 2008: 176–77, for a dissenting view, arguably supported by Catapano 2017: 114. This issue does not strongly concern me here. If one should agree that the Two Modes represent a development in the presentation of the Five Modes and think it likely that it is, therefore, a student or a follower of Agrippa who is responsible for this development, then one can take the term "Agrippan" to refer to problems with their ancestry in the work of Agrippa's school, rather than problems with their ancestry in the work of one philosopher called Agrippa.

rendered equally convincing, or are shown to be equally well supported, so that it would be illegitimate to assert the truth of either.[23] I think that the crucial aspect of the procedure of the Agrippan modes is that they in fact indicate a specific kind of equipollent opposition: one in which the opposing claims, in fact, turn out to be completely arbitrary.[24] In such cases, the opposing claims are equally convincing in that neither has *anything* in its favour, and so one can be asserted with just as much right as the other. I think that this description applies to Sextus' characterisation of both the Five Modes and the Two Modes, which I will now summarise briefly, starting with the Five.

The first, the mode of disagreement, applies when 'undecidable disagreement about the matter proposed has come about' (*PH* I:165). If the disagreement is undecidable, at least on the basis of the evidence currently available, the reasonable thing to do is to suspend judgement accordingly. The second mode, the mode of infinite regression, suggests that when the evidence provided in support of some claim in fact tends towards an infinite regress of supporting evidence, it then offers no real support as 'we have no point from which to begin to establish anything' (*PH*:166). Given that the claim in question on the matter at hand is effectively unsupported, an opposing claim can be asserted as equally convincing, so the reasonable thing to do again is to suspend judgement on the matter.

The third mode, that of relativity, at least as it is described by Sextus, appeals to the relativity of varied perceptions and thoughts concerning the matter at hand to motivate a suspension of judgement over the veracity of any particular perspective (*PH* I:167). A natural way to read Sextus' account of this mode is as suggesting that, given that some object can appear one way to Perceiver A and another way to Perceiver B, there is no way to know how the object really is, and that we must therefore suspend judgement on the matter.[25]

---

23. Of course, it need not be *p*'s strict negation but merely some claim which is incompatible with P and which therefore implies ¬*p*.
24. It is not obvious that this is the case with the Ten Modes, by contrast.
25. The mode of relativity looks as though it can represent the approach of the Ten Modes in general (see *PH* I:39). On Fogelin's reading, addressed shortly, the mode of relativity appears to have precisely the same function as that of dispute. Hankinson agrees, suggesting that 'Relativity, at least in its Agrippan context, should perhaps not be treated as a separate Mode at all' (Hankinson 1995: 185). Sienkewicz, rightly, it seems to me, suggests that either relativity reduces to the mode of disagreement, or, it in fact, renders disagreement impossible. This would be the case if, rather than the mode of relativity indicating the possibility of disagreement by calling to the fact that attention that the same object can appear one way to Perceiver A and another way to Perceiver B, it instead amounted to the claim that the same object *is* one way, in accordance with the relation it bears to Perceiver A, and *is* another way, in accordance with the relation it bears to Perceiver B (Sienkewicz 2019: 147–53). A different reading of the mode of relativity, as specifically targeting apparently self-supporting propositions, is provided in Brennan and Lee 2014 and has received support from Bett (2019: 119). I do not think that it is necessary to elaborate on these alternatives here. See Dunphy 2020b: 266–69, for a brief discussion.

The fourth mode is the mode of hypothesis, which applies in those instances where some Dogmatic interlocutor asserts the truth of something 'which they do not establish but claim to assume simply and without proof' (*PH* I:168). This mode points out that the claim in question appears completely arbitrary since no attempt has been made to support it. It is, therefore, no more convincing than an opposing assertion that might be made equally arbitrarily, so it is reasonable to suspend judgement on the matter.[26]

Finally, Sextus describes the mode of reciprocity, which covers the familiar, problematic scenario in which the evidence upon which some claim relies for its support includes, at some point, that claim itself, so that its justification is viciously circular (*PH* I:169). Like the mode of infinite regression, this is taken to undercut the value of that evidence, so that the claim in question is effectively unsupported. An opposing claim can again, therefore, be equally convincingly asserted so that the reasonable thing to do is to suspend judgement on the matter. This is only a rough account of the Five Modes, and it obscures a number of important interpretative issues, but it will suffice as a starting point for the remainder of this account.[27]

Readers familiar with the *Posterior Analytics* have tended to notice that the combination of the modes of hypothesis, reciprocity, and infinite regress coincides with Aristotle's account of the challenge to the possibility of knowledge through demonstration.[28] As Aristotle's account suggests, it looks as though there is a specific sceptical problem which can be generated by the application of these three modes together, one which can be used to ask of any claim p whether it has been merely arbitrarily asserted, corresponding to the mode of hypothesis, or whether it depends for its support on some other claim E1. If the latter, then the focus then switches to E1. If this latter claim has been asserted arbitrarily, then this presumably nullifies the support that it offered to p. If, on the other hand, E1 is supported by some claim E2, then the investigation continues. Should this chain of supporting claims eventually repeat, so that E2 turns out to rely upon E1, or indeed p, for its support, then the apparent support for p is thought to be undermined by the circularity of the argument. This corresponds to the mode of reciprocity. If the chain neither terminates somewhere arbitrary nor repeats, then the apparent support is thought to be undermined by the unacceptability of an infinite regress. Thus, together, these three modes look as though they pose a Sceptical challenge to the justification of any claim whatsoever, precisely the way I suggested

---

26. It is worth noting in passing here that Hegel always translates the mode of "hypothesis" as "presupposition" (*Voraussetzung*).
27. Barnes 1990 and Sienkiewicz 2019 are extended studies of the Five Modes. A good discussion is also provided in Heidemann 2007: 42–55.
28. Aristotle 1984: 72b5–73a20. Aristotle's defence of the possibility of immediate knowledge is not under investigation here. It is safe to assume that the Sceptics were not convinced.

earlier: by showing that the opposing claims in question are equipollent because, even if they appear to be supported, they turn out to be ultimately arbitrary.

This combined or systematic use of three of the Five Modes as they appear in the *Outlines* is attributed to Sextus by Jonathan Barnes, among others,[29] and it clearly corresponds to what is today discussed either as the "epistemic regress problem",[30] or, acknowledging its ancestry in the presentation of the Five Modes, the "Agrippan trilemma".[31] This problem continues to receive significant attention in contemporary epistemology, where no clear consensus has formed concerning its adequate solution.[32] Although I will suggest later on that the general form of the trilemma occurs in a number of distinct problems, the text of *PH* I:164–69 reads as though it is problematising the providing of evidence in support of claims in the manner which now occurs in discussions of the epistemic regress problem.

Given that engagements with the systematic combination of three of the Five Modes both predate and postdate Sextus' work, it is not surprising that there has been a tendency on behalf of philosophers to separate the modes making up the trilemma of the epistemic regress problem from the modes of disagreement and of relativity when engaging with the Five Modes. Thus, for example, Robert Fogelin distinguishes these two from those making up the trilemma by referring to the former as 'challenging modes' and the latter as 'dialectical modes' (Fogelin 1994: 116). The thought governing this division is that the challenging modes, rather than being primarily intended to motivate a suspension of judgement on their own, call attention to an actual or merely possible difference of opinion on whether or not it is the case that *p*. In doing so, they give rise to an inquiry into the evidence that might be put forward in support of holding that *p*. This inquiry is accordingly referred to the dialectical modes, which, at least according to Fogelin, is bound to result in a suspension of judgement, since he holds that 'no justificatory program seems to show any prospect of solving the Agrippa problem' (Fogelin 1994: 193). As I indicated in the previous section, this seems to be Sextus' opinion as well.

This way of isolating the trilemma within the context of Sextus' account seems to me both to have been the most influential and to be the most elegant

---

29. See Barnes 1990: 118.
30. See, for example, Cling 2008: 401–21, Kajamies 2009: 523–34, or Aikin 2011: 8–43.
31. See, for example, Fogelin 1994: 114, or Williams 1999: 183. Both Fogelin and Williams suggest that their choice of title reflects an emphasis that the problem is a trilemma between three equally problematic justificatory alternatives, suspecting that referring to the problem as the epistemic regress problem involves a misleading emphasis upon only one of these. I am not particularly worried about this and will continue to talk about the epistemic regress problem.
32. Klein suggests that '[m]any contemporary epistemologists take the epistemic regress problem as *a*, if not *the* central problem, in epistemology' (Klein 2007: 1).

way of recombining the material of the Five Modes.³³ It is the problems that take these modes as a trilemma which will be my focus in discussing the general nature of Agrippan problems shortly. It is worth acknowledging, however, that there is no clear indication in Sextus' text that the Five Modes are to be divided in this fashion, and when Sextus does suggest that the modes might be used collectively, he mentions all five.³⁴ His use of the Agrippan modes, however, does occasionally suggest their trilemmatic application.³⁵ Still, a lengthier investigation of Sextus' own views on this matter goes beyond my concerns here. It is enough to have shown that the possibility of extracting this trilemma from the Five Modes exists and that it operates the way that I have suggested: by showing that, for any claim that p, $\neg p$ can be asserted equally convincingly because, despite appearances, the claims in question are, in fact, indistinguishable from arbitrary assertions. In the case of hypothesis, this involves no more than just pointing out that an opposing claim can be equally as groundlessly put forward. In the case of reciprocity, this is achieved by showing that, despite the appearance of some support for p, this support in fact reduces to simply asserting p, so that again, $\neg p$ can be equally convincingly asserted. In the case of the infinite regress, this is achieved by showing that the apparent support on offer is continuously postponed, so that it never becomes clear that the Dogmatist in question is doing more than arbitrarily asserting p.

Sextus is explicit in claiming that 'every object of inquiry can be referred to these modes' (*PH* I:169), and, as I have already indicated, although he cannot rule out the possibility that some argument might be put forward in favour of a claim that turns out not to be vulnerable to the Five Modes, he thinks that the Sceptics are yet to encounter such an argument.

After his account of the Five Modes, Sextus describes the Two Modes in the following manner:

> Since everything apprehended is thought to be apprehended either by means of itself or by means of something else, [the Two Modes] are thought to induce puzzlement about everything by suggesting that nothing is apprehended either by means of itself or by means of something else.
>
> That nothing is apprehended by means of itself is . . . clear from the disagreement which has occurred among natural scientists over, I suppose, all perceiv-

---

33. Franks, famously, has suggested that the Agrippan modes making up the trilemma play a vital role in the development of German Idealism (Franks 2005: 8–10). That is a broader claim than the one under investigation in this book, which is merely that the Agrippan modes provide the format for one specific problem with which Hegel engages at the beginning of his *Logic*.

34. See *PH* I:170–77. This passage is held to be difficult to interpret, and the tendency has been to reject it as incoherent (see, for example, Barnes 1990: 114). A sophisticated reading is provided by Sienkiewicz (2019: 157–66), although even this discusses the interrelations only of four of the Five Modes, with the author finding the mode of relativity to be incompatible with the others.

35. See *PH* II:20, for example.

able things and intelligible things—a disagreement which is undecidable, since we cannot use either something perceivable or something intelligible as a criterion because anything we may take has been disputed and so is unconvincing.

And for the following reason they do not concede either that anything can be apprehended by means of something else. If that by means of which something is apprehended will itself always need to be apprehended by means of something else, they throw you into the reciprocal or infinite mode; and if you should want to assume that that by means of which another thing is apprehended is itself apprehended by means of itself, then this is countered by the fact that, for the above reasons, nothing is apprehended by means of itself. (*PH* I:178–79)

As I suggested earlier, I think that this can be read as a restatement of the alternatives of the trilemma located in the Five Modes.[36] The simplest way to express this is to suggest that the rejection of the possibility of apprehending something immediately, or by means of itself, corresponds to the application of the mode of hypothesis, while the rejection of the possibility of apprehending something mediately, or by means of something else, corresponds to the application of the modes of reciprocity and infinite regress. Just as the argument of the trilemma appeared to pose a problem for the justification of any claim whatsoever, here the Two Modes are held to "induce puzzlement about *everything*". However, there are two idiosyncrasies of the presentation of the Two Modes that must be addressed, although I shall attempt to do so as briefly as possible. The first of these is the apparent absence of the mode of hypothesis from the account of the Two Modes, and the second is the appeal to the problem of the criterion in the first of the Two. Happily, they can be dealt with together. My contention is that neither idiosyncrasy causes a problem for the claim that the Two Modes express the same kind of problem as the Five.

As stated, the first idiosyncrasy is that there is no explicit mention of the mode of hypothesis in the statement of the Two Modes. Instead, it looks as though Sextus references the mode of disagreement when rejecting the possibility of immediate knowledge. This might imply that if there is a trilemma present in the Two Modes, it consists of disagreement, reciprocity, and infinite regress.[37] Barnes considers this a weakness in the presentation of the Two Modes, complaining that 'they ignore the hypothetical mode—which . . . is a mode of the first importance to the Pyrrhonists' (Barnes 1990: 119). Of course, I agree with Barnes that the mode of hypothesis is of the first

---

36. Janáček goes further, suggesting that the presentation of the Two Modes provides the first genuinely systematic account of the use of the Agrippan modes: 'I believe that here is where we first find the model according to which the five loosely bound modes receive a logical order' (Janáček 2008: 176).

37. This is how it has commonly been taken. See, for example, Barnes 1990: 117–18, Woodruff 2010: 226, or Sienkiewicz 2019: 166.

importance. As I have sketched the epistemic regress problem earlier when discussing the Five Modes, the Agrippan modes function by drawing attention to the justificatory arbitrariness of claims, and it is the mode of hypothesis that most directly emphasises this. The modes of reciprocity and infinite regress, as I have portrayed them, function by stripping away the illusion of support, and rendering the claim in question indistinguishable from just another arbitrary hypothesis. In this sense, one might say, hypothesis is the most fundamental of the modes.

The tendency among interpreters of the Two Modes who have not been content to regard them as a flawed presentation of the Sceptic's arguments has been to connect Sextus' use of disagreement here to the matter of claims that are put forward as having some special foundational or self-supporting character, rather than being merely arbitrary hypotheses or relying on some other claims for their support. Specifically, the dominant interpretation of this passage is that while the modes of reciprocity and infinite regression function, in the second of the Two Modes, just as they do in the formula of the epistemic regress problem which one extracts from the Five Modes, the function of disagreement as it occurs in the first of the Two Modes is to introduce another, distinct problem: the problem of the criterion.[38] This is the second idiosyncrasy mentioned previously.

The problem of the criterion is a distinct problem from the epistemic regress problem. The latter targets the attempt to provide evidence in support of a claim, while the former targets the suggestion that a claim can be recognised as true because it is authorised by a criterion of truth.[39] Although they are different problems, however, they both make use of the three modes of the trilemma. Accordingly, I shall go on to suggest that both are instances of what I will call Agrippan problems. For now, though, I will provide a brief explanation of the problem of the criterion and explain why it is thought to be invoked in the context of the Two Modes.

Among the Sceptics' Dogmatic opponents, appealing to a criterion in order to argue that a particular claim was true without needing to support it with further evidence was a common strategy.[40] Whether the criterion in question is formulated in terms of the human subject making the claim, in terms of the relevant cognitive faculty, in terms of the nature of an appearance or argument which gives rise to a claim, or in terms of some other possibility, the general character of this procedure involves appealing to a criterion, where that criterion is a principle which can be used to distinguish truth from falsity.

---

38. Various versions of this interpretation have been defended. See, for example, Hankinson 1995: 189–91, Catapano 2017, or Sienkiewicz 2019: 167–77.
39. Here I am following Cling (2009: 333).
40. Sextus addresses various Dogmatic accounts of purported criteria of truth in *PH* II:48–79.

A good criterion, accordingly, is one that accurately sorts true claims from false ones.

The problem of the criterion works by questioning whether or not the criterion to which a Dogmatist has appealed in order to characterise a claim as one that can immediately be recognised to be true is, in fact, a good one, or why we should suppose that it accurately sorts true claims from false ones. As Sextus would put it, it prompts a disagreement about the criterion. It appears that the way in which one would justify the choice of a particular criterion is to refer to claims which are known to be true and which the criterion accurately sorts. These claims, of course, cannot be the same as the original claim, on pain of circularity or reciprocity. But if the Sceptic asks how it is that these other claims are known to be true, then the Dogmatist cannot appeal again to the same criterion, again on pain of circularity. Should the Dogmatist simply assert the validity of a particular claim *or* a particular criterion without being able to authorise or evidence it, then it is no more than an arbitrary hypothesis. And if the Dogmatist is forced to cycle through a non-repeating, never-ending sequence of claims and criteria, this is suggestive of an infinite regress. Sextus provides a brief statement of the problem of the criterion, explicitly referring it, as I have here, to the modes of the trilemma, in *PH* II:20.[41]

That Sextus is referring to his treatment of the problem of the criterion in the account of the Two Modes is clear from his account of the first of those modes. There, as I have already indicated, he suggests that a disagreement about something that is held to be apprehended by means of itself, be it a matter of perception or of thought, will be undecidable, 'since we cannot use either something perceivable or something intelligible as a criterion because anything we may take has been disputed and so is unconvincing' (*PH* I:178).

Clearly, the text here suggests that the challenge from the Sceptic to the Dogmatist who holds that a certain claim can be apprehended by means of itself in virtue of the fact that it is authorised by what they suppose to be the criterion of truth, is to inquire into the reasons for accepting that criterion. The argument will be that the case for the criterion will result in an undecidable disagreement because the Sceptic will refer the case to the modes of the trilemma in exactly the manner sketched above. If the disagreement surrounding the criterion is undecidable, we have no compelling reason to accept that the

---

41. 'In order for the dispute that has arisen about criteria to be decided, we must possess an agreed criterion through which we can judge it; and in order for us to possess an agreed criterion, the despite about criteria must already have been decided. Thus the argument falls into the reciprocal mode and the discovery of a criterion is blocked—for we do not allow them to assume a criterion by hypothesis, and if they want to judge the criterion by a[nother] criterion we throw them into an infinite regress.'

Again, since a proof needs a criterion which has been proved and a criterion needs a proof which has been judged, they are thrown into the reciprocal mode' (*PH* II:20).

claim in question is, in fact, a genuinely self-supporting or foundational one. This account, coupled with the more straightforward applications of the modes of reciprocity and infinite regress in the case of things which are held to be apprehended by means of something else, constitutes the dominant interpretation of the manner in which the Two Modes are held "to induce puzzlement about everything", or to prompt one to a suspension of judgement over any given claim. It seems to me to make good sense of the text of the *Outlines*.

I think that it is worth emphasising that, in the application of the problem of the criterion to what is put forward as self-supporting claims, it becomes clear that the mode of hypothesis is not, in fact, absent from the system of the Two Modes in Sextus since the text of *PH* II:20 explicitly makes use of it.[42]

In addition, the suggestion might be made that the mode of hypothesis is also more directly implicit in the statement of the first of the Two Modes because, if the claim in question were indeed merely an arbitrary assertion, it would obviously be in equipollent opposition to any incompatible alternative.[43] The only kind of unsupported claim that therefore needs dealing with is the kind which is alleged to have a special, foundational status which distinguishes it from a merely arbitrary assertion, and so it is this kind of claim which receives focus in the statement of the mode. This strikes me as a plausible reading, but even if it were to be rejected, the mode of hypothesis is still present (a) in the invocation of the problem of the criterion in the first of the Two Modes as we have just seen in that, and (b) at least according to the interpretation I offered earlier, the modes of reciprocity and infinite regress operate by showing that apparently supported claims are, in fact, indistinguishable from arbitrary hypotheses. It would be a mistake, therefore, to suppose that the mode of hypothesis is absent from the Two Modes.

It seems clear then that the Sceptics making use of the Two Modes intended them to target both claims put forward on the basis of other claims, and those put forward as self-supporting, and thereby to cause trouble for justification in general, in a manner that contemporary epistemologists would categorise as an application of the epistemic regress problem. It also seems, on the basis of the text of Sextus' *Outlines*, that their preferred methodology for targeting putatively self-supporting claims was to invoke a different problem, the problem of the criterion, in order to supplement their application of the epistemic regress problem. I do not intend to raise any criticisms about this procedure here. However, if it were to be suggested, on the basis of the account of the Two Modes, that a supplementary appeal to the problem of the criterion is *required* in order for a Sceptic applying the epistemic regress problem to

---

42. This point is also common to the accounts of the Two Modes, which I have labelled the dominant interpretation. See Hankinson 1995: 191, Catapano 2017: 117, and Sienkiewicz 2019: 171–72.
43. See Hankinson 1995: 189–90, for a suggestion to this effect.

arrive at a suspension of judgement in the face of a claim which is held to be foundational or self-supporting, then I would disagree.

I would instead like to suggest a simpler reading of the Two Modes: one that need not commit the Sceptic simultaneously to appeal to two different problems in order to ensure the strength of their procedure. The suggestion is that the Two Modes can be thought of as a straightforward restatement of the modes of the trilemma but this time as a dilemma.[44] Here, the reference to the undecidable dispute in the account of the first of the Two Modes indicates that undecidable dispute is always possible in the case of something that has been put forward without any support since such a claim is indistinguishable from an arbitrary assertion, even if the Dogmatist making the claim claims that it is somehow immediately known or foundational. Therefore, the first mode, which states that nothing can be apprehended by means of itself, really expresses the mode of hypothesis, since, as Sextus says elsewhere, 'nothing ought to be assumed all by itself' (*AL* II:373). The second mode, which states that nothing can be apprehended by means of something else, problematises any support that might be provided, by pushing that support either toward reciprocity *or* towards an infinite regress. The Two Modes, therefore, express a dilemma between the arbitrariness of an unsupported claim and the arbitrariness of fundamentally inadequate attempts at support.

I think that this account is suggested by *PH* II:85, which, as Karel Janáček points out, is an instance of the application of the Two Modes to Dogmatic disputes concerning the existence of truths.[45]

> There is a disagreement about truths among the Dogmatists; for some say that some things are true, and some that nothing is true. And it is not possible to decide the disagreement; for if you say that some things are true, you will not be found convincing if you say it without proof . . . and if you actually want to bring a proof . . . if you say that the proof is true you fall into the reciprocal argument and in addition you will be asked for a proof of the fact that it is true—and another proof for that, and so on *ad infinitum*. (*PH* II:85)

This simplified application of the Two Modes does seem amenable to the idea that the disagreement here is a symptom of the presence of arbitrary hypothesis. It also avoids necessitating an additional discussion of the problem of the criterion in the case of the first mode.[46]

---

44. To this extent, the account of the Two Modes might be said to anticipate Kajamies' claim that the epistemic regress problem can be expressed, at its simplest, as a "duo" (Kajamies 2009: 533–34).
45. See Janáček 2008: 180.
46. This is not to dispute the dominant interpretation of *PH* I:178–79, which ties the first of the Two Modes to the problem of the criterion. It is merely to suggest that, at least on one occasion in Sextus' works, he appears to apply the Two Modes in this more straightforward manner, without needing to invoke a second problem.

On the basis of this discussion of the Agrippan modes, it seems to me that the most important kind of sceptical problem that we inherit from Sextus, and the Pyrrhonian Sceptical tradition can be expressed at its simplest in terms of a dilemma, as it is in the case of the Two Modes. On the one hand, one confronts the apparent arbitrariness of a claim that is made without any support and, on the other hand, the apparent arbitrariness of a claim whose support can be shown to be fundamentally inadequate. And in fact, in the account just provided, I have already discussed two distinct problems which appeal to this dilemma: the epistemic regress problem and the problem of the criterion.[47]

I will call these problems which share the same structure, derived from the Agrippan modes, "Agrippan problems". And the epistemic regress problem and the problem of the criterion are not, I think, the only two. Before going further, however, I would like to briefly address a matter of terminology. I am by no means the first person to notice that different problems make use of the Agrippan modes. Howard Sankey, for example, suggests that the problem of the criterion is an instance of 'a more general form . . . sometimes known as *Agrippa's Trilemma*' (Sankey 2011: 562). I am not inclined to adopt this usage because, as I have already noted, the same term is often used to refer specifically to the epistemic regress problem.[48] Andrew Cling offers an excellent analysis of the epistemic regress problem and the problem of the criterion and suggests that they are both instances of what he refers to as 'the paradox of reasons' (Cling 2009: 338), where this term indicates various problems concerning justification which force one towards the Agrippan modes. In light of this Pyrrhonian heritage, I refer to problems of this kind simply as "Agrippan problems".

Cling also, accurately, in my view, indicates that the epistemic regress problem and the problem of the criterion do not exhaust the range of Agrippan problems. He suggests that such problems might target proposals for 'evidence that a proposition is true; a criterion of truth that sanctions a belief . . . an epistemic principle that implies that a belief would be a case of knowledge or justified belief; an account of how the state of affairs described by a

---

47. Although things are simpler with the epistemic regress problem, the problem of the criterion can also be expressed in terms of a dilemma: either (a) a particular claim *or* a particular criterion is asserted merely arbitrarily, or (b) inadequate attempts are made to authorise claims and criteria, where those attempts result in circular or infinitely regressive reasoning which ultimately provide no real authorisation.

48. One might also be uncomfortable with insisting on the "trilemma" formulation; on the one hand, because, as I have suggested in light of my reading of the Two Modes, it might, at its simplest, be expressed as a dilemma, and on the other hand because the sheer variety of responses to the epistemic regress problem that have now been developed by epistemologists can render the term "trilemma" rather misleading (Aikin [2011: 46], for example, suggests that it might, in fact, be a '*hexalemma*').

proposition is possible; factors that would make a belief valuable whether or not it is true, likely to be true, or reasonably believed to be true . . . ' (Cling 2009: 338). And it is worth noting that Agrippan problems are not confined to epistemology. The same troubling alternatives of an arbitrary "foundation" or endless repeating or non-repeating grounds occur in the context of metaphysical explanation, both historical and contemporary.[49] Still another example of an Agrippan problem, I think, occurs in what is sometimes described as the "paradox of autonomy" in the context of discussions of Kant's moral philosophy. This problem concerns Kant's case for understanding the moral law as something that is arrived at as an act of self-legislation rather than being some ready-made source of authority that is externally imposed on humanity by nature or by God. The difficulty, roughly, is that if the moral law is something that one has a *reason* to impose on oneself, then it seems that its authority derives precisely not from self-legislation but from the reasons to which one appeals in order to justify it (which must themselves be justified, etc.), but, on the other hand, if no reason can be given for imposing the moral law, then its self-imposition looks merely arbitrary in a way which would seem to undermine the authority Kant clearly attributes to it.[50]

Agrippan problems, then, seem to crop up across various philosophical disciplines and historical periods, in a manner that presumably would not greatly surprise Sextus, who thinks that 'every object of inquiry can be referred to these [Agrippan] modes' (*PH* I:169). As I have already indicated, I think that Hegel's problem of beginning, too, is best understood as a distinctive Agrippan problem, but the articulation of this claim must wait until Hegel's engagement with Pyrrhonism and the history of the problem of beginning have been introduced over the remainder of this chapter and the next.

I think that it is worth ending this section with a brief sketch of the structure of an Agrippan problem, in order to bring out the hallmarks of their characteristic dilemma more clearly and to indicate the kinds of responses to which they typically give rise. This should facilitate easier comparison between Agrippan problems. In Section 3.2, I will present Hegel's problem of beginning according to the same model, in order to support the interpretative claim that it should be understood as an Agrippan problem as well. Such a model

---

49. Franks (2005: 19, n.11) suggests that the Agrippan modes occur in both epistemological and metaphysical variants in Schelling's 1795 *Of the I as the Principle of Philosophy*, for example. Schaffer 2009 includes a prominent contemporary defence of metaphysical foundationalism, while Cameron 2022 explores the viability of forms of metaphysical infinitism and holism. Where Hegel stands on this matter is subject to ongoing dispute. His remarks about the Concept as '*absolute foundation*' (*WL* 508/6:245) suggest to me that he endorses a *kind* of metaphysical foundationalism, but such interpretations have recently come under a lot of pressure from Kreines (2015: 24-25, 258-65). I cannot address these arguments here.

50. See Kleingeld and Willaschek 2019: 2–4, for a good summary of work on the Kantian "paradox of autonomy".

involves presenting an Agrippan problem in the form of three propositions, all of which are *prima facie* attractive but jointly incompatible. The specific Agrippan problem I will present here is the epistemic regress problem, and the model follows, in simplified form, Cling's (2009: 334) presentation. The three propositions are as follows:

(R1) It is possible that there is some claim which is supported by another claim.
(R2) Supporting claims must themselves be supported.
(R3) Infinite regresses of supporting claims, whether repeating or non-repeating, do not provide genuine support.

Although any two of these propositions are compatible, it should be clear that all three taken together are not. Accordingly, it is necessary to reject one of them. The major approaches to the epistemic regress problem follow this strategy and are reasonably well-known. One can reject (R1), which amounts to scepticism. Sextus, as I have shown earlier, rejects (R1) in a carefully undogmatic fashion, contending that no claim that the Sceptics have yet inquired into has, in fact, been genuinely supported.[51] If one does not wish to adopt a Sceptical position, one faces a dilemma: one can reject (R2) and hold that some specific claims can be immediately known, without support from elsewhere, or one can reject (R3) and hold that either that circular chains of evidence or non-circular, infinitely regressing chains of evidence can, in fact, offer genuine support.[52]

1.1.4 Summary

In the foregoing discussion of Pyrrhonism on its own terms, I have defended the following principal interpretative claims: firstly, I have suggested that the Sceptical way of life as it is presented by Sextus has as its primary component a particular model of inquiry, centred on the construction of equipollent arguments for opposing claims. Secondly, I have claimed that this model of inquiry is rooted in the Sceptics' attempt to believe only what it is rational to believe, and the attempt to relieve the disturbance they feel at the prospect

---

51. That the Pyrrhonian Sceptics endorse (R2) is clear from Sextus' expression of the first of the Two Modes (or the mode of hypothesis from the Five). That they endorse (R3) is clear from the second of the Two Modes (or the modes of reciprocity and infinite regress from the Five).
52. Another response worth mentioning here is to set out the dilemma—reject (R2) or (R3)—and then refuse to accept the exclusive disjunction. Thus Haack (1993) and, more recently, Aikin (2011) have, in different ways, attempted to solve the epistemic regress problem by suggesting that genuine support must combine immediacy and the provision of further reasons. As I shall suggest in Section 3.3.1, rejecting the exclusive disjunction in the dilemma will also be key to Hegel's solution to the Agrippan problem under investigation in this book: the problem of beginning.

of believing incorrectly. Thirdly, I have argued that the reason that Sceptical inquiry results in suspension of judgement about every topic, so that the Sceptics hold no beliefs, is that they find that, in the course of their inquiries, cases for opposing claims always turn out to be equipollent. Fourthly, I have shown that the means by which the Sceptics carried out these inquiries are the various sets of modes and spent some time showing that the Agrippan modes function by showing that any claim which is put forward as being justified can, in fact, be shown to be merely arbitrary. Finally, I have suggested that the Agrippan modes can be combined to form a number of different "Agrippan problems", the defining characteristic of which is a dilemma between a merely arbitrary assertion and the arbitrariness of a claim which appeals to other material for its justification but where this justification is ultimately unsatisfactory.

I turn now to a discussion of Hegel's engagement with Sextus and the Pyrrhonian Sceptical tradition, in order to further prepare the ground for a reading of the beginning of his *Logic*, which emphasises the Pyrrhonian nature of the problem with which he grapples there.

1.2 HEGEL AND PYRRHONISM

There are, I think, three "Pyrrhonisms" in Hegel's work, at least in principle separable from one another, even if they are not always clearly distinguished in his texts. Firstly, there is Hegel's engagement with what he takes to be the essential aspects of Sceptical argumentation: the "principle of scepticism", which claims that "to every argument an equally convincing argument can be opposed", the "abstract" nature of this opposition, the various modes by which the Sceptics bring about this equipollent result, their extensive work in producing such oppositions across the scope of the various philosophical and extra-philosophical disciplines, and the result of their inquiry in suspension of judgement about everything. This aspect of Hegel's engagement with Pyrrhonism is at work not only in his various explicit engagements with the Sceptical tradition, but also in discussion of Scepticism in the introduction to the *Phenomenology*, his characterisation of the negative or dialectical moment of the account of speculative thought which is essential to his *Logic*, and, more specifically, as I shall go on to argue, his approach to the problem of beginning at the start of the *Logic*. This aspect of Pyrrhonian Scepticism is especially important for Hegel since, as I shall detail in Section 1.2.1, he takes it to have the resources to rebut any metaphysical claim not made from the position of a genuinely "speculative" philosophy, of the kind that he himself endorses.

Secondly, in "On the Relationship of Scepticism to Philosophy", and at greater length in his *Lectures on the History of Philosophy*, Hegel provides a fuller account of historical Pyrrhonism as he understands it. This account includes the argumentative material just mentioned but also situates it in the context of a particular historical configuration of spirit's understanding of itself, its freedom, and its relation to objects, the central aspect of which, as Hegel sees it, is the individual Sceptic's rejection of any account of objective reality composed of determinate, fixed objects, in favour of an account only of appearances, in which the only certainty is of oneself as a perceiving subject before whom things appear, only to be negated by opposing appearances (*VGP* 460–61/19:358–59).[53] The argumentative material can clearly be separated from this broader account of Pyrrhonian Scepticism, however, as Hegel's discussions of it in the *Phenomenology* and the *Logic* demonstrate. Indeed, Hegel himself seems to make such a distinction when he describes Scepticism in this broader sense as an unappealing 'paralysis . . . an incapacity for truth which can only come to certainty of itself' (*VGP* 460/19:359), with which he contrasts the argumentative content of Scepticism as a '*thinking* scepticism', which 'is quite another thing . . . it is the demonstration, of everything determinate and finite, that it is unstable' (*VGP* 460-61/19:359), a project in principle quite independent of this subjective "paralysis" to which historical Pyrrhonism lends itself, in Hegel's opinion.

Thirdly, the course of the argument of the *Phenomenology* also includes the examination of a specific shape of consciousness that Hegel calls 'scepticism' (*PhG* §202–6/3:159–63). This shape is so named because of the resemblance elements of it bear to historical Pyrrhonism as Hegel understands it. Its treatment, however, occurs in the context of the immanent criticism of various shapes of consciousness, none of which is Hegel's own position. And since the *Phenomenology* is also not a work of history of philosophy, for all that Hegel draws on historical resources in his treatment of consciousness, one also should not presume that the "scepticism" of the *Phenomenology* is identical to Hegel's own understanding of historical Pyrrhonian Scepticism. The shape of scepticism in the *Phenomenology* occupies a specific place in the development of the "Self-Consciousness" chapter, where it names a shape of consciousness that views the objects of its cognition merely as 'vanishing magnitudes' (*PhG* §202/3:160), observing the ways in which claims about objects in earlier shapes of consciousness had tended to be negated and coming to abandon the making of such claims altogether in favour of an attitude

---

53. Hegel is following Sextus to some extent here, who famously claims that 'the standard of the Sceptical way of life is what is apparent' (*PH* I:22). I have not discussed this aspect of Sextus' presentation of Pyrrhonism in any great detail in the account above, although it is undeniably important. I justify the omission on the grounds that the sketch of Pyrrhonism presented above emphasises those elements which are most significant for Hegel's engagement with Sceptical argumentation, and that this element does not strike me as so very crucial for those aspects of Sceptical argumentation upon which I have focused. See Forster 1989:14-16, for some discussion of Hegel's attitude towards this aspect of Sextus' Pyrrhonism.

of undisturbedness (*ataraxia*), which it takes to constitute its freedom (*PhG* §203–05/3:160–63). This sceptical shape of consciousness, Hegel suggests, is certain only of itself, in distinction to the flux of equally valid opposing claims it thinks can be made about the world around us. Hegel will go on to illustrate that this self-certainty, since it ultimately consists in nothing other than the very awareness of the array of mutually negating appearances it perceives around it, undermines its own undisturbedness and 'goes back and forth from the one extreme of self-equal self-consciousness to the other of contingent, confused, and confusing consciousness', with the contradiction between the two ultimately giving rise to what Hegel calls 'the unhappy consciousness' (*PhG* §205-06/3:163), but a discussion of this material falls beyond the purview of this book.[54]

The "Pyrrhonism" most relevant to the argument of this book is, unsurprisingly, the first of the three just elaborated, and Hegel's remarks on this topic will receive the most attention in the remainder of this chapter and this book as a whole. To the extent that Hegel's broader assessment of Pyrrhonian Scepticism as a historical philosophical movement is also relevant to his assessment of the strengths and weaknesses of Sceptical lines of thought relevant to the problem of beginning it will also receive some attention, but not a great deal. The third "Pyrrhonism"—the specifically sceptical shape of consciousness examined in the "Self-Consciousness" chapter of the *Phenomenology*—for all that it clearly exhibits elements which reflect Hegel's understanding of Pyrrhonian Scepticism, occurs in a context that seems to me to be sufficiently far removed from the concerns of this book that I have chosen not to discuss it at all in what follows.

In the remainder of this chapter, I will do two things. Firstly, I will discuss what seem to me to be the crucial aspects of Hegel's philosophical engagement with Pyrrhonism, particularly with its distinctive form of inquiry involving the Agrippan modes. Secondly, I will briefly address the development that takes place in Hegel's appreciation of the challenge offered to speculative philosophy by Pyrrhonian Scepticism, between his 1802 essay "On the Relationship of Scepticism to Philosophy", his *Phenomenology*, and his mature, systematic works.

1.2.1 Key Aspects of Hegel's Understanding of Pyrrhonian Inquiry

Striking across Hegel's various engagements with Pyrrhonian Scepticism is his interpretation of what Sextus called 'the principle of Scepticism' in *PH*

---

54. See Röttges 1987: 31-57, Stewart 2000: 142-64, or Gabriel 2009: 170-82, for example, for discussions of the sceptical shape of consciousness in the *Phenomenology*.

I:12: 'opposed to every argument is an equal argument'.[55] Hegel accords this principle a central role in his interpretation of Pyrrhonism in both "On the Relationship of Scepticism to Philosophy" (*VSP* 325/2:230) and the *Lectures on the History of Philosophy* (*VGP* 468/19:372-73), and takes it to cause real problems for philosophical, and especially metaphysical claims that are not arrived at by an exercise of specifically speculative reason, of the kind Hegel himself elaborates in his own works.

Sextus, as I have indicated in Section 1.1.2, is careful to insist that this principle is not the expression of a general law about opposing claims and determinations, but rather merely a report of the results of every inquiry the Sceptics have conducted so far. Hegel, however, tends to treat it precisely as Sextus does not, calling it 'something universal' (*VGP* 469/19:374). He thus takes the various Sceptical phrases to be expressions of a general and secure position on the nature of claims to which an apparently incompatible claim can be opposed, suggesting that, in such circumstances, 'Scepticism ... proves with certainty the untruth [of all opposing claims]' (*VGP* 462/19:362).[56]

In translating what, for Sextus, is at most a reliably reached result after the application of the Sceptical modes to a particular set of opposing claims, into a general principle about all possible such oppositions, Hegel finds in Pyrrhonism confirmation of a view that he himself endorses: that claims and thought-determinations, understood from a certain "ordinary" or "natural" perspective as fixed and "finite" in terms of their meaning and their implications, and compared "externally" with one another in order to see whether they are compatible, ultimately drive one to a sceptical conclusion about their truth. Hegel expresses this view in the following manner:

> [O]rdinary understanding or ordinary consciousness ... holds fast to the given, the fact, the finite (whether this finite is called "appearance" or "concept") ... the Sceptical modes show ordinary consciousness the instability of such certainties ... Scepticism likewise calls upon appearances and finite things for help, and from their diversity and the equal right of all of them to count as valid, from out of the antinomy to be discerned in the finite itself, it discerns their untruth. (*VSP* 332/2:240)

---

55. As Forster (1989: 65, n.5) points out, Sextus does not always require that there be *arguments* for there to be an equipollent opposition. Merely immediately asserted opposing propositions would also constitute an equipollent opposition.

56. In fairness to Hegel, while his tendency is to treat this principle as a universal principle, he does occasionally acknowledge that Sextus himself does not quite take it this way. It seems that, in Hegel's eyes, this caution on Sextus' part, in his insistence on supplementing such principles with "it seems to me, for every claim I have examined so far", or similar caveats, is evidence of a "sickening" pedantry and timidity on the Sceptic's behalf, and should not be accepted (see *VSP* 338/2:249, for example).

With this talk of taking opposing claims as "finite", or "one-sided", as he often puts it, Hegel is characterising the ordinary tendency to suppose that concepts and claims exclude one another so that something is either finite, or infinite, for example, but cannot be both at once.[57] Holding hard and fast to the assumption that such exclusive conceptual oppositions, 'the strict either/ or' (*EL* §32Z), accurately capture the structure of all thought, Hegel thinks, will always invite a sceptical rebuttal of the case for whichever side of the opposition one holds to, and a demonstration that the cases for the two sides are equipollent.

In his discussion of the Sceptic's principle of equipollence, however, Hegel is not only going beyond Sextus by taking the principle to have a universal scope. He is also suggesting that it indicates a kind of metaphysical position to which the Sceptics are, in his opinion, committed.[58] This claim, clearly present in the passage just quoted, to the effect that the objects which are thought of or which appear to us exhibit an "instability", or are themselves "antinomial", effectively attributes to Pyrrhonism a metaphysics of flux, whereby the objects of cognition are understood to be indeterminate or constantly shifting, with this metaphysical claim offering an explanation as to why any attempt to judge some object as *this*, not *that*, will be vulnerable to a sceptical rebuttal.

A curious feature of this reading is that it is quite possible that earlier Sceptics, whose works are mostly lost to us, may have thought something similar to the position Hegel ascribes to Sextus. The "Aristocles passage", in which Pyrrho is asked about the nature of things, is famously ambiguous concerning whether his answer is a metaphysical claim about the indeterminacy and instability of things, or a more recognisably "Sceptical" claim about the indeterminacy and instability of our attempts to know about the nature of things.[59] A similar ambiguity can be found in what we know of Aenesidemus' characterisation of Scepticism.[60] What is clear, however, is that Sextus

---

57. It is worth acknowledging that while Sextus, for the most part at least (there is a question about oppositions between "objects"), seems to consider equipollent oppositions only between items with propositional form, Hegel takes Scepticism to apply to concepts or categories themselves. I will not be addressing the topic of how it is that Hegel's logical work addresses concepts on their own terms, prior to incorporating them in judgements, here.

58. In fact, Hegel seems to suggest that the principle of Scepticism, understood in a metaphysical context, runs directly counter to a metaphysical statement of the principle of non-contradiction (see *VSP* 325/2:230). This is a peculiar reading indeed, since nothing in Sextus' discussion of equipollent opposing claims suggests that the appropriate response in the face of such claims is to take both to be true, rather than just suspending judgement and continuing to inquire. I will take no stand here on whether or not Hegel is best understood as genuinely rejecting the principle of non-contradiction, taken as a metaphysical, or semantic, or logical principle. See Ficara 2021, 137–41, 189–93, for a good discussion of this topic in relation to Hegel's engagement with Scepticism.

59. See Bett 2018: §3, for a good overview of this ambiguity.

60. See Hankison 2010: 115–17, for a brief discussion of the relationship between Aenesidemus' Scepticism and Heraclitean metaphysics.

explicitly rejects precisely the attribution of this kind of metaphysics to the Sceptics (*PH* I:210–12).⁶¹

Hegel's take on the Sceptic's tendency to find equipollent cases for and against opposing claims may differ, then, in a number of ways, from Sextus' own conception of "the principle of Scepticism", but his account of how it is that the Sceptics conduct their inquiry and demonstrate the validity of this principle, on the other hand, is much closer to Sextus. He clearly recognises that the various Sceptical modes are the primary means by which the Pyrrhonists reach their sceptical conclusions. And he also seems to acknowledge that it is the Agrippan modes in particular that are especially wide-ranging and effective when it comes to this task. He takes them to 'proceed against . . . scientific categories [and] against the thinking of the sensuous, against the determination of the latter through concepts' (*VGP* 470/19:375), and as early as 1802, he concludes that 'there are no more suitable weapons against dogmatism' (*VSP* 335/2:245).⁶²

Hegel is also clearly in agreement with the case I made in Section 1.1.3 for understanding the Two Modes as a simple, dilemmatic expression of the systematic application of the Agrippan modes, remarking that 'one sees that they are nothing new, but rather the preceding [Five Modes], brought to a more general form' (*VSP* 335/2:244). And in fact, when Hegel characterises what he sees as the fundamental vulnerability of all non-speculative metaphysics to the argument of the Five Modes, he expresses this 'deficiency' as '(α) in part the demonstration,—[which regresses] into the infinite; (β) in part the presuppositions,—[an alleged] immediate knowledge' (*VGP* 479/19:388). I think that this dilemma is clearly that expressed in the Two Modes, as I have explicated them earlier.⁶³ It suggests that a claim or a conception is defended either as an instance of immediate knowledge, for which no support is offered, and which is thus indistinguishable from an arbitrary assertion, or else

---

61. Hegel does, in fact, distinguish the metaphysical position he attributes to Scepticism from earlier ancient Greek philosophers who are taken to endorse a metaphysics of flux and indeterminacy, but not, as Sextus does, by distinguishing the merely epistemological nature of the Sceptics' claims from any metaphysical interpretation. Rather Hegel emphasises that, for the Sceptics as he understands them, the objects which are so unstable and indeterminate are to be understood as appearances, or only for self-consciousness (see *VGP* 460-64/19:358-64, for example). This is not to suggest that such appearances are of "things in themselves" whose nature might be quite different, but rather that reality itself is understood as being for self-consciousness, according to the Sceptics as Hegel understands them. The metaphysics he attributes to them therefore has the character of a "subjective idealism".

62. Röttges (1987: 117-57) seems to suggest that each of the Five Modes is reconfigured in Hegel's general refutation of Pyrrhonian Scepticism. I cannot discuss this intriguing idea here, however, since Hegel's more general answer to the Sceptic is not at stake here but rather only his solution to the problem of beginning. Readers interested in Hegel's broader refutation of Scepticism should also consider Trisokkas 2012: Chs.8–12, which claims to discover such a refutation in Hegel's treatment of judgement in the *Science of Logic*.

63. This becomes clearer if one remembers that Hegel always renders Sextus' "hypothesis" as "presupposition" (*Voraussetzung*), as I mentioned earlier.

it is defended as an instance of mediated knowledge, held on the basis of other claims or conceptions which support it but where this support turns out to be infinitely postponed, in circular or non-circular fashion, and thus fails to offer any real support at all, leaving it also indistinguishable from an arbitrary assertion. It is this kind of dilemma, characteristic of what I have called Agrippan problems, which forms the most powerful argumentative tool of the Sceptics, as Hegel reads them.

A careful reader of Sextus will most likely object both to Hegel's tendency to take the principle of equipollence to be universal, and to attribute to it a metaphysical significance, if not to his appreciation of the significance and power of the Agrippan modes. But I am not principally interested in criticising Hegel's reading of Sextus here so much as in exploring its significance for his own thought. And the really striking thing about the features of Hegel's construal of Sceptical inquiry examined so far is that they indicate that Hegel takes Pyrrhonism to accomplish one of the tasks that he himself sets out to achieve in his Objective Logic: the task of providing a thoroughgoing critique of all "abstract" accounts of fundamental logical and metaphysical categories, which I first mentioned in Section 0.1.[64]

This critical project is directed at any philosophical approach which, in Hegel's view, constrains its activity to the kind of thinking which he labels "understanding" (*Verstand*), where this indicates the grasping of some content as something determinate, and holding fast to this conception 'and its distinctness over against others' (*EL* §80), so that one can see which other contents it is compatible and incompatible with, and use these to conceptually carve up the world accordingly. Hegel is, of course, not opposed to the activity of understanding, seeing it on the contrary as one of the essential '*moments* of every *logical reality* . . . every concept or every truth' (*EL* §79A). His criticism is directed at philosophical projects which are restricted *only* to understanding, thereby ignoring what Hegel takes to be the two other crucial forms to which pure thought can lend itself, as well as the possibilities for logic and metaphysics which he takes to accompany these forms. These additional two forms properly belong to the kind of thinking Hegel labels "reason" (*Vernunft*).[65] The first of these is negation, which Hegel describes

---

64. In the Introduction to his *Logic*, Hegel, considering the traditional task of metaphysics to grasp the fundamental nature of being by means of a system of categories or thought-determinations, claims that his Objective Logic is 'the true critique of such determinations' (*WL* 42/5:62). Hegel claims explicitly that his logic accomplishes the same task as a completed scepticism in *EL* §78A. Forster (1989: 37) also addresses the overlap that Hegel sees between these two projects.

65. In the context of the account of the mind that Hegel offers in the *Philosophy of Spirit*, these forms of thinking could be discussed as faculties (*EG* §467), but I follow Nuzzo (2010: 12–17) in thinking that this is inappropriate in the context of the *Logic*, the subject matter of which is more abstract, being concerned with forms of possible thought in general, considered a priori, rather than with the specifics of the human mind.

as the 'dialectical' moment of logic, whereby a thought-determination is confronted with its opposite (*EL* §81). The second is the unifying of opposing determinations in a higher concept which contains within itself the opposition of the previous ones. Hegel calls this the '*speculative* or '*positively rational*' moment of logic (*EL* §82).[66] The higher, opposition-encompassing concept to which such thinking gives rise can again be grasped in isolation by the understanding, and so, roughly, Hegel's Objective Logic proceeds, until Hegel takes himself to have arrived at the concept of "the Concept", 'which contains all the earlier determinations of thought as sublated within itself' (*EL* §160Z), whereupon both the critical task of exposing the limitations of the one-sided or merely "intellectual" (*verständig*) grasp of the categories, and the positive task of exhibiting the categories and their relations of mutual implication and negation in systematic form have been accomplished.[67]

In fact, what Hegel calls the second moment of logic—negation—can, it seems, be considered either from the perspective of reason or from that of the understanding. In the case of the former, "dialectical reason", one category, "finitude", for example, considered on its own terms, is found to imply or immanently give rise to its opposite: "infinity".[68] In this context, Hegel calls the dialectic 'the moving soul of the scientific progression' (*EL* §81A). In the case of the latter, however, the negative moment, Hegel thinks, 'constitutes *Scepticism*' (*EL* §81). In this case, the opposing category does not emerge immanently from the consideration of the first, but instead, the first category is held fixed, and another, incompatible concept is introduced "externally", with the usual Sceptical method of showing that equally good cases can be made for assenting to either conception by appeal to the modes. The method of negation differs between Scepticism and Hegel's Objective Logic, then, but he is clearly of the opinion that both projects can, in principle, be carried out exhaustively, so that all logical categories are examined and criticised, either in Sceptical or dialectically and speculatively rational fashion. Hence, he describes Scepticism as amounting to 'the dialectic of all that is determinate',

---

66. Hegel famously uses the term "sublation" (*Aufhebung*) to refer to this overcoming and, at the same time, preserving of a conceptual opposition. He discusses his use of this term in *WL* 81-82/5:113-15. What I provide in this section is, of course, only a very rough sketch of Hegel's use of *Verstand*, *Vernunft* and the role of *Aufhebung* in the methodology of his science of logic. A more thorough examination of these topics belongs to a study which has as its focus the methodology of Hegel's *Logic*, according to which it proceeds after its beginning, while this study is focused merely on that beginning.

67. I should briefly note here that I endorse the usual provisos accompanying such a schematic presentation of the procedure of Hegel's *Logic*: i.e., that it does not represent a "method" in its own right which can be brought to bear on any content one chooses but from which it is itself distinct, and that such presentations are properly understood only as characterising in general terms the kind of transitions to which the content of logic—the categories—themselves have given rise, described retrospectively after the investigation.

68. See *WL* 101–20/5:139–66, for Hegel's account of the emergence of the concept of the (qualitative) infinite from the concept of finitude.

and as effectively 'directed against the thought of the understanding, which lets determinate differences count as ultimate' (*VGP* 461/19:359–60), just as his own logic is.[69]

This suggestion, to the effect that Pyrrhonian Scepticism accomplishes, in an alternative manner, the critical task of the Objective Logic, is borne out by some of Hegel's remarks about the Agrippan modes. In his *Lectures on the History of Philosophy*, Hegel states that the Sceptics' use of the Agrippan modes demonstrate 'an awareness of the categories—a high awareness' (*VGP* 477/19:388). Later on, he goes further, suggesting that,

> It does Scepticism credit, to have arrived at this awareness of the negative and to have so determinately thought the forms of the negative . . . These modes turn on the Concept, the essence of determinateness itself, and are exhaustive against the determinate. (*VGP* 480/19:394)

Here Hegel is stating explicitly that an exhaustive Sceptical inquiry accomplishes the same as the critical task of the Objective Logic: the complete negation of all one-sided conceptions of determinate categories. This is not to say, however, that he takes Scepticism also to accomplish the positive task of the Objective Logic, i.e., of elaborating a system of categories, showing how higher concepts unify oppositions between earlier ones, nor of arriving at the Concept as the totality in which all finite concepts are grounded. This is to say that although, as I have indicated, Hegel does attribute a kind of metaphysical position, having as one of its corollaries the critique of one-sided conceptions of the categories, to the Sceptics, it is clearly not the same position as the speculative metaphysics founded on the Concept which he himself develops and endorses, even though the latter has the very same corollary.[70] Instead, the only conclusions that Hegel takes the Sceptics to draw from the metaphysics of indeterminacy which he attributes to them are merely negative: suspension of judgement about any particular claim made about the world, and perhaps an attitude of undisturbedness accompanying this suspension.

I think that the fact that Hegel takes Pyrrhonian inquiry, conducted exhaustively, to accomplish one side of the project of his Objective Logic, and to do so also by means of negation, albeit understood only from the perspective of the understanding, is behind his frequent claims to the effect that his speculative philosophical project in the *Logic* contains, in some sense, Scepticism within itself. Thus he will claim, for example, that 'the logical Concept is itself just as much this dialectic, for the true knowledge of the idea is this negativity,

---

69. Hegel goes on to say that 'The rational, as known [i.e., by logical thinking], does the same against the determinate as what Scepticism wants to do' (*VGP* 482/19:397).

70. Of course, Hegel's own metaphysics also does not construe all of its objects only as appearances, as he takes the metaphysics which he attributes to the Sceptics to do.

which is just as much native to Scepticism' (*VGP* 461/19:360). And as early as 1802, Hegel is characterising the philosophical project that he is developing as 'a philosophy which is neither Scepticism nor Dogmatism, and is thus both at once' (*VSP* 322-23/2:227). Put straightforwardly, Hegel's claim here seems to be that everything that is of value in Pyrrhonian inquiry is also accomplished by his own speculative philosophical project, but that the latter *also* provides a positive, systematic, logical, and metaphysical science.[71]

As I have already indicated, Hegel is clearly open, unlike some commentators, to the idea that Pyrrhonian Sceptical inquiry could be "completed", where this means that the Sceptic could genuinely come to suspend judgement about everything.[72] He acknowledges the possibility of such a 'completed scepticism' as a 'negative science' in which the 'nullity' of all dogmatic 'presuppositions' would be demonstrated in his *Encyclopaedia* (*EL* §78A), and in his *Lectures on the History of Philosophy*, he describes Pyrrhonism as 'the art of dissolving all that is determinate, to show it in its nullity' (*VGP* 460/19:358). But insofar as such a project fails to acknowledge the possibilities Hegel sees in dialectical and speculative reason—of overcoming oppositions by means of unifying them in higher-order concepts, and thus deriving a system of interrelated categories—it is, therefore, for all his praise of the ancient Sceptics, a severely limited one in Hegel's eyes.

There are four principal and related limitations that Hegel sees in Scepticism, three of which I will address here and the fourth in the next section.[73] The first is straightforwardly that Scepticism itself remains restricted to the thinking of the understanding, even in its project of the thoroughgoing negation of claims and conceptions defended by others. 'Scepticism conducts itself only as understanding', Hegel says, considering conceptual oppositions only externally, and thereby missing the possibility that the negative result of its inquiry could also be understood as positive, as 'nearer to infinite affirmation, the self-relating negativity [of the Concept]' from the perspective of speculative reason (*VGP* 461/19:360).[74] This passage also introduces the

---

71. See Heidemann 2007: 132–36, and 324–27, for discussions of this 'internal Scepticism' which Hegel attributes to his own speculative philosophy and of the way in which he takes this to 'immunise' his project against sceptical objections. I discuss this briefly in the next section of this chapter.

72. Compare Ribeiro 2002, mentioned earlier, which contends that the Sceptic's claim to suspend judgement about *everything* must be understood as the expression of an aspiration.

73. See Forster 1989: 36–43, for a lengthier discussion of the criticisms Hegel directs towards Pyrrhonian Scepticism more broadly. I am in broad agreement with Forster that many of the limitations that Hegel perceives in Pyrrhonism are a result of it failing to measure up to the standards of his own speculative philosophy. This is, of course, not a standard that the Sceptics would have recognised. In Section 1.2.2, I suggest that Hegel became increasingly aware of the inadequacy of insisting on those standards without justifying them before the Sceptic.

74. Curiously, Hegel does on occasion seem to suggest that the ancient Sceptics go some way beyond this limitation, in the direction of genuinely "speculative" metaphysical insights, as his brief allusion to Sextus' discussion of space in *Against the Physicists* illustrates (*VGP* 481/19:396). Usually, however, he considers the Sceptics to be restricted merely to the resources of the understanding.

second limitation, already addressed to some extent: that Scepticism's result is *merely*, or only "abstractly", negative. Scepticism, in remaining stuck at the level of the understanding, Hegel thinks, concludes only in a form of negation that does not indicate any way forward for the inquiry.[75] The Scepticism which proceeds by externally introducing opposing determinations and concluding with suspension of judgement, rather than exploring how a determination might immanently negate itself, he suggests, is the

> Scepticism, which sees in the result always only *pure nothing*, and abstracts away from the result that this nothing determinately is the nothing *of that from which it results* . . . Scepticism, which ends with the abstraction of nothingness or emptiness, can go no further from this, but rather must wait and see whether something new will present itself, and what, in order to throw it into the same empty abyss. (*PhG* §79/3:74)

This "abstractly negative" approach which concludes in the mere nothingness of the Sceptic's universal suspension of judgement is contrasted with Hegel's preferred method of "determinate negation", whereby some concept, or some other content, is seen to negate itself and give rise to its own opposite, with which it is then united.[76] As Hegel elaborates the possibilities of this alternative model of negation:

> [Speculative] philosophy does not stop at the merely negative result, as is the case with Scepticism. The latter misjudges its result, in that it keeps hold of it as a mere, i.e., as an abstract, negation. In that the dialectic has the negative as its result, so is this, precisely as a result, at the same time positive, for it contains that from which it results as sublated within it, and is not without it. This, however, is the fundamental determination of the third form of the logical, namely of the *speculative* or positively rational. (*EL* §81Z2)

In this contrast between the Sceptic's abstract negation and Hegel's determinate negation, a third limitation of Sceptical inquiry, as Hegel understands it, becomes clear. Since Sceptical inquiry into any particular determination concludes merely negatively, furthering the inquiry in the way required if it is to be exhaustive is a matter of "seeing whether something new will present itself". As Hegel characterises the prospects of a 'completed Scepticism'

---

75. Hegel seems to agree with Epistemon, the scholastic character in Descartes' dialogue *The Search for Truth by means of the Natural Light*, who says of the Pyrrhonists that 'the fruits which they themselves have derived from their philosophical method have been so meagre that they have been wandering about aimlessly all their lives' (Descartes 1984: II, 413–14).

76. See Hentrup 2018 for a good discussion of the relation between the determinate negation which characterises the "self-completing scepticism" of Hegel's *Phenomenology* and the abstract negation which characterises Pyrrhonian inquiry. I have more to say about the notion of determinate negation in Section 4.2.2.

in the *Encyclopaedia*, it would be an 'unpleasant' task, having 'to find the finite forms [to be negated] only empirically and unscientifically, and to take them up as given' (*EL* §78A).[77] As Hegel sees it, in speculative logic, since further concepts arise as a result of the determinate negation of earlier ones, '*an immanent connection and necessity* enters into the content of science' (*EL* §81A), securing the completeness and rigour of the investigation of the categories. The Sceptic, meanwhile, has to rely on their ongoing experience of objects in the world, or the presentation of new claims from their Dogmatic interlocutors, in order to extend the scope of their suspension of judgement. In comparison with the necessity which he thinks characterises the progression of his logical project, then, Hegel claims that 'Scepticism, on the contrary, exercises its dialectic contingently', merely responding as the material 'comes up before it' (*VGP* 461/19:360).

I have suggested in this section that Hegel is optimistic about the success of the Sceptics' critical project. He supposes that the Agrippan modes, expressed at their simplest in the dilemmatic form of the Two Modes, provide an unanswerable challenge to any claim made on the basis of the understanding, which is typical of ordinary or "natural" thought, as well as a great deal of philosophy. I have also indicated that Hegel seems to take the force of Sceptical argumentation further than Sextus did, supposing the principle of Scepticism to have a universal scope, and to indicate a kind of metaphysics of indeterminacy. Putting the inaccuracies of this reading aside, I have suggested that it allows Hegel to conceive of Pyrrhonism as accomplishing the same critical or negative task as he sets himself in his Objective Logic, by slightly different means. Despite this, I have also suggested that Hegel perceives a number of serious limitations in the Sceptical project as he understands it. He thinks that it constrains itself needlessly to the kind of thinking he calls "understanding", and that as a result of this, the negation it provides of one-sided conceptions of the categories has a merely abstractly negative result: the nothingness of the Sceptic's suspension of judgement. And because of this merely negative result, Hegel thinks, the Sceptics must proceed only "empirically" and "unscientifically" in their inquiry, rendering the path to a completed Scepticism long, "unpleasant", and haphazardly dependent upon whichever concepts happen to be presented to them.

Having set out what I take to be the most significant elements of Hegel's understanding of Sceptical inquiry, seeing briefly how that inquiry relates to his own conception of speculative, logical thinking, and having introduced some of the significant limitations that Sceptical inquiry, in Hegel's opinion, has, I am now in a good position to introduce the final, and perhaps most

---

77. In his *Science of Logic*, Hegel alludes to the 'bother' involved in the Sceptics' way of demonstrating exhaustively the antinomial nature of all finite concepts (*WL* 158/5:217).

significant, limitation that Hegel perceives in Pyrrhonism: that however effective it might be in rebutting logical and metaphysical claims or conceptions of the categories put forward at the level of the understanding, its arguments do not, in fact, threaten the positive claims of the speculative logic and metaphysics that he himself will develop and defend. Yet Hegel's appreciation of the challenge offered by Pyrrhonism to his own philosophical project is one that altered as that project developed, so it is to the evolving nature of Hegel's appreciation of this challenge that I now turn.

1.2.2 The Evolution of Hegel's Appreciation of the Challenge of Pyrrhonism

During his early works in Jena, which include "On the Relationship of Scepticism to Philosophy", Hegel is explicitly of the opinion that, since he takes himself to be operating with a notion of speculative reason which can encompass oppositions between logical categories, as well as an idealist metaphysics which supposes reality itself to be structured in such a way that it encompasses and unites categorial oppositions, a Scepticism which operates by calling one-sided conceptions into question by appealing to equipollent oppositions offers no real problems for him.

This attitude is clear in his 1802 discussion of the Agrippan modes, where he claims that,

> [T]hey are completely useless against [speculative] philosophy . . . turned against dogmatism they appear from the side where they belong to reason, setting the other part of the necessary antinomy alongside the one asserted by dogmatism,—against philosophy on the other hand, [they appear] from the side where they belong to reflection. Against the former they must thus be victorious; but before the latter they must fall apart or be dogmatic themselves'. (*VSP* 335/2:245)

As I explained in the previous section, Hegel understands speculative reason to contain the key elements of Sceptical argumentation within itself. Dietmar Heidemann has helpfully labelled Hegel's strategy an 'integrative antiscepticism' which seeks to 'immunise' his project against any Sceptical objection (Heidemann 2007: 134–36). The basic strategy of this integrative antiscepticism is clearly present in "On the Relationship of Scepticism to Philosophy", where Hegel expresses his fundamental metaphysical contention that what is, is "the rational", where this encompasses all opposing, finite categorial determinations.[78] Because of this feature of his metaphysical position, Hegel

---

78. This use of "the rational" is clearly on the way to what Hegel will later call "the Concept".

thinks, the Agrippan modes cannot challenge it, or can challenge it only by mischaracterising its nature and treating it as itself finite, in which the use of the modes itself becomes "dogmatic", as Hegel suggests in the previous passage, by assuming, without argument, that there can *only* be finite, externally opposed conceptions of metaphysical categories. Against such a position, Hegel claims that,

> [T]he rational is not an unproven presupposition . . . against which the opposite could with equal right be presupposed unproved, for the rational has no opposite . . . [the mode of hypothesis] involves the concept of a ground and a consequent, according to which one is grounded by the other; [but] because there is no one opposed to another for reason, both oppositions made on the basis of foundations and the infinitely continued demand for a ground, [the mode of infinite regress], fall away; neither that demand nor this infinity is of any concern to reason. (*VSP* 336-37/2:247)

The alternatives of the dilemma characteristic of Agrippan problems are both rejected here as gaining no purchase on a philosophical thinking that grasps the nature of reality as encompassing and uniting the determinations which the Sceptic would oppose to one another in order to argue that the cases for them are equally arbitrary.[79] It would be possible to spend a great deal of time evaluating the prospects of this claim of Hegel's, but that task goes beyond what I want to achieve in this book.[80] Instead, I want to go on to suggest that Hegel did not remain completely satisfied with the adequacy of this response to Pyrrhonian Scepticism, and that this change bears significantly on the problem with which he engages at the beginning of his *Logic*.

For all that the details of Hegel's metaphysics develop a great deal after his early work in Jena, he never abandons the basic thrust of this claim: that, properly understood, the results of speculative reason are immune to Sceptical criticism.[81] There is, however, a significant development in his attitude

---

79. As Forster (1989: 110) puts it, 'Hegel believes that the claim of his philosophy . . . has no negation and indeed no coherent alternatives'.

80. See Trisokkas 2012: 332–40 for a defence of the claim that Hegel would go on, in the third book of his *Logic*, to satisfactorily refute this kind of Sceptical problem by providing a speculative theory of judgement which demonstrates how opposing determinations can be unified in a manner that undercuts the demand that grounds or reasons, be they foundational or infinitely regressive, be provided in order to decide between the opposing determinations.

81. Thus, in his *Lectures on the History of Philosophy*, delivered in Berlin in the 1820s, we find the same claim being made:

> Scepticism finds its application against the finite. But however much power these moments of its negative dialectic have against what is really the dogmatic conviction of the understanding, it is just as much *powerless against the speculative*. For as far as the speculative idea itself is concerned, it is precisely not something determinate, has not the one-sidedness of a proposition, is not finite; rather it has the absolutely negative in itself, the opposition within itself . . . There is nothing for Scepticism to do (*VGP* 481-82/19:397).

towards the challenge posed by Scepticism to his own speculative philosophy that takes place after 1802.[82] This development is best understood as a response to an obvious inadequacy of Hegel's antisceptical strategy as it is presented in "On the Relationship of Scepticism to Philosophy".

The issue is that Hegel appears, in his early works, to simply *assume* the validity of a form of speculative reasoning in which Sceptical argumentation and its constitutive oppositions are contained and superseded. But of course, a Sceptic is under no obligation to accept the validity of this special form of reasoning without question.[83] As the matter stands, a Pyrrhonist is bound to treat Hegel's claims about a notion of philosophical reason which encompasses and unites conceptual oppositions as little more than an arbitrary assertion, and to oppose to it with equal right the claim that there is no valid form of such reasoning, nor a coherent metaphysics of "the rational", in Hegel's sense. Even if Hegel is in fact right, then, about the immunity of speculative philosophy, properly understood, against Sceptical objection, he has not yet presented a convincing case in favour of his position and remains in that sense vulnerable to Sceptical rebuttal from a position "outside of" or opposed to his own philosophical standpoint.

By the time that he comes to write his *Phenomenology of Spirit*, however, and certainly by the time that he writes the first edition of his *Science of Logic*, Hegel has clearly shifted position. In both the preface and the introduction to the *Phenomenology*, it is clear that one of Hegel's central preoccupations in that work is the justification of his speculative philosophical standpoint to an interlocutor who does not recognise, or is sceptical of, its legitimacy. In that context, he explicitly acknowledges that it will not do to simply assert that his own position is correct and immune to Sceptical objection, since '*one* bare assurance is exactly as valid as another' (*PhG* §76/3:70). Instead, a case must be made for it which does not already assume the legitimacy of a peculiar model of speculative reason, or indeed an idealist metaphysics.[84] This is one of the primary goals of the *Phenomenology*, which I will discuss in Section 4.2.3. Similarly, in his *Encyclopaedia*, Hegel notes straight away that it is unsatisfactory to begin with '*presuppositions* or *assurances*' (*EL* §1). Later, he acknowledges that '[t]he ancient Sceptics generally called every philosophy

---

Hegel makes the same point in his *Encyclopaedia Logic* (*EL* §81Z2).

82. See Röttges 1987: Chs. 1–3, or Heidemann 2011, for more detailed treatments of the development of Hegel's attitude towards Scepticism between 1802 and his mature systematic works than the one provided here.

83. As Heidemann puts it, 'An obvious objection would be that sceptical doubt does not coincide with dialectical negation because the conception of dialectical negation presupposes the truth of dialectical logic, something the Sceptic calls into doubt' (Heidemann 2011: 96).

84. Westphal has argued persuasively that Schulze's satirical *Aphorisms on the Absolute* played a part in prompting Hegel to write his *Phenomenology* as a justification for the speculative standpoint from which his philosophical work would be carried out (Westphal 2020: 2).

dogmatic to the extent that it set up definite doctrines. In this wider sense, genuinely speculative philosophy also counts as dogmatic for Scepticism' (*EL* §32Z), which I take as additional evidence in favour of thinking that Hegel has come to recognise that there are still typically Pyrrhonian Sceptical objections which he must overcome in elaborating his systematic philosophy.

This is to suggest that both the project of Hegel's *Phenomenology* and his later, mature works, principally the *Science of Logic*, are written from a perspective which acknowledges that Hegel can presuppose neither the validity of a notion of speculative reason, nor an idealist metaphysics which understands the fundamental nature of reality to unify opposing finite determinations within itself, nor, indeed, if he is to satisfy the determined Pyrrhonian Sceptic, *anything at all*. A key part of Hegel's strategy, as should be clear from the sketch of the contents of the *Logic* I provided in 0.1, is to proceed in such a fashion that the Concept, as a fundamental conceptual and metaphysical principle which encompasses all of the opposing, finite categories, and the legitimacy of his account of speculative reason itself, are among the *results* of his logical project rather than being dogmatically presupposed at its beginning.[85] This strategy means that a great deal still depends on constructing the *beginning* of that project, from which those results are reached, in a way that is not itself open to Sceptical objection.[86] In Section 3.2, I will suggest that Hegel is sensitive to just this concern, as he thinks that a specific Agrippan problem, the problem of beginning, needs to be solved in order to overcome Sceptical objections to the beginning of his logical project.

1.3 CONCLUSION

In this chapter, I have introduced some of the fundamentals of Pyrrhonian inquiry, paying special attention to the Agrippan modes, and suggested Sextus' discussion of the Two Modes yields the basic, dilemmatic form of what I call "Agrippan problems". I have also introduced what I take to be the fundamental elements of Hegel's engagement with Pyrrhonian Sceptical argumentation, which, I have suggested, includes a sensitivity to the nature of Agrippan problems as I have spelled them out in Section 1.1.3. Finally, I have

---

85. During his earlier works in Jena, Hegel seems not to have developed the idea of treating the foundation of a philosophical science as a result that can be demonstrated. In *Faith and Knowledge*, for example, he suggests that the 'highest idea' should 'alone begin philosophy' (*GW* 67/2:302). Hegel clearly changes his mind about this. He will later criticise Schelling, for example, for thinking that the highest principle of a philosophy can simply be asserted at the beginning like an axiom, 'without proving that it is the truth' (*VGP* 825/20:435), since such a procedure clearly invites sceptical objections to the case for such a beginning. I discuss this further in Section 2.3.4.

86. A great deal also depends, of course, on the moves Hegel makes between the beginning and the results of his logical investigation, but those are not my concern here.

suggested that, in his *Phenomenology* and in his mature systematic works, Hegel comes to see that, even if the details of his system of philosophy, properly developed and understood, prove to be immune to Sceptical rebuttal, he needs to make a case for that system which is not itself vulnerable to the Sceptic. The beginning of his *Logic*, I will go on to argue, is a key element of Hegel's attempt to make such a case.

Before I provide an in-depth account of Hegel's discussion of the beginning of the *Logic* in chapter 3, the next chapter provides additional background material which should be useful for that discussion, in the shape of a commentary on the brief history of the problem of beginning with which Hegel opens his essay, "With what must the beginning of the science be made?"

Chapter Two

A Short History of the Problem of Beginning

2.0 INTRODUCTION

As I indicated in the introduction to this book (Section 0.3.2), Hegel inserts a brief historical interlude early on in his discussion of the problem of beginning in "With what must the beginning of the science be made?" Its purpose is presumably to clarify what he is doing in that essay by locating its task in the context of the history of philosophical work on the topic. That being said, the brevity of Hegel's presentation of this material risks, or so it seems to me, contributing to a reader's confusion rather than clarifying the matter for them, at least if it is read in isolation. In this chapter, therefore, I will attempt to expand on Hegel's historical sketch of the problem of beginning, supplementing it with brief discussions of some of its significant figures and approaches, and supporting my interpretation of this very short section of Hegel's text with the examination of remarks on this history that Hegel makes elsewhere, primarily in his *Lectures on the History of Philosophy*.[1] I should acknowledge, however, that Hegel's sketch of the history of the problem of beginning covers an immense amount of ground, and that even a chapter-length extension of that discussion involves, at times, deeply inadequate discussions of the various historical philosophers Hegel considers and of his opinion of their work. I have endeavoured to provide enough information for the interested reader to explore each aspect of this chapter in greater depth, should they wish to, but I cannot do much more than this here. A *long* history of the problem of beginning according to Hegel would require a book in its own right.

---

1. For some other helpful but briefer discussions of this material, see Rosen 2014: 76–82, Stekeler-Weithofer 2019: 244–47, and Krijnen 2021: 52–57.

This chapter will follow the structure of Hegel's sketch. Accordingly, I begin by discussing the topics which Hegel refers to as the "objective beginning" and the "subjective beginning", where "beginning" here indicates something like "the fundamental metaphysical principle", which has historically been taken, according to Hegel, to be of either an objective or subjective character. Secondly, I discuss what I call the "methodological beginning", by which I mean the concern for where one ought to begin developing a systematic metaphysics if the account is to be properly justified. Thirdly, I discuss at greater length what Hegel calls 'the modern perplexity about the beginning' (*WL* 45/5:65), which involves a brief characterisation of approaches to the problem of beginning in the work of Descartes, Kant, Reinhold, and Fichte.[2] In the final part of the chapter, I attempt to spell out how Hegel's approach to the problem of beginning differs from those of his German Idealist forebears (and contemporaries), as a prelude to the in-depth discussion of Hegel's treatment of the problem of beginning in the next chapter.

I should point out at the outset that Hegel does not explicitly name any philosophers or schools in his historical sketch of the problem of beginning, so the identifications and examples that I provide here, although I provide a rationale in each case for my interpretation, cannot be taken to capture exactly who Hegel has in mind in any given remark with absolute certainty. However, I think that, even if it should be the case that I am mistaken in identifying certain specific elements of this historical sketch, this should not necessarily undermine the more general narrative of the history of the problem of beginning that I reproduce here, nor show that the account of Hegel's own, distinctive approach to the problem of beginning which I begin to elaborate in the final section of this chapter, and continue in the next, is mistaken.

2.1 THE OBJECTIVE BEGINNING AND THE SUBJECTIVE BEGINNING

Hegel starts by acknowledging attempts to provide a beginning in the sense of identifying a fundamental metaphysical principle, 'the beginning of *all things*' in the sense of their absolute foundation, or that upon which everything else ontologically depends (*WL* 45/5:65). If there is a "problem of beginning" in this sense, it is that of figuring out what is in fact the fundamental metaphysical principle, since, of course, there are competing candidates. Hegel mentions some familiar ones of an "objective" character: Thales'

---

2. These have as their focus, however, Hegel's critical understanding of the work of his forebears. I make no claim to do Descartes, Kant, Reinhold, Fichte, or Schelling justice on their own terms here.

water, the Neoplatonist "one", Anaxagoras' *nous*, and 'idea', 'substance', and 'monad' (*WL* 45/5:65).

Whom Hegel has in mind in regard to the last three candidates mentioned here is not obvious. Pirmin Stekeler-Weithofer, not unreasonably, takes Hegel to be thinking of Plato, Spinoza, and Leibniz respectively.[3] There are alternatives that one might consider, however. Hegel's use of "idea" here is in all likelihood a reference to Plato, but he also discusses Aristotle's 'speculative idea' at some length elsewhere (*VGP* 353–55/19:153–55). Aristotle is also a good candidate for being one, or perhaps the primary, philosopher Hegel has in mind when he talks about "substance" here, since his discussion of Aristotle's metaphysics in his *Lectures on the History of Philosophy* uses the term 'absolute substance' to refer to the principle of the latter's metaphysics more than once (*VGP* 353–62/19:151–68).[4] And finally, Diogenes Laërtius, whose *Lives of the Eminent Philosophers* Hegel certainly read and relied upon, says that the monad is 'the first principle of all things', according to the views of the Pythagoreans (Diogenes Laërtius 2018: VIII, 25).[5] I think that it is at least plausible that it is these ancient metaphysical projects and their foundations that Hegel is addressing here.

One might think that such a reading has an advantage over accounts that take Hegel to be grouping philosophers as chronologically distant as Thales and Leibniz together, especially if one takes Hegel to suppose that the history of the topic of beginning takes a decisive turn with the work of Descartes and the inauguration of modern philosophy, as his remarks about the "modern perplexity about the beginning" might seem to suggest. I would not put too much store by such an argument, however. Even if Descartes represents a significant step in the history of thinking about the topic of beginning, for Hegel, this might not prevent later modern thinkers failing, by his lights, to appreciate the significance of the Cartesian revolution, as I will suggest in what follows.[6] Ultimately, however, exactly whom Hegel has in mind when he talks about the objective beginning is less important than what he takes to be inadequate about the approach, but before discussing its inadequacies, it

---

3. See Stekeler-Weithofer 2019: 244.
4. See Tahko 2013: 51–52, for the suggestion that, according to Aristotle, metaphysics or "first philosophy" studies being qua being, and 'the question of being is just the question of substance'. In fact, although Hegel does not make it explicit at the beginning of his *Logic*, I take it that his discussion of objective and subjective "beginnings" is intended to recall the topic of "first philosophy" and the nature of the priority of its subject matter.
5. For Hegel's discussion of this point in his *Lectures on the History of Philosophy*, which admittedly draws mostly from Sextus and Aristotle, see *VGP* 120–21/18:241. Hegel seems to have used *Einheit* and not *Monade* in his lectures, but that is no strong reason to think that he couldn't have used the other term elsewhere, when working on the *Logic*.
6. It is in a related sense, I think, that Rosen takes Spinoza to represent 'a step backwards from Descartes' in Hegel's eyes (Rosen 2014: 78).

is worth also introducing the other sense of "beginning" that he discusses in this context.

Hegel also addresses, in same part of the text, the notion of a "subjective beginning", which would play much the same role—that of the fundamental metaphysical principle on which everything depends—but where this is taken to be of a distinctively "subjective" character. In this case the beginning would be a principle which 'refers to the nature of cognition . . . - thinking, intuition, sensation, I, subjectivity itself' (*WL* 45/5:65).

The nature of the fundamental principle differs in such cases, clearly, from those cases representative of the objective beginning, but the nature of the approach that Hegel has in mind seems to be the same. Thus, the metaphysics to be elaborated in the case of the subjective beginning will take objects to be ultimately grounded upon sensation, or upon consciousness, rather than an objective principle like water or substance, but the elaboration of this subjective metaphysics does not seem to differ in methodology: it will be a question of considering the various objects making up the world and moving from them to identifying, e.g., the "I", as their fundamental ground, and illustrating how everything depends on that ground.

The question of whom Hegel has in mind when he addresses the subjective beginning is even harder to determine than in the case of the objective beginning.[7] It might not be unreasonable to suppose that Hegel is referring to more recent philosophers like Kant and Fichte here, especially since his criticisms of the alleged "subjectivism" of their metaphysical positions are well known.[8] Yet there is good reason to suppose that these philosophers, Fichte in particular, are among the targets of Hegel's discussion of the more "modern" concern about beginning, which I will discuss in Section 2.3. This suggests that one should perhaps look further back in history for examples of what Hegel considers a fundamentally subjective beginning.

Among the plausible candidates for philosophers Hegel has in mind when he discusses the subjective beginning are, I think, the members of several of the major philosophical schools of the Hellenistic Period. I have already described, in Section 1.2.1, Hegel's appraisal of Pyrrhonian Scepticism as having 'completed the perspective of the subjectivity of all knowledge and put, universally, the expression of *appearance* in the place of being' (*VGP* 460/19:358). Yet Hegel does not attribute a fundamentally subjective

---

7. Stekeler-Weithofer suggests that Hegel is referring to Descartes, Locke, Hume, Kant, Fichte, and to himself, in his commentary on this passage (Stekeler-Weithofer 2019: 244). The account I give in this chapter differs, clearly, from Stekeler-Weithofer on this point.

8. Hegel is of the opinion that both Kant's and Fichte's positions are problematically subjective from very early on in his philosophical career, and he never seems to revise this evaluation. See, for example, *GW* 67/2:301–2 and *D* 156/2:94, for early versions of the charge of a problematic subjectivism directed at Kant and Fichte respectively. These charges remain unaltered in their substance in Hegel's later *Lectures on the History of Philosophy*.

philosophy to the Sceptics alone. Indeed, in relation to the Stoics, Epicureans, *and* Sceptics he claims that 'the principle . . . was subjective', in that '[t]he principle of all these philosophies is the pure relation of self-consciousness to itself' (*VGP* 406/19:251), before adding, more specifically, that he thinks that the fundamental principles of Stoic and Epicurean philosophies, respectively, are 'thinking' and 'sensation' (*VGP* 408/19:253).

As with candidates one might consider for the philosophers Hegel has in mind when discussing the objective beginning, however, I do not think that there is a strong argument for taking the discussion of the subjective beginning to refer only to premodern philosophers, even if this lends Hegel's short history of the problem of beginning a tidier, more chronological presentation.[9] After, all, when discussing the Academic Sceptics, whom he also supposes to operate on the basis of a fundamentally subjective principle, Hegel claims that '[t]he general standpoint of the Academics is that they express the truth as a subjective conviction of self-consciousness, which agrees with the subjective idealism of more modern times' (*VGP* 450/19:336). These modern "subjective idealists", by which Hegel appears to mean primarily Berkeley, and perhaps slightly more peculiarly, Hume (*VGP* 735/20:270), might presumably also be assigned to the category of the subjective beginning, just as philosophers like Spinoza and Leibniz might be taken as exemplars of the objective one.[10]

The identity of the philosophers Hegel has in mind when he discusses the objective beginning and the subjective beginning, then, is difficult to determine. Yet more important than identifying a specific philosopher for each of Hegel's examples of such "beginnings" is the question of what it is that is lacking in the approaches in question, or of what it is in the treatments of the topic of beginning 'in more recent times' (*WL* 45/5:65) the importance of which earlier philosophers were not alert to, according to Hegel.

Briefly, however, it is worth noting in passing that I do not here take Hegel to be opposed to the philosophical project of identifying a fundamental principle capable of supporting a systematic science of metaphysics. His remarks in the third book of his *Logic* identifying the Concept as the '*absolute foundation*' of all of the logico-metaphysical categories examined in the Objective Logic are at least open to such an interpretation (*WL* 508/6:245).[11] Idealist that he is, he would presumably reject any characterisation of the fundamental

---

9. I think it is clear that Hegel does chart a roughly developmental narrative throughout the history of Western philosophy but only a rough one. Readings which attempt to directly map the development of the argument of the *Science of Logic* onto Hegel's chronological treatment of the history of western philosophy are bound, I think, to run into insurmountable difficulties.

10. See also *GW* 154/2:394–95, where Hegel claims that, 'According to the task of philosophy, as it was determined through the tradition of Locke and Hume, the world should be computed and henceforth explained from the standpoint of the subject'.

11. Although, as I noted in Section 1.1.3, such interpretations are contested.

principle as merely "objective" or merely "subjective" in character, but the exclusively objective or subjective character of the principles in question here is perhaps not the primary criticism that Hegel levels at these earlier approaches.[12]

The primary criticism that Hegel will level at these examples of projects focused upon an objective or a subjective beginning is that, in their 'need' to identify 'what the *truth*, what the *absolute ground* of everything is' (*WL* 45/5:65), they pay insufficient attention to the justification of the metaphysical system they propose, or to the question of where the elaboration of such an account, on the part of the thinker, ought to begin. Instead, Hegel suggests, the topic of where one begins to elaborate a metaphysical system and its fundamental principle is treated, according to this approach, as a merely 'accidental way to introduce the exposition, [which] remains disregarded and indifferent' (*WL* 45/5:65). But, of course, if the beginning of the exposition is considered philosophically insignificant, no guarantee of the validity of the exposition is being provided; this is a deficiency which seriously impacts the convincingness of the project as a whole.

Hegel's criticism is simply a version of the quintessentially Pyrrhonian Sceptical rejection of the development of philosophical theories on problematically arbitrary grounds. And certainly if one takes Hegel to be primarily concerned with premodern metaphysics here, then the role of Scepticism in the development of this criticism presents itself very clearly. This is because the influence of Pyrrhonism is commonly taken to have played a significant role in the downfall of the dominant premodern approach to metaphysical knowledge, an approach which does, in fact, have a story to tell about how knowledge of an "objective beginning", for example, is acquired but one which would strike the Sceptics, as well as philosophers as varied as Descartes, Hume, Kant, and Hegel, as insufficiently self-critical.

Most of the major premodern projects of identifying an objective beginning, in Hegel's sense, for all of the differences in their first-order metaphysical commitments, seem to share a broadly empiricist, abstractionist account of how we come to knowledge of first principles.[13] Roughly, this is to say that

---

12. In his early work at Jena, by contrast, Hegel's preference for Schelling's systematic philosophy over that of Fichte is expressed most clearly in terms of the more adequate way in which the former establishes a fundamental principle which is both subjective and objective at the same time or consists in the "absolute identity" of subject and object (*D* 155/2:94).

13. This is not to deny that there might not be some cases where the story is rather more complicated. See Black 2014 and Ogden 2021 for discussions of the possible opposition between abstractionism and emanationism in the works of Avicenna, for a good example of such a case. Rosen (2014: 76) acknowledges the dominant Greek picture of philosophy 'as an ascent from everyday life to the forms or categories that constitute the structure the whole', but then suggests that, at least sometimes, 'Plato and Aristotle speak as if the forms and categories are directly accessible to theoretical intelligence'. I cannot explore this issue further here.

the assumption is that knowledge begins with immediate sensory information, like instances of which are combined by memory or by the imagination, in turn facilitating a further degree of abstraction, when these contents are grasped conceptually or intellectually. Only after abstracting general or universal conceptual determinations from what is originally given in sensory experience, goes the thought, it is possible to inquire into fundamental grounds or first principles.

The assumption I have just sketched very briefly and inadequately is clearly operative at the opening of Book Alpha of Aristotle's *Metaphysics*, which would set the methodological terms for a great deal of premodern metaphysical inquiry. There Aristotle gives an abstractionist account of the move from sensory information to 'experience' which is produced by memory before noting that 'science and art come to me *through* experience ... when from many notions gained by experience one universal judgement about similar objects is produced'. Reflecting in still more abstract terms on such universal judgements, thinks Aristotle, allows us to ask after and theorise 'the first causes and principles of things' (Aristotle 1984: 980a28–982a18), the science of which is metaphysics. And although Aristotle is clear that the subject matter of this science is not dependent on the objects of less abstract disciplines but rather the reverse since it is concerned with that upon which everything else depends (as their "objective beginning", Hegel might say), this procedure clearly makes our metaphysical knowledge ultimately dependent on our empirical knowledge.[14] And if there are reasons to entertain sceptical concerns about empirical knowledge then, according to such abstractionist accounts, this would appear also to endanger the metaphysical positions we have developed on this empirical basis.

This approach to metaphysics as the science of fundamental principles or objective beginnings, which supposes that such a science must develop by way of abstraction from empirical knowledge, is clearly expressed in the popular mediaeval slogan *nihil est in intellectu nisi prius fuerit in sensu*: there is nothing in the intellect that was not first in the senses.[15] And Hegel is perhaps quicker than many contemporary historians of philosophy would be to conclude that scholastic philosophy as a whole is founded on a 'generalisation of the Aristotelian writings' which yields 'no scientific progress' (*VGP* 552/19:551).

---

14. This sketch passes over many of the significant details of Aristotle's account of how we come to knowledge of first principles without commenting upon them. For more detailed discussion, see Ferejohn 2009 or Zuppolini 2016, for example.

15. In his *Encyclopaedia*, Hegel briefly appears to endorse a version of this slogan, which is surprising, given what I take to be his clear commitment, expressed elsewhere, to conceiving logic as an a priori science. I cannot discuss this matter here, but I am confident that this apparent tension can be relieved.

As is well known, this broadly empiricist picture of the generation of metaphysical knowledge began to be forcefully challenged in the aftermath of the translation into Latin and then the popularisation of Sextus' Sceptical works in the sixteenth century.[16] Much of Sextus' presentation of the Aenesideman modes, as Hegel is well aware, principally target attempts to claims to knowledge on the basis of sensory experiences, often by appeal to the apparent relativity of such experiences.[17] Sextus also explicitly levels Sceptical arguments against any attempt to construe sensory experience as the criterion of truth.[18] With the spread of these texts in Europe, the dominant, scholastic approach to the development of metaphysical claims came under a great deal of pressure from sceptically inclined philosophers like Montaigne and Sanches. Indeed, Sanches' occasional appeals to the relativity of perceived objects and perceiving subjects in order to cast doubt upon cases of presumed empirical knowledge clearly recall material from the Ten Modes (as presented by Sextus and by Diogenes Laërtius).[19]

Hegel, I think it is clear, is sympathetic to the idea that an empiricist methodology will result in sceptical consequences for metaphysics. He notes, '[i]n that perception is supposed to remain the foundation of that which counts as truth, so universality and necessity appear as something *unjustified*, as a subjective contingency, a mere habit, the content of which can be thus, or otherwise' (*EL* §39). Although it is the sceptical consequences of modern empiricism that he primarily has in mind in making this remark, the criticism that the content of an immediate empirical judgement might just as well be otherwise, with its overtones of Pyrrhonian equipollence, can presumably be taken to target any philosophical project which begins by simply accepting the validity of the deliverances of sensibility. Indeed, Hegel commends Pyrrhonian Scepticism over Humean scepticism here, precisely because he takes the former to adopt a critical attitude towards sensibility itself (*EL* §39A).

The significance of the impact of Pyrrhonian arguments against attempts to develop scholastic metaphysical systems on partially empirical grounds

---

16. See Popkin 2003: 17–43, for a classic discussion of the revival of Pyrrhonian Sceptical materials in European thought in the fifteenth and sixteenth centuries.

17. See *PH* I:38-140, in particular. The first eight of the Ten Modes are all focused on prompting a suspension of judgement about perceptual judgements by appeal to cases of relativity among human perceivers, perceived objects, and the combination of these two (the last of the Ten Modes seem to be concerned more specifically with value judgements).

18. See, for example *PH* II:49–56, where Sextus argues against the idea that the senses can function as the criterion of truth, by pointing out that 'the senses are moved in contrary ways by external objects': honey tasting now sweet, and then bitter, a tower appearing now round, then square, etc. And an attempt to provide a further criterion to decide between such conflicting cases points towards the familiar Agrippan options of merely arbitrarily asserting one arbitrarily or slipping into a regress of criteria and perceptions. See also *AL* I:344–47.

19. See Sanches 1988: 213–14, or 246–54, for example. The primary target of Sanches' *Quod Nihil Scitur*, I should acknowledge, is rather the Aristotelian account of demonstrative knowledge, which I have not discussed here.

is clearly appreciable in the speed with which Descartes, in the first of his *Meditations*, dismisses sensory experiences as an inadequate means for developing a scientific metaphysics (Descartes 1985: II, 12–13). It is the unsatisfactoriness of uncritically empiricist approaches to metaphysics which prompts Descartes to adopt a radically new approach in comparison to the scholastic metaphysicians who preceded him. While Aquinas, for example, supposed that knowledge of the existence of God as a fundamental metaphysical principle is inferred on the basis of our empirical experience of the world around us, in the fashion of a cosmological argument, Descartes thinks that basic metaphysical truths such as the Cogito and the existence of God are immediately available to the intellect.[20] It is thus Descartes who most clearly begins to remodel the science of metaphysics in the style of a system of geometry, whereby one is entitled to begin immediately with fundamental principles (if they withstand various sceptical tests) and derive further claims from these a priori, in the fashion of a proof, as I briefly noted in Section 0.1.[21]

Descartes' claims to immediate, intellectual knowledge of God and of the existence of the self as a thinking thing will also ultimately look problematic, from Hegel's point of view, but I suspect that Descartes is, despite this, the high point of pre-Kantian work on the problem of beginning, considered in the context of Hegel's short sketch of the history of that problem. In fact, Descartes' work, rather more than that of some later proponents of "objective" and "subjective" beginnings, arguably belongs among the projects Hegel will discuss in terms of the "modern perplexity" about beginning, so I will hold off from further discussion of Descartes until the next two sections of this chapter. Here one might simply note (a) that in insisting that a scientific metaphysics not rely on premises or axioms that are open to sceptical refutation, as he does in the First Meditation, and (b) that in elaborating a basically realist metaphysics, yet apparently on the basis of the certainty of Cogito, Descartes exhibits a perhaps uncommonly strong concern to elaborate metaphysical claims in a way that is at no point open to sceptical objections, and might appear to be operating on the basis of a fundamental principle that is

---

20. Hegel is clearly alert to this, acknowledging that 'the so-called immediate intuition, inward revelation of modern times belongs here' at the beginning of Descartes' philosophy (*VGP* 658/20:129).

21. See Carreiro 2009: 11–17 and 168–75, for instructive comparisons of Aquinas and Descartes on the nature of human cognition, and of knowledge of God's existence, respectively, which bring the radicality of Descartes' break with the Aristotelian, scholastic tradition nicely into focus. See, e.g., *VGP* 690/20:167, for Hegel's acknowledgement of the significance of Descartes' redevelopment of the science of metaphysics according to the geometrical model. This is not to say that the method of demonstration was not applied to metaphysical topics by Aristotelian and scholastic philosophers, of course, but the account of the knowledge of the first principles is clearly rather different. A lengthier discussion of the differences between Descartes' methodology and that of the scholastics goes beyond what I can accomplish here.

neither straightforwardly objective or subjective.[22] Both of these, I will suggest in what follows, are crucial aspects of the modern treatments of the topic of beginning which Hegel discusses at the opening of the *Logic*.

Even if elements of Descartes' approach appear to set him apart from the discussion of merely "objective" and "subjective" beginnings, however, this is again not to deny that, after Descartes, philosophers might, in Hegel's opinion, develop a more dogmatic, and merely subjective, metaphysics, as in the case of Berkeley, or slip back into empirically deriving the fundamental determinations of metaphysics, even if they are then held to be objective and treated in systematic fashion, as Hegel accuses Wolff of doing (*VGP* 729–30/20:260–61), or simply asserting fundamental principles as axioms, in a manner that looks problematically arbitrary, as Hegel criticises Spinoza for doing.

Spinoza's practice of beginning with definitions and axioms, the truth of which is taken to be self-evident, amounts to a particularly glaring example of an attempt to develop a science of metaphysics on grounds which, Hegel thinks, are problematically open to sceptical rebuttal.[23] He claims that 'Spinoza begins, in his mathematical, demonstrative method, from definitions . . . and these are really assumed, presupposed, not derived; he knows not how he came to them' (*VGP* 690/20:167) and refers to this method as 'the deficiency' of Spinoza's philosophy (*VGP* 679/20:172).[24] The reasoning, I take it, is clear. In fact, it is an application of the Agrippan mode of hypothesis: even more so than an attempt to derive a fundamental metaphysical principle on the basis of appeals to sceptically questionable deliverances of sensible experience, merely asserting basic principles and claiming that they are self-evident without providing any argument or reasons in their favour opens one to the typically Pyrrhonian riposte which asserts opposing principles with equal right and calls the entire metaphysical edifice, Spinozist or otherwise, into question.

To conclude this section, then, I think that it is safe to say that, regardless of whom exactly it is that Hegel has in mind when he discusses the objective and the subjective beginning, his criticism of the approach is the same in both cases. He rejects metaphysical projects which "disregard" the question of where one ought to begin the exposition of a philosophical system in favour

---

22. One might think that, in insisting on the primacy of the Cogito, Descartes might belong to the tradition of the "subjective beginning", in Hegel's eyes. The discussion of Descartes in Section 2.3 should show that this is not the case.

23. Like Descartes, however, it is not clear that Spinoza can be easily assigned to the tradition either of the "objective" or "subjective" beginning, since Hegel also takes the latter to be an 'Idealist', in the sense of one who affirms 'the unity of thought and being' (*VGP* 675/20:161).

24. See also *D* 105/2:37, for an earlier version of Hegel's criticism of Spinoza's method of beginning. See Schmid 2021, for an informative discussion of Spinoza's dismissive attitude toward the importance of meeting sceptical objections.

of an over-hasty and under-critical concern to identify "the absolute ground of everything", whether this ground is understood as objective or subjective in its nature (*WL* 45/5:65), and whether it is dubiously derived empirically, from sensible experiences on the basis of abstraction, or merely arbitrarily asserted as an axiom. Having indicated the substance of his criticisms of these approaches, I will proceed to discuss the next aspect of the topic of beginning that Hegel discusses: the methodological concern for where the exposition of a philosophical system ought to begin.

2.2 THE METHODOLOGICAL BEGINNING

By "methodological beginning", I mean to pick out precisely what Hegel thought was problematically lacking in the previous two approaches to the topic of beginning: an awareness of the inadequacy of paying insufficient attention to the question of where one ought to begin the elaboration of a systematic philosophical project, if it is not to be rejected on the basis of sceptical criticisms to the effect that the case in its favour rests on problematically arbitrary grounds.[25] The subject matter of this kind of beginning need not be characterised in terms of ontological priority, as the objective and the subjective beginnings were, but in terms of methodological priority when it comes to the study of what has ontological priority.[26]

It is arguably somewhat artificial to distinguish this third approach to the topic of beginning in Hegel's historical sketch in the *Logic*, since he discusses it here explicitly only as what is missing in those philosophical projects which are concerned *merely* with either an objective or subjective beginning as discussed in the previous two sections. This approach is also what, when combined with a concern to identify a "beginning" in the sense of a fundamental metaphysical principle, characterises, at least in part, the "modern perplexity" about beginning that Hegel will focus on, but I think that it can be briefly

---

25. Krijnen (2021: 55-56), interestingly, seems to take Hegel to *endorse* the view that a concern for the 'way of introducing the exposition' (*WL* 45/5:65) is to be disregarded. This, in part, I think, is because Krijnen takes Hegel to be referring here to contingent facts about how an individual philosopher might come to think about the matter of the (objective or subjective) beginning, rather than whether or not the (methodological) beginning of the exposition itself is justified. It seems, to me, however, that Hegel's tone is clearly *critical* of those who disregard the way in which the exposition is introduced, or view this as a merely accidental matter, and this is presumably because he is not here talking about merely contingent aspects of the beginning of an individual philosopher's investigation, but the universal requirement that the elaboration of a systematic metaphysics and its fundamental principle begin from somewhere that is itself justified.

26. This is not to deny the possibility that the methodological beginning could ever coincide with the beginning in terms of a fundamental principle, however. Fichte, for one, seems to endorse precisely this idea.

treated in its own right, all the same.²⁷ The primary historical example of a philosopher who exhibits a concern for the methodological beginning is, of course, Descartes, who attempts to begin the elaboration of a scientific metaphysics from grounds that are not open to sceptical objections, as he understands them, and to achieve this by way of the application of a methodological doubt.²⁸ I think it is clear that Descartes' approach exerts a strong influence on Hegel's work at the beginning of his *Logic* in just this respect.

The task that Descartes sets himself, as the narrator of his *Meditations*, is that of 'the general demolition of my opinions'—'to demolish everything completely and start again right from the foundations . . . [in order to] establish anything at all in the sciences that was stable and likely to last' (Descartes 1985: II, 12). This attempt to rid oneself of dogmatic assumptions and begin from somewhere not open to sceptical objections, I will suggest in Section 3.3.1, is also operative at the beginning of Hegel's *Logic*, and Hegel's various accounts of the "presuppositionless" nature of the beginning of that logical project clearly recall his characterisation of Descartes' procedure—a procedure whereby 'presuppositions . . . are given up; only proof is sought', as Hegel describes it (*VGP* 659/20:130).²⁹

It is not only Descartes one might consider in the context of the methodological beginning, even if it seems that it is he who exerts the most obvious influence on Hegel in this regard. Hegel sometimes exhibits a tendency to construe whichever historical philosopher he is discussing as elaborating a systematic philosophy, or even a systematic metaphysics, even where this is perhaps a questionable interpretative strategy, as in the case of Sextus, as I discussed in Section 1.2.1. This tendency is also evident in his attribution of a kind of "subjective idealism" to Hume, whom Hegel reads as having 'completed Lockeanism' (*VGP* 739/20:277) by making empirical experience

---

27. See Krijnen 2021: 52–53, for a helpful discussion of metaphysical and what I am here calling "methodological" beginnings in Hegel's *Logic*, in connection to Rickert's distinction between "ontological" and "gnoseological" beginnings.

28. See VGP 657/20:127, for Hegel's take on the difference between Cartesian and Pyrrhonian Scepticism. There, Hegel also explicitly attributes to Descartes the significance of 'renouncing all presuppositions taken as immediate and true'. This is just to say that (a significant part of) Descartes' importance lies in the attempt to avoid the Agrippan mode of hypothesis, which Hegel always translates as "presupposition".

29. The Cartesian influence on the beginning of Hegel's *Logic* is emphasised in Houlgate's work on the beginning of Hegel's *Logic* (Houlgate 2005: 32, 39; 2006: 31-32). Stern, however, has criticised this line of interpretation, suggesting that Hegel is better read as anticipating later, American pragmatist criticisms of Cartesian methodology (Stern 2009: 218-37). It seems to me that, at least in the context of the beginning of the *Logic*, Houlgate is clearly in the right here, not only because of the resemblance Hegel's account of the beginning of the *Logic* bears to his discussions of Descartes in his *Lectures on the History of Philosophy*, but also because, in his 1831 *Lectures on Logic*, Hegel *explicitly* invokes Descartes when discussing the beginning of the logical science (*VL* 71/84). There is a larger discussion to be had about whether Hegel's metametaphysical commitments are better read with an emphasis on the rationalist tradition which preceded him, or on later, pragmatist innovations which Hegel might be taken to anticipate, but this is not the place for it.

the foundation of all philosophical knowledge, even as he draws sceptical conclusions from this move. Yet, presumably, it is not necessary to read philosophers like Sextus and Hume in this manner. One might instead take them merely to proceed with piecemeal investigations of philosophical topics, alert to the issue of the justification of philosophical claims about the matter at hand and beginning in every case with concerns about how such claims are in fact justified, yet without any aspirations to locate an objective or subjective beginning in the sense of a metaphysical principle, or to develop a systematic perspective on its basis. Even if this possibility is not one to which Hegel pays a great deal of attention, it is presumably a real one, and might also be counted as an instance of the concern for the methodological beginning.

When Hegel criticises those proponents of an objective or subjective beginning for leaving the beginning of the elaboration of the system which is ultimately grounded on such a fundamental principle unjustified, then, it is the importance of a methodological concern for where one begins to elaborate such a system that he is emphasising. And whether this methodological beginning proves to be the beginning of the elaboration of a philosophical system that is grounded on a fundamental principle or whether it comes apart from such a project and plays its role in a less ambitious, less systematic philosophical project, taking it seriously is clearly what is required in order to not run into a sceptical rebuttal of one's philosophical project right away.

One might think that an appropriate concern for the methodological beginning of the philosophical science, coupled with an interest in identifying a fundamental metaphysical principle, be it objective or subjective by nature, should be all that is required by the more modern investigations into the matter of beginning with which Hegel is primarily concerned. It seems to me, however, that there are two distinct elements which Hegel takes to be essential to the "modern perplexity" about beginning, and which distinguish it from earlier attempts to identify an objective or a subjective beginning. One is precisely this concern for a methodological beginning, for the justification of those initial claims on the basis of which one either elaborates a systematic philosophy, as, for example, Descartes' does in making his initial cases for the Cogito and for the existence of God in the first three Meditations, or one elaborates a less ambitiously systematic set of philosophical claims, as, for example, Sextus does in setting out the Sceptical way of life in identifying the equipollence of opposing dogmatic claims, or Hume does in suggesting that those ideas are not legitimately used for which no original sensory impression can be identified. Of course, that a philosopher takes the topic of the methodological beginning seriously does not mean that the methodological beginning that they propose is a satisfactory one. And Hegel is operating with particularly demanding standards when it comes to precisely this topic, since, as I have already indicated in Section 0.1, he thinks that metaphysics, which he takes to coincide with logic, should take the form of an a priori, demonstrative science which *proves* that its results are necessarily true.

The second element of the "modern perplexity" concerns the distinctively German Idealist idea that the fundamental principle of a systematic metaphysics should be conceived of as both objective and subjective and should come first in the order of the elaboration of the system. These two elements, how they relate to one another, and what Hegel makes of notable attempts to satisfy the demands of both of them, I discuss in the next section.

2.3 THE MODERN PROBLEM OF BEGINNING

'Only in more recent times', says Hegel at the opening of "With what must the beginning of the science be made?", 'has the awareness arisen, of the difficulty of finding a *beginning* in philosophy' (*WL* 45/5:65). This "modern perplexity about the beginning" seems to have two principal motivations, according to Hegel's analysis. Firstly, it is in part the result of the increasing prominence of methodological questions about how a given thinker, or how thought, can legitimately begin to gain purchase on the subject matter of a systematic philosophy. This points us towards the methodological revolution in metaphysics initiated by Descartes, which I briefly discussed earlier, since it is with Descartes that philosophers most obviously start to ask 'the question of with what to begin' (*WL* 45/5:65) in earnest.

Secondly, Hegel also says that modern work on the problem of beginning 'emerges from a further requirement' that several of the major philosophical projects of modern philosophy after Descartes fail to satisfy, by his lights:

> If earlier abstract thought was primarily only interested in the principle as *content*, in the progress of culture it was driven to pay attention to the other side, to the conduct of *cognition*, accordingly the subjective activity was grasped as an essential moment of the objective truth, and this thereby leads to the requirement that method and content, *form* and *principle* be united. Thus the *principle* should also be the beginning, and what is the *Prius* for thought should also be the *first* in the *course* of thinking. (*WL* 46/5:66)

The "earlier abstract thought" mentioned here applies to both "objective" and "subjective" beginnings discussed earlier, since both are concerned with identifying a principle in terms of some content upon which everything else is grounded, whether objective atoms or subjective perceptions, for example. Hegel's claim appears to be that, over the course of the development of modern European philosophy, as a result of the increased attention to the methodology and the justification of metaphysical claims, from Descartes' engagement with sceptical arguments, or from Kant's critical investigation of the capacities and limitations of our cognitive faculties, for example, it has become apparent that it is necessary to treat metaphysics, or the nature of being, and cognition, or the nature of thinking, together.[30] But Hegel then suggests a consequence of this realisation: that, if the philosophical project in question is to amount to a demonstrative science, and if being and thought are to be treated together, then the fundamental metaphysical principle must also be the first principle of philosophical thought, and should come first in the order of the elaboration of the system.

There are really two components to this second requirement then. One calls for some kind of idealism: for treating thinking and being together, or, as Hegel might put it, for treating logic as metaphysics. The fundamental principle of such an idealist philosophical system is thus not to be considered as merely objective or merely subjective but as encompassing both characteristics. Since this component extends far beyond the topic of beginning to broader questions about the nature of the metaphysical positions developed by Hegel and some of his predecessors, I can only treat it in an extremely cursory fashion in what follows. The second component, more closely related to the topic of this chapter, supposes that the fundamental principle of an idealist philosophical system must be given first, and indubitably, at the beginning of the elaboration of the system in question. I will suggest in Section 2.4 that Hegel endorses the first of these two components but not the second. Firstly, however, it is worth providing some more detail concerning Hegel's characterisation of the "modern perplexity about the beginning" and the philosophers he has in mind at this point in his discussion.

Hegel suggests that this requirement—for a beginning which places its specifically idealist principle first in the order of exposition—was neglected by those too busy 'dogmatically demonstrating [an objective] principle' and by those who are occupying themselves with 'sceptically finding a subjective criterion against dogmatic philosophising' (*WL* 45/5:65). And I have already discussed his critical attitude towards such methodologically dogmatic, and merely objective or subjective beginnings, in Section 2.1. Whom, then, is Hegel thinking about when he writes about this "modern perplexity about the beginning" and its attendant requirements?

---

30. Depending on exactly how it is understood, this might look rather more controversial today than it did in Hegel's time, since metaphysical idealism is by no means the dominant position in contemporary Western philosophy. Charting and evaluating the fall of Hegel's narrative concerning the emergence and triumph of idealist philosophy goes far beyond what I can achieve here, however. In the remainder of this section, it will suffice to acknowledge that Hegel affirms this requirement and criticises others for falling short of it. Hegel's arguments for metaphysical idealism, and for the way in which he understands the position to have emerged over the course of modern philosophy, are topics for another study.

2.3.1 Descartes

An obvious candidate, I have already suggested, is Descartes. That Descartes takes the issue of a methodological beginning seriously I have acknowledged in the previous section. And in his *Lectures on the History of Philosophy*, Hegel remarks that 'with Descartes we really arrive at a self-standing philosophy which knows . . . that self-consciousness is an essential moment of the truth' (*VGP* 653/20:120). In Descartes' defence of the indubitability of the Cogito, then, one seems to encounter both a concern for the methodological beginning of a scientific metaphysics and a fundamental principle which comes first in the order of the exposition and, in Hegel's opinion, at least, is neither merely objective nor subjective. As Hegel puts it, characterising Descartes' position,

> "I think", this thought immediately incorporates my being; this, he says, is the absolute foundation of all philosophy. The determination of being is in my "I". This connection itself is the first. Thought as being and being as thought, that is my certainty, "I"; in the famous *Cogito, ergo sum*; thought and being are thus inseparably connected. (*VGP* 659/20:131)

Yet Descartes only goes so far, both in the direction of an adequate methodological beginning and in the direction of the kind of idealist account of a first principle that Hegel seems to be interested in here. In the first case, in Descartes' account, the Cogito, and, indeed, the existence of God, are, as I have already noted, metaphysical truths that are immediately available to the intellect. Yet Hegel, perhaps following Kant to some extent, is not convinced by appeals to rational or intellectual intuition. He notes that 'the so-called immediate intuition, inward revelation of modern times belongs here' when discussing the beginning of Descartes' philosophy (*VGP* 658/20:129). Yet when discussing the problem of beginning in his *Logic*, he suggests that appeals to 'inner revelation, faith, intellectual intuition, etc.' are merely evidence of an attempt to 'be exempt from *method* and logic' (*WL* 45–46/5:66).[31] However a fundamental principle is to be identified, then, Hegel seems to want to reject any appeal to the notion that it might be immediately and indubitably available to the mind by way of an intellectual intuition.[32]

---

31. See also *EL* §§71–76, where, after criticising Jacobi's defence of immediate, intuitive knowledge of God, Hegel suggests that this amounts to a return to Cartesian philosophy with its 'unproven presuppositions, assumed to be unprovable' (*EL* §77).

32. This represents a difference from Hegel's earlier work in Jena, where he seems to think that some kind of 'transcendental intuition' is necessary for speculative philosophy (*D* 109–11/2:41–43). Houlgate (2006: 125–26) maintains that the mature Hegel does in fact endorse a kind of intellectual intuition, insofar as he takes the thought of indeterminate immediacy with which the *Logic* begins to amount to direct, immediate knowledge of being itself. I cannot discuss this claim here, but it seems to me that more would need to be done to explain why, if this is Hegel's view, he is so explicitly critical of the idea of an intellectual intuition of being in "With what must the beginning of the science be made?".

When it comes to the idealist, or objective and subjective character of the fundamental principle of the system, Descartes' approach also appears to be limited, according to Hegel. This is because, for all that Descartes identifies being with thought in the case of the Cogito, he does not proceed to derive a system of logic and of metaphysics on the basis of this principle. Instead, the Cogito serves to identify the character of the kind of intellectual intuition that Descartes thinks provide basic metaphysical knowledge:

> I am certain that I am a thinking thing. Do I not therefore also know what is required for my being certain about anything? . . . So I now seem to be able to lay it down as a general rule that whatever I perceive very clearly and distinctly is true. (Descartes 1985: II, 24)

It is with this criterion in hand that Descartes turns to his first proof of the existence of God in his Third Meditation, and it is really God who then serves as an objective, fundamental metaphysical principle from which a scientific metaphysics can be developed. As Jeffrey Bell (2021: 54) helpfully puts it, for Descartes, '[d]emonstrations . . . begin with what is primary in the order of things, namely *God*, rather than the *Cogito*'. Hegel is clearly aware that, in this respect, Descartes' account of the beginning falls short of what he is discussing as "the modern perplexity about beginning": he compares him unfavourably with Fichte who also begins with the immediate certainty of the I but represents progress in comparison to Descartes precisely in that he attempts to derive all fundamental logico-metaphysical determinations from this point (*VGP* 660/20:132).[33] There is a case to be made, then, for seeing elements of Descartes' work in Hegel's discussion of the modern problem of beginning, but those elements only go so far. The next step in the direction of this "modern perplexity", I think, comes from Kant.

2.3.2 Kant

Descartes clearly represents significant progress on the way to Hegel's modern problem of beginning. But I think that much the same should be said about Kant. Kant, like Descartes, is concerned to develop metaphysics as a science and, in so doing, to ensure that there is no opportunity for a sceptic to rebut the metaphysical claims in question by arguing that an equally good case can be made for opposing claims. Similarly to Descartes, Kant views the

---

33. Spinoza, in making extension and thought both attributes of God, arguably goes further in the direction of idealism that Descartes, in Hegel's eyes, but it is clear that his axiomatic approach to systematic philosophy excludes him from Hegel's discussion of the "modern perplexity about the beginning", which demands a more careful account of why the first principle is not vulnerable to sceptical objections.

dominant metaphysical tradition of his day (Wolffian rationalism) as problematically dogmatic and thinks that this opens the door to scepticism: 'the dogmatic use of [reason] without critique . . . leads to groundless assertions, to which one can oppose equally plausible ones, thus to scepticism' (*KRV* B22–23).³⁴ And similarly to Descartes, Kant thinks that efforts must be made to purge metaphysics of dogmatism and its vulnerability to sceptical rebuttals, for the sake of 'the advancement of metaphysics as a well-grounded science' (*KRV* Bxxxvi).

But Kant does not adopt a version of the Cartesian method of doubt, however. Nor does he agree with Descartes and later rationalists that metaphysics can proceed on the basis of axioms, known immediately by intellectual intuition.³⁵ Kant's approach to the matter of the methodological beginning is to insist that before the science of metaphysics is developed, a preparatory discipline is required: a critique of our cognitive faculties in order to see what kinds of genuine a priori knowledge are possible for human beings.³⁶ The results of this discipline, Kant suggests, will be the identification and validation, a priori, of principles on the basis of which an undogmatic scientific metaphysics can be developed (*KRV* A11/B24–25).³⁷

Kant's conception of such a scientific metaphysics, once set on secure grounds by the project of critique, otherwise largely resembles traditional rationalist conceptions of such a science, with Kant insisting that metaphysics 'must prove its conclusions strictly *a priori* from secure principles' (*KRV* Bxxxv), and that it exhibit systematic unity, or that all of its claims exhibit 'interconnection based on one principle' (*KRV* A645/B673).

If Kant does not make a suspect appeal to a faculty of intellectual intuition in addressing the matter of the methodological beginning of the science of metaphysics, he may also be taken to go further than Descartes in the direction of the other requirement that Hegel imposes on such a discipline: that its fundamental principle be understood as neither merely objective nor merely subjective. This aspect of Kant's idealism is perhaps clearest in his discussion of the traditional discipline of general metaphysics or ontology: the

---

34. See Forster 2008: 16–20, for a discussion of the influence of Pyrrhonism on Kant's account of the ways in which the dogmatic use of reason leads to sceptical results.

35. Kant explicitly rejects the idea that philosophy can proceed on the basis of axioms at *KRV* A732/B760. He rejects the idea that humans have a capacity for immediate, intellectual intuition at *KRV* B307, among other places.

36. Kant sometimes uses "transcendental philosophy" to refer to this preparatory project of critique, but this term he also uses rather more flexibly. See Förster 2012: 100–6, for a discussion of the changes in the way Kant uses "transcendental philosophy".

37. Thus Kant goes on to claim that his critique of theoretical reason yielded the basic principles of the metaphysics of nature, while his critique of practical reason yielded the basic principle of the metaphysics of morals (*KU* 20:202). These two metaphysical disciplines make up Kant's conception of a systematic science of metaphysics (*KRV* A841/B869). See Schafer (forthcoming), for further reflections on Kant's philosophical methodology and the relation between critique and metaphysics.

identification of the fundamental categorial structure of reality. Dissatisfied with Aristotle's account of fundamental metaphysical categories, which he considers to err both in failing to properly *derive* the categories on the basis of a principle and in identifying at least some categories empirically, on the basis of sensible experience (temporal and spatial categories, as well as the category of motion) (*KRV* A81/B107), Kant derives a table of twelve quantitative, qualitative, relational, and modal categories from forms of judgement which he adapts from traditional, "general" logic (*KRV* A67–83/B92-116). This procedure, Kant thinks, allows him to derive *all* fundamental categories a priori 'and according to a principle, namely that of the faculty for judging in general' (*P* 4:308).[38]

Yet as well as exhibiting what he considers to be genuine scientific rigour, Kant's derivation of the categories from the forms of judgement means that he takes these categories not as having an immediate ontological significance but rather to be the fundamental categories of human understanding and, in this sense, to have a subjective dimension.[39] Kant follows this so-called "metaphysical deduction" of the categories with what he calls their "transcendental deduction", the purpose of which is to show that one is also entitled to take these categories to apply legitimately to objects in the world (*KRV* A85/B117). Putting the question of the details and validity of Kant's transcendental deduction aside, its putative results are well known: Kant takes the categories to have both subjective and objective validity, or to provide the fundamental categorial structure both of thought and of objects, with two important caveats.[40] The first is that the categories can only legitimately be known to apply to objects of possible experience (*KRV* B166) so that theoretical metaphysical knowledge, too, is also restricted to objects of possible experience. The second is that objects of possible experience must be conceived of as appearances and not as things in themselves (*KRV* A238-39/B297-98). These caveats are results of Kant's "two-stem" conception of human cognition, which claims that concepts and sensible intuitions in combination are

---

38. The case of Kant's metaphysical deduction of the categories is a curious one, in that it clearly belongs to the project of critique, which is to say, critically examining our cognitive capacities and their limits and thereby discovering the principles on the basis of which a system of metaphysics can be developed, yet in claiming to derive, a priori, a system of fundamental categories on the basis of a single, certain principle, the metaphysical deduction appears to correspond more closely to the model Kant endorses for the development of a scientific metaphysics than that of the project of critique. This peculiarity, coupled with the importance attributed to Kant's metaphysical deduction by the early German Idealists, probably goes some way towards explaining why Kant's line between critique and metaphysics would become increasingly blurred by the idealist philosophers of the 1790s.

39. Kant assigns the task of deriving a system of basic categories of objects, which typically belongs to the discipline of ontology, to "transcendental logic"—the discipline of determining 'the origin, the domain, and the objective validity' of such basic concepts of objects (*KRV* A57/B81).

40. As Hegel expresses Kant's position, 'The thought determinations or *concepts of the understanding* make up the *objectivity* of experiential cognition' (*EL* §40).

required for the cognition of any determinate object at all (*KRV* A50-52/B74-76), and of his transcendental idealism, which I take to be the claim that, since all of the objects we experience are given in space and time, and since Kant argues that space and time are a priori intuitions belonging to our faculty of sensibility rather than determinations of the objects themselves, our experience of objects is always of objects according to a form imposed on them by our minds and thus of objects only as they appear to us, rather than as they are in themselves (*KRV* B69).[41]

Both aspects of Kant's "modern" approach to the topic of beginning—his methodological concern for establishing metaphysical principles in a manner not open to sceptical rebuttal and his idealist conception of fundamental principles as combining objective and subjective dimensions—seem to go further that Descartes' did towards what Hegel discusses as the "modern perplexity about the beginning". And yet, Hegel will also direct criticisms at both of these aspects of Kant's project.

Against the first aspect, Hegel is famously critical of the attempt to preface metaphysics with a separate project of critique, since the attempt to critically examine our cognitive faculties itself already relies upon the use of those faculties. He compares it on more than one occasion to the attempt not to enter the water before one has learned how to swim.[42] James Kreines has convincingly shown that this objection from Hegel is intended to generalise to any attempt to insist that metaphysics be preceded by some propaedeutic discipline, be it epistemological, semantic, or otherwise, since in each case such a project immediately raises the question of the legitimacy of the claims made in that propaedeutic discipline, and threatens, in a regressive fashion, to demand a further preparatory, critical inquiry into the legitimacy and limits of claims made in that first propaedeutic discipline in turn, and so on.[43] In such a case, as Kreines puts it, 'we could never begin to philosophise' (Kreines 2015: 13). Hegel's approach to the methodological beginning, accordingly, is not to appeal to a preparatory project of critique.[44]

---

41. Despite these caveats, I think it is clear that Kant is still interested in developing a metaphysical system along broadly Wolffian rationalist lines. See de Boer 2020 for a strong case for such a reading of Kant's First Critique.
42. See *EL* §§10A, 41Z, or *VGP* 772/20:334, for example.
43. See Kreines 2015: 13–14, 140–42.
44. In the *Encyclopaedia*, Hegel suggests (a) that philosophical thinking requires both that the necessity of its results and its ability to arrive at genuine knowledge of objects must be properly justified, (b) that this treatment of philosophical knowing must itself fall *within* the properly philosophical discipline itself, and therefore, (c) any attempt to provide a '*preliminary*' explication', like Kantian critique, designed to provide such justification, is undermined by the fact that would itself be an 'unphilosophical' discipline, falling short of the standards required of a genuinely scientific philosophy, and thus that it would be only 'a web of presuppositions and assurances . . . of contingent claims against which the opposite could be assured with equal right' (*EL* §10). Here then, Hegel is clearly suggesting that he takes the Kantian project of a propaedeutic discipline of critique to invite a Pyrrhonian Sceptical rejoinder.

The second aspect of the approach to the topic of beginning as it occurs in Kant's work—the identification of fundamental principles that are both objective and subjective in nature and the demand that a fundamental principle come first in the order of the elaboration of the system—demands more discussion that I can provide here. The same goes for Hegel's critical attitude towards Kant's position on this topic. All that I will do is to indicate the rough nature of the primary criticism that Hegel directs towards Kant on this score. Detailed evaluations of Kant's position, Hegel's understanding of Kant's position, and the legitimacy of the criticisms he directs towards that position must be (and, indeed, already have been) accomplished elsewhere.[45]

It is clear that, by Hegel's lights, Kant's idealism is an inadequate one. Although he acknowledges that Kant's categories are treated both as subjective, since they are the categories of the understanding, and as objective, insofar as they are the categories any object of possible experience must conform to, Hegel objects the way in which Kant restricts the objectivity of the categories to appearances.

[T]he Kantian objectivity of thinking itself is only subjective insofar as thoughts, according to Kant, despite being universal and necessary determinations, are *only our* thoughts and differentiated from what the thing *in itself* is by an insurmountable gulf. In contrast, the true objectivity of thinking consists in this: that thoughts are not merely our thoughts, but rather at the same time the *in itself* of things. (*EL* §41Z2)[46]

Accordingly, despite the obvious influence of Kant's idealism on the position that Hegel develops in his *Logic*,[47] it is clear that what Kant himself calls his 'formal idealism' (*KRV* B519) falls short of unity of the subjective thought and objective being that, Hegel suggests, characterises the "modern perplexity about the beginning". In fact, Hegel suggests that, in withholding from claims to metaphysical knowledge about things in themselves, Kant has replaced the 'objective dogmatism' of the rationalists with a 'subjective dogmatism' interested only in conditions of the possibility of experience, with the result that the question of what is true in and for itself has been given up (*VGP* 771/20:333).[48]

What is more striking and more important for my purposes here than Hegel's criticisms of the nature of Kant's idealism is the fact that Kant does

---

45. See the detailed discussions in Bristow 2007, or Sedgwick 2012, for example.
46. See also *EL* §60Z1, or *VGP* 770-73/20:330-39.
47. See *WL* 514–16/6:254–56, for example, where Hegel explicitly discusses the influence of Kant's account of the synthetic unity of apperception on his own account of the Concept.
48. See also *WL* 516/6:256, for Hegel's rejection of Kantian idealism on the grounds that it is problematically subjective and that it takes a fundamental logical category as 'something merely *formal* that, because it abstracts from content, does not contain truth.'

not seem to fully endorse Hegel's second requirement for a modern treatment of the problem of beginning: the demand that this idealist metaphysics begin directly from a single fundamental principle. This is already clear from the brief discussion of Kant's idea of a propaedeutic project of critique which should preface metaphysics and discover the latter's first principles, provided above, since a project which aims to discover fundamental principles clearly does not begin with them. And despite the fact that Kant goes some way, if not as far as Hegel wants, towards identifying principles which are taken to be both objective and subjective in nature, it is not at all clear that Kant endorses the idea that a scientific metaphysics must be grounded in a *single*, fundamental principle.

Yet, it is exactly this issue—of whether Kant supposes that a scientific metaphysics should proceed on the basis of a single, fundamental principle, and of whether he takes this requirement to attach also to the preparatory project of critique—that drives the developments in post-Kantian idealist approaches to the topic of beginning, which, I think, provide the real background to Hegel's comments about the "modern perplexity" about this topic. The first step in this narrative, only a very brief and inadequate version of which can be presented here, is Reinhold's development of Kant's transcendental philosophy during the period of what the former called his "Elementary Philosophy".[49]

2.3.3 Reinhold

Hegel himself, I should note, tends not to acknowledge the importance of Reinhold in the development of early post-Kantian idealism, usually restricting his engagement with Reinhold's work to criticisms of Reinhold's later "rational realism".[50] Still, there is now wide agreement that Reinhold's Elementary Philosophy represents a decisive step between Kant's critical philosophy and the systematic philosophical projects of Fichte, Schelling, and Hegel.[51]

Various of Kant's own remarks on the relationship between critique and metaphysics, the nature of a properly scientific discipline, and the role of a fundamental principle, are taken by Reinhold to present a problem for the develop-

---

49. Reinhold famously repeatedly revised his position, from criticising Kant to Kantian transcendental idealism, to his own attempt to improve on Kant's approach in his Elementary Philosophy, to adopting Fichte's position, to his later "rational realism", under the influence of Bardili, and further still in the direction of reflections on the philosophy of language. See Bondeli 1995 for a thorough treatment of Reinhold's work on the problem of beginning across several stages of his philosophical development.
50. See, for example, *D* 179–92/2:121–36, or *WL* 48/5:69. Hegel passes over Reinhold's early philosophy almost in silence in his *Lectures on the History of Philosophy* (*VGP* 800/20:387).
51. See Beiser 1987: 226–65, Pinkard 2002: 96–104, Franks 2005: 211–59, or Förster 2012: 154–61, for some notable discussions of Reinhold's impact on the development of German Idealism.

ment of a broadly Kantian metaphysics in an unequivocally scientific format capable of convincing any sceptical interlocutor: that of identifying a single, foundational principle upon which a systematic metaphysics is to be grounded.

Besides his claim to have derived the categories according to a principle of judging in general, Kant also remarks, for example, that systematic cognition should exhibit 'interconnection based on one principle' (*KRV* A645/B673). Such remarks *can* be read as suggesting that Kant thinks that a systematic, scientific metaphysics must be derived from a single, foundational principle, but such a reading is far from the only available one. Kant claims to have derived the categories "in accordance with" a principle, but this is not obviously the same as "from" a principle, which would more clearly imply the principle in question plays a foundational role. And several of Kant's remarks concerning the demand that systematic cognition exhibit interconnection based on one principle take place in his discussion of the regulative use of the transcendental ideas in empirical cognition rather than straightforwardly in a discussion of metaphysics. Furthermore, it is there that Kant shows himself to be quite open to the idea that sometimes such a unifying principle is not given at the beginning of the investigation but must itself be discovered by a 'hypothetical use of reason' (*KRV* A647/B675). If it is fair at all to apply Kant's remarks here concerning the nature of systematic cognition to his conception of a scientific metaphysics, then, given the need that Kant sees for a propaedeutic project of critique in relation to the latter, it would be surprising if Kant also thought that metaphysics was a matter of deriving a system from a principle that was '*in itself certain* and given' (*KRV* A646/B674).[52]

Kant also, however, in his *Critique of Practical Reason*, remarks that a reader persuaded by his derivation of determinations of the will from moral principles should find the syllogistic nature of his analytic of practical reason and its points of similarity with the structure of his analytic of theoretical reason (which, Kant suggests, proceeds in the opposite direction, from determinations of experience to theoretical principles) pleasing,

> for they rightly occasion the expectation of perhaps being able some day to attain insight into the unity of the whole pure rational faculty (theoretical as well as practical) and to derive everything from one principle—the undeniable need of human reason, which finds complete satisfaction only in a complete systematic unity of its cognition. (*KPV* 5:91)

This, certainly, sounds rather more as though Kant is interested in identifying a single principle from which an entire philosophical system can be derived,

---

52. See also *KPV* 5:89, where Kant remarks that 'the analytic of pure theoretical reason . . . had to begin from *intuition* . . . only then progress to concepts . . . and could end with *principles* only after preparation by way of both these'.

even if it is not straightforwardly given at the beginning, and requires the work of critique to identify. And yet, the matter is still not so clear. Kant's remarks here concerning what sounds as though it is, in his view, a reasonable expectation, and indeed, an "undeniable need of human reason", namely to ground the entirety of a systematic philosophy in a single, foundational principle, recall very clearly, I think, his descriptions in the *Critique of Pure Reason* of the problematic tendency of human reason to seek 'with every right' an unconditioned which it cannot ever genuinely know, in order to explain everything else, 'thereby demanding the series of conditions as something completed' (*KRV* Bxx).[53] Kant's various remarks, which seem to suggest the model of a scientific metaphysics as a system derived from a single, foundational principle, then, are, at the very least, open to alternative interpretations.

It is clear that Reinhold, however, straightforwardly takes all such remarks of Kant's to identify a crucial criterion for a scientific philosophical project: that it take the form of a complete system strictly derived from a single, absolutely fundamental principle. And, perhaps rather questionably, he seems to take Kant's expression of the 'supreme principle of all synthetic judgements' (*KRV* A158/B197) to amount to such a fundamental principle for a science of metaphysics (Reinhold 1978: 68). Yet this principle itself is established by means of Kant's critical work in the *Critique of Pure Reason*, and when Reinhold considers this work, he does not find that it itself satisfies this scientific criterion:

> Whenever Kant speaks of philosophy as a *science*, he himself requires *systematic form*, thoroughgoing unity of manifold cognitions under one principle . . . If the critique of pure reason should already be a strict, proper science, which, then, would be the principles that, in connection with a single highest principle, constitute its foundation? (Reinhold 1978: 116–17)

Reinhold accordingly sets out, in the various works in which he advances his Elementary Philosophy, to remedy this perceived limitation in Kant's critical philosophy by arguing for what he takes to be basically Kantian conclusions, but in a manner that derives all of its various claims in systematic form on the basis of a 'first and universally accepted principle of all philosophy' (Reinhold 2003: 3).[54] Of course, this involves a suspect reading of Kant, since (a)

---

53. See also *KRV* A299-338/B355-96, or A751-83/579-611.

54. The objection which Hegel directs towards the Kantian preparatory project of critique in comparing it to attempting to learn to swim before entering the water, if it is a successful one, would presumably also apply to Reinhold's project of an Elementary Philosophy. The response that Reinhold would give to such criticism would doubtless be to appeal to what he takes to be the self-evident nature of the first principle of the Elementary Philosophy, but I think that it is fair to assume that this would not convince Hegel any more than it convinced Schulze, Maimon, or any other of Reinhold's critics in the 1790s.

it is not clear, even in Kant's remarks concerning the role of first principles in a proposed systematic metaphysics which would follow his critical work, that he always conceives them as foundations from which all of the determinations of the system can be derived, and (b) even if Kant in fact does think that this is how a systematic metaphysics should be presented, it is clear that he, *contra* Reinhold, does not take this criterion to apply to the preparatory work of critique.[55] Nor can he think any putative fundamental principle of philosophy should come first in the order of thinking as absolutely certain and self-evident, since it is precisely the role of the project of critique to discover principles, rather than begin with them.

Yet it is not Reinhold's possible misunderstandings of Kant that are the focus of this section.[56] I am rather interested in the development of the problem of beginning as Hegel understands it, and despite his neglect of Reinhold's importance, I think it is clear that he is sympathetic to at least a certain aspect of the line of interpretation that Reinhold inaugurates. This is suggested by his repeated remarks to the effect that Kant fails to properly demonstrate the validity of his system of logico-metaphysical categories precisely because he does not derive them from a fundamental principle, even if Hegel tends to credit Fichte rather than Reinhold with originating this claim (*EL* §42A, *VGP* 799/20:386).

Concerns about Reinhold's interpretation of Kant aside, it is clear that Hegel's "modern perplexity about the beginning" really takes shape in Reinhold's revisions to Kant's critical philosophy. Reinhold exhibits a clear methodological concern for the validity of the beginning of a philosophical, systematic science and argues that the appropriate response on this issue is to identify a fundamental principle with which thought can begin, which is absolutely certain, and from which all of the determinations of an idealist system of philosophy can be derived. Thus what I called second aspect of Hegel's modern problem of beginning—that a scientific philosophy begin from a single idealist principle—provides the dominant answer to the first— the methodological concern for a beginning that is not vulnerable to sceptical challenges—precisely by attempting to identify a principle that is universally accepted and self-evident. Reinhold's candidate for such a principle he refers to as "the principle of consciousness": 'representation is distinguished in consciousness from the subject and from the object and is related to both' (Reinhold 2003: 144). On the basis of this principle, Reinhold thinks, it will be possible first to provide a thorough philosophical account of consciousness and particularly of the nature of representation, and that on the basis of *this*

---

55. See de Boer 2021 for a discussion of whether Kant's project of critique should itself be considered a science, and of what criteria it would then have to meet.
56. See Förster 2012: 154–58 for a brief but informative discussion of Reinhold's interpretation of Kant, focused on the role of the provision of a fundamental principle.

account, it should then be possible to found a scientific metaphysics, along with the various other philosophical disciplines.[57] Yet establishing the validity of such a fundamental principle is no straightforward task, as Reinhold is aware. He remarks:

> That which has to stand at the *head* of . . . all philosophical explanations and proofs, cannot be demonstrated through a proof drawn from any part of philosophy whatever, nor through any philosophy, neither previous nor yet to come. (Reinhold 1978: 77)

The absolutely fundamental principle from which all other philosophical claims will be derived, Reinhold points out here, cannot itself be derived or proved on the basis of philosophical reasoning, since then its status as the first, absolutely fundamental principle is undermined, and with it the security of the system to be derived on its basis. Yet the alternative, Reinhold acknowledges, cannot be to merely assert the principle, if this is simply to stipulate that it is valid, or simply to "define" it, since this is to render it indistinguishable from an arbitrary assertion, and a fundamental principle must be 'distanced from . . . all *arbitrariness*' (Reinhold 1978: 81). Reinhold has effectively constructed a dilemma here (one that Fichte will repeat): a fundamental principle, placed at the beginning of a philosophical system, on the one hand, cannot be proved without raising the question of the status of what is appealed to for its proof and thereby undermining its status as absolutely fundamental; yet on the other, it cannot merely be defined and placed at the beginning, as this looks problematically arbitrary. This is Reinhold's modern problem of beginning.

Reinhold is concerned to show that his principle of consciousness does not fall into either side of this dilemma. After rejecting the possibility of proving the first principle, in the passage I quoted earlier, he adds that,

> the principle of consciousness is so little a *definition*, that it much rather qualifies thus only as the *first fundamental principle* of all philosophy, because it presents a concept of which no definition is possible . . . the principle of consciousness . . . is determined *through* what the principle expresses, namely the *facts of consciousness* . . . My first, fundamental principle expresses, as the *principle of consciousness*, only the *fact*, through which the concept of representation is defined . . . It grounds this definition [of representation] without itself being grounded through another. Its ground is consciousness. (Reinhold 1978: 78–80)

In Reinhold's view, it is the content of consciousness itself which immediately grounds and determines the fundamental principle of philosophy,

---

57. See di Giovanni 2000: 9–19, for a critical examination of these aspirations of Reinhold's.

distinguishing it from a mere definition, in the sense of an arbitrary assertion. Reflection on the nature of conscious experience itself, which is not itself a principle, of course, irresistibly gives rise, according to Reinhold, to the principle of consciousness. He thus appeals only to 'the self-explanatory fact of consciousness', which 'determines the principle of consciousness immediately, [and] which is not itself open to further analysis, nor to being reduced to simpler elements than those indicated by it itself' (Reinhold 1978: 83).

The problem of beginning that Reinhold attempts to solve by appealing to the notion of a fundamental principle determined immediately by the nature of consciousness itself is, I think, clearly an Agrippan problem. More specifically, it is an instance of the regress problem, which I discussed in Section 1.1.3. Reinhold is concerned to avoid, on the one hand, the arbitrariness implicit in continuing to appeal infinitely to further and further reasons in order to prove a given philosophical claim and, on the other, the arbitrariness of merely asserting something without reasons to support it. In Reinhold's case, and in the cases of several major German Idealists after him, concerns about the regress problem tend in the direction of an attempted foundationalist solution, which is to say, an attempt to locate a fundamental claim which can be recognised immediately to be justified, without the need to support it with any further claims, and yet which is clearly distinct from a merely arbitrary assertion.[58] Indeed, as I have indicated, Reinhold develops this kind of foundationalist solution into a criterion for the scientificity of a philosophical system based on his (at times questionable) reading of Kant and seeks to show that the justification, or even the proof, of all of the philosophical claims of such a system can ultimately terminate satisfactorily in the principle of consciousness because it is determined self-evidently by consciousness itself.

In the light of the demand that philosophy take the form of a unified system, derived from a single fundamental principle, if it is to genuinely prove its claims, it is clear that the stakes of the regress problem and its solution are very high. And the regress problem was very much in the philosophical air at the time that Reinhold composed the texts making up his Elementary Philosophy, although perhaps due less to a great deal of explicit engagement with Sextus' presentation of the Agrippan modes than to the influence of Jacobi's work on the development of post-Kantian philosophy.[59] I cannot discuss

---

58. This approach amounts to rejecting (R2), in the account of the regress problem I provided in Section 1.1.3. Alternative possibilities, such as the idea that metaphysical infinitism might be a plausible position, for example, which have some defenders today, do not seem to have occurred to the German Idealists. The dominant assumption, at least, seems to be that the regress problem must be solved in a foundationalist manner.

59. Pinkard, for one, suggests that Reinhold is following Jacobi in his fascination with the regress problem (Pinkard 2002: 98) and that, in Reinhold's work, this results in the attempt to establish Kantian positions on a single, secure, foundational principle.

Jacobi's work, important as it is, in any detail here.[60] His own response to regress-style worries about the justification of philosophical claims seems to be to cease attempting to answer the sceptic's demands for justification and to appeal to a '*natural faith* of reason' (Jacobi 1994: 553) which accepts the ultimate dependence of ordinary objects on God without sceptical questioning and without the attempt to provide a rigorous proof. This approach, clearly, will not be acceptable to a reader like Hegel who is precisely interested in developing a scientific metaphysics that can answer the sceptic, and Jacobi seems to be one of the principal targets of Hegel's remark that the importance of the problem of beginning is 'completely denied by those who begin, as if out of a pistol, from their inner revelation, faith, intellectual intuition, etc., and who wanted to be exempt from *method* and logic' (*WL* 45–46/5:65–66).[61]

Whether or not Hegel acknowledges it then, it seems as though it is with Reinhold that what Hegel refers to as the "modern perplexity about beginning" really comes together, as a particularly acute version of the regress problem, as it occurs in the context of the attempt to elaborate a systematic philosophical science on the basis of a fundamental principle which comes first for thought. To reiterate this point: in Reinhold's Elementary Philosophy, one encounters an explicit methodological concern for where one ought to begin the elaboration of a scientific metaphysics, coupled with the demand that such an elaboration proceed by derivation from a single, absolutely certain fundamental principle which solves the regress problem and which will give rise to a system of determinations both of thought and of objects, which is to say, an idealist system.[62] This seems to be exactly the modern problem of beginning that Hegel describes in "With what must the beginning of the science be made?"

And yet, with Reinhold, exactly what is so problematic about this formulation of the problem of beginning also comes clearly into focus. By insisting that a systematic science of metaphysics be derived from a single, absolutely certain principle, which also comes first in the order of the exposition, Reinhold guarantees that any sceptically inclined interlocutor will be quick to inquire into whether Reinhold's candidate for an absolutely certain first principle is really so certain as he claims, whether it is really self-evident, or really clearly distinguishable from a mere arbitrary assertion. And if reasons are found for thinking that such a candidate fundamental principle is, in fact,

---

60. See Franks 2005: Chs. 2–3, or Förster 2012: Chs. 4–5, for excellent discussions of the impact of Jacobi's thought on the reception of Kant and the development of German Idealism.

61. Compare this with *VGP* 768/20:327, where Hegel suggests that Jacobi's appeal to immediate knowledge based on faith 'indicates a lack of all criticism, all logic'.

62. It should be acknowledged that the Reinhold of the Elementary Philosophy maintains Kant's distinction between appearances and things in themselves, however. I will not address this topic here, but I take it that many of the criticisms Hegel directs towards the "merely subjective" character of Kant's idealism he would also direct towards the idealism of Reinhold's Elementary Philosophy.

not self-evident but little more than an arbitrary assertion or a hypothesis, then the sceptic will suspend judgement concerning its validity and with it the entire systematic edifice Reinhold seeks to erect on its basis. And indeed, exactly these kinds of sceptical arguments were soon directed at Reinhold's presentation of his Elementary Philosophy.[63]

This is not the place for an extended discussion of the criticisms that were directed at Reinhold's principle of consciousness, as an attempt to solve the modern problem of beginning as I have described it here.[64] All the same, it is worth acknowledging that some of these criticisms were, and, in fact, are, widely seen as successful. Schulze is probably the most significant of Reinhold's contemporary critics on this score. In his *Aenesidemus*, he develops a series of criticisms of Reinhold's case for the principle of consciousness, and while some are rather less persuasive,[65] others seem to amount to genuine problems for Reinhold's case. Schulze notably argues, for example, that Reinhold's case for the principle of consciousness being universally accepted and self-explanatory looks suspect, since it is not clear what is involved in the activities of "distinguishing" the representation from and "relating" it to the subject and the object, to which the principle appeals (Schulze 1996: 54–58). Perhaps even more problematically for Reinhold, Schulze argues that the

---

63. Noticing that Reinhold's presentation of a systematic philosophy, derived from a single, fundamental principle, is, among other things, an attempt to provide a scientific proof of its results which is not vulnerable to the regress problem, should not be confused with the questionable claim that critics of Reinhold like Schulze deployed a particular regressive argument in order to refute the principle of consciousness. This argument would suggest that Reinhold's principle itself gives rise to a certain regress because it states that any representation is distinguished by the subject from both the subject and the object, yet this implies that the consciousness of the subject and the object on which the principle relies can only be saved from contradicting the principle itself if they, too, are distinguished as representations from a subject and an object, which must then, in turn, also be so distinguished, and so on. But as Franks (2005: 219–24), Messina (2011), and Breazeale (2016) have shown, it is not clear that Schulze actually levels this argument at Reinhold, and Reinhold, anyway, seems to think that our knowledge of the subject and the object in his principle of consciousness is not representational. This kind of regressive argument, and its presence or absence in the works of Reinhold, Schulze, and Fichte, is not my focus here. Rather it is the classical Agrippan regress problem, as it applies to German Idealist attempts to develop a scientific metaphysics, and their attempts to provide a foundationalist solution, which I am interested in.

64. Breazeale (2016) provides a good overview of Schulze's criticisms of Reinhold on this score, of Fichte's consideration of their efficacy in turn, and of the significant secondary literature that exists on this score. See Imhoff 2016: 104–9 for a brief discussion of Maimon's critical attitude towards Reinhold's principle of consciousness.

65. The significance of Schulze's first charge, that the principle of consciousness cannot amount to the highest principle of a philosophical system because it itself must stand under the principle of non-contradiction (Schulze 1996: 52–53), is to some extent contested. Breazeale (2016: 159), following Fichte's review of *Aenesidemus*, suggests that this criticism is misguided in that it fails to observe the distinction between a 'real or material' first principle and a 'merely formal or logical one', and points out the principle of consciousness is not derived from the principle of non-contradiction, even if it must not violate that formal principle. Since it is the derivation of a philosophical system that is at stake, for Reinhold, Schulze misses the mark. Fichte himself, in his *Foundation of the Entire Wissenschaftslehre*, seems to think that formal principles, too, can be derived, albeit not directly, from the fundamental principle which he himself endorses (Fichte 2021: 187, 207–10).

attempt to ground the principle on the "fact" of conscious experience itself is to render the principle itself an abstraction, known a posteriori. Yet if it is known a posteriori, then it is difficult to see how Reinhold can hold it up as universal, certain, and necessary, as he seeks to (Schulze 1996: 62–63).

If criticisms from Schulze and other readers of Reinhold were largely seen as successfully undermining the validity of Reinhold's principle of consciousness, Reinhold's statement of the modern problem of beginning and his general approach of attempting to ground a scientific philosophical project, including a scientific metaphysics, in a single, fundamental principle, and thus to provide a foundationalist response to the regress problem as it applied to such a project, was not nearly so quickly abandoned. It is clearly present in Fichte's 1794 *Wissenschaftslehre*, which Hegel pays far more attention to than he did Reinhold's Elementary Philosophy.

2.3.4 Fichte (and Schelling)

The regress problem as it occurs in the face of any attempt to derive a systematic, scientific metaphysics is clearly recognised by Fichte, who expresses both it and the form of his preferred foundationalist solution, clearly echoing Reinhold on both counts, in its simplest, dilemmatic form: 'We have to seek out the absolutely first, simply unconditional foundational principle of all human knowledge. [But] it cannot be *proved* or *defined* if it is to be the absolute first, foundational principle' (Fichte 2021: 200). Fichte, just as Reinhold did, captures the basic form of an Agrippan problem in his expression of the regress problem that any attempt to develop a systematic science of metaphysics according to this post-Kantian model must overcome if it is to be successful. An attempt to "prove" the first principle requires showing that it itself can be derived from further grounds, raising the spectre of a regress, as well as undermining the claim that it is really the absolute first principle in any case. Merely "defining" the principle, however, looks as arbitrary as Spinoza's axiomatic approach to the beginning and will not convince the sceptic.

Fichte's statement of the problem of the beginning, more than Reinhold's, appears to be the example that Hegel has in mind in his discussion of the "modern perplexity about the beginning" in "With what must the beginning of the science be made?" In fact, he credits Fichte, rather than Reinhold, both with arriving at the model for a systematic science of metaphysics and with acknowledging the regress problem facing it. 'The Fichtean philosophy has the great advantage and importance of having established that philosophy must be a science derived from the highest fundamental principle, from which all determinations are necessarily derived' (*VGP* 802/20:390), he notes approvingly in his *Lectures on the History of Philosophy*, shortly before he exactly reproduces Fichte's expression of the regress problem from the *Foundation of the Entire Wissenschaftslehre*, which I just quoted (*VGP* 803/20:391).

Fichte's attempted solution to the modern problem of beginning is not to appeal, as Reinhold did, to a principle which is supposedly immediately evident when reflecting empirically on any case of conscious representation. He is accepting of Schulze's charges that the principle of consciousness cannot be immediately self-evident, since its fundamental terms are ambiguous, and that the principle is ultimately an abstraction from empirical representations.[66] Fichte's approach is rather to argue that one's knowledge of the proposition "I am" is immediately certain in a manner that no empirical representation can be, since the "I" is actively posited by itself in thinking itself, in a manner presupposed by any empirical representing of the kind consideration of which allowed Reinhold to arrive at his principle of consciousness. Fichte claims that this activity of the "I" in positing itself amounts to a kind of intellectual intuition of a fundamental principle that should be understood not as a fundamental *fact* (*Tatsache*) but instead as a fundamental *action* (*Tathandlung*).[67] As Fichte puts it, the fundamental principle which 'stands at the summit of the *Wissenschaftslehre*' is '*The I originally posits its own being purely and simply*' (Fichte 2021: 205).[68]

From this principle, Fichte attempts to strictly derive all of the fundamental determinations of theoretical and practical reason in the form of a system.[69] This includes the fundamental logico-metaphysical categories, hence Hegel's appreciative remark in the *Encyclopaedia* that 'it remains the deep merit of the *Fichtean* philosophy to have reminded us that the *thought-determinations* are to be demonstrated in their *necessity* and that they are essentially to be *derived . . .* from thinking itself' (*EL* §42A).[70] And Fichte clearly conceives of his attempt to derive the fundamental categories from the I's self-positing activity as a solution to the perceived arbitrariness of Kant' own metaphysical

---

66. See Fichte 2000: 139–41. See Frketich 2021: 68–69, for example, for a brief discussion of these points.

67. Förster characterises Fichte's rehabilitation of intellectual intution—the claim that our knowledge of the proposition "I am" is of fundamentally different kind to our knowledge of any other proposition since, in intuiting oneself, one is not passively receiving the intuition but actively producing oneself—as a 'discovery . . . unprecedented in the history of philosophy' (Förster 2012: 163). The fundamentally practical nature of Fichte's account of intellectual intuition is surprisingly downplayed by Hegel in his discussion of Fichte in "With what must the beginning of the science be made?"

68. See Schnell 2021: 79–90, for a good discussion of Fichte's case for this fundamental principle in the *Foundation of the Entire Wissenschaftslehre*.

69. Förster (2012: 182–220) provides a masterful summary of Fichte's attempt to provide such a complete philosophical system on the basis of his fundamental principle in the *Foundation of the Entire Wissenschaftslehre*.

70. As I indicated in the discussion of Descartes earlier in this chapter, Hegel takes Fichte to have exceed Descartes precisely in that Fichte genuinely derives the content of his science of metaphysics *from* the "I", where Descartes did not.

deduction.[71] Also noteworthy is that fact that Fichte conceives of this system of determinations as ultimately culminating in the derivation of its fundamental principle again. As he puts it:

> A foundational principle has been exhausted when a complete system has been erected upon it, that is, when the principle in question necessarily leads to *all* the propositions that are asserted [within this system] and when *all* these propositions necessarily lead back to that foundational principle. (Fichte 2021: 176)

Fichte claims that this circular procedure—of deriving all of the propositions of a philosophical science from its foundational principle and then finding that this derivation concludes in a return to such a principle—amounts to a proof of the completeness, or systematicity of the science.[72] I will explain in Section 3.4.1 that I take Hegel to also endorse this criterion for a systematic metaphysical science. My focus here, however, is on Hegel's attitude towards Fichte's proposed solution to the modern problem of beginning, understood as a version of the regress problem, as I have presented it here.

As I noted in Section 0.3.4, Hegel dedicates some time to a critical discussion of Fichte's claim that it is necessary to begin with the immediate knowledge of the "I" as a fundamental principle toward the end of "With what must the beginning of the science be made?" Here Hegel states that Fichte's proposed beginning follows from the idea 'that from the first truth all the following ones must be derived, and also from the requirement that the first truth be something familiar, and still further, something *immediately certain*' (*WL* 53/5:76). On the basis of this latter requirement the "I" presents itself as something with which we are immediately and more fundamentally familiar with than any other representation.

But, Hegel notes, while the "I" can indeed be expressed, as Fichte expresses it, as 'the simple certainty of itself' and nothing more, it is '*at the same time* something concrete, or the "I" is, much more, the most concrete—the consciousness of itself as an infinitely manifold world'. The details of this concrete experience that I have of myself as the subject of the experience of an infinitely diverse world, with its various complex relations and contingencies, argues Hegel, cannot be what functions as an absolutely certain, intellectually

---

71. See Fichte 2021: 206, where Fichte positions his fundamental principle as the key to the deficiencies of Kant's metaphysical deduction and relates it to both Descartes and Reinhold. See Bruno 2018: 78–79, for some discussion of this point.

72. See Fichte 2021: 173. Fichte's remarks on circularity have led to differences in interpretation similar to those which have arisen surrounding Hegel's remarks on the same. Just as some interpreters have, mistakenly in my opinion, as I shall argue in Section 3.4.1, taken Hegel to appeal to the circularity of his *Logic* in order to justify beginning with pure being, some readers of Fichte have taken Fichte's appeals to circularity to count against the interpretation of Fichte as the foundationalist *par excellence* with his indubitable, intellectually intuited principle of a self-positing I. See Breazeale 2013: 272–300, for a convincing case in support of Fichte's foundationalist credentials in this context.

intuited fundamental principle from which all the claims of a scientific metaphysics are derived. Therefore, considering the idea that the "I" could be the 'beginning and ground of philosophy', Hegel states that this first 'requires the separation of this concrete [content]—the absolute act whereby the "I" is purified by itself and enters consciousness as the abstract "I"' of Fichte's fundamental principle. Hegel thinks that this purification of the "I", which he takes Fichte to commit to in distinguishing the absolute, pure "I" from the apperceptive "I" of ordinary experience, amounts to a problem for Fichte's approach. The problem, he says, is that 'this pure "I" is now *not* something immediate, nor the familiar, usual "I" of our consciousness' (*WL* 53/5:76). But it was precisely this immediate familiarity and certainty to which Fichte could appeal, according to Hegel, in making the case for treating the self-positing I as the first, fundamental principle of his philosophical system. In order to *prove* that the purified, self-positing "I" is absolutely certain, Hegel suggests, Fichte would have to demonstrate its validity by deriving it from the content of the concrete, ordinary "I" with which everyone is immediately familiar.[73] Otherwise, even though the principle is 'defined as *intellectual intuition*', it 'appears . . . as an arbitrary standpoint'. And even if Fichte were to carry out such a demonstration, the self-positing "I" would itself no longer be the absolutely first principle in such a case (*WL* 53-54/5:76).[74]

The nature of this criticism, I think, is fairly clear, even though I have not discussed and cannot discuss here whether it really hits its mark or even whether it accurately portrays Fichte's case for his first principle. Instead of prosecuting that case, which must be accomplished elsewhere, I will turn to another aspect of Hegel's discussion of the modern problem of beginning, one that, it seems to me, expresses a deeper opposition to the approach to that problem of the kind offered by Fichte. I take it that Hegel is expressing this line of thought when he writes:

> It can be demanded of the system, as an organisation of propositions, that the absolute on which the reflection is grounded be presented . . . as the highest or absolutely fundamental proposition. But such a demand already carries in itself its own nullity; since a proposition, posited through reflection, is for itself something limited and conditioned and needs another for its grounding, etc. *ad infinitum*. (*D* 103/2:36)

This passage could be read as a straightforward rejection of the possibility of a foundationalist solution to the regress problem as it applies to the attempt

---

[73]. I take it that this is a nod towards the necessity of the kind of project that Hegel carries out in his *Phenomenology of Spirit*.

[74]. Xiong (2022: 101–2) also provides a brief discussion of these criticisms directed towards Fichte's principle in "With what must the beginning of the science be made?"

to develop a systematic, scientific metaphysics, but I do not think that such a reading is quite warranted. Rather than rejecting the possibility of grounding all of the categories of a scientific metaphysics in a foundational principle, I think that Hegel is rather directing criticism at the idea that such a principle should take the form of a fundamental *proposition*. Thus, in his *Lectures on the History of Philosophy*, he reiterates the claim that the attempt to provide a fundamental principle in the form of a proposition will always be vulnerable to the regress problem, since that proposition will either look like a merely arbitrary 'presupposition' or will 'require [further] proof' itself, in which case it is not fundamental, as further grounds must be adduced for it, *ad infinitum*. But he then adds that 'the Concept [however] is this self-movement, not, as with a proposition, a wanting to rest—nor is it the case that the proof [of the Concept] brings forth another ground or middle term, or is another movement, rather it is that movement itself' (*VGP* 482/19:398).

I will return to this claim further in Section 2.4, but I will say here that it seems plausible to me to read Hegel here as claiming to have identified a fundamental principle upon which to ground a system of logico-metaphysical categories—"the Concept"—but also as arguing that it must not be expressed in the form of a proposition, since a fundamental proposition will always remain vulnerable to the sceptical objection that it requires either further grounds for its justification or is itself a merely arbitrary hypothesis,[75] while this "self-movement" of the Concept escapes this dilemma.

Before going any further, I think that it is also worth briefly saying a word about Hegel's perspective on the relationship between Fichte's fundamental principle and his idealism. Fichte conceives of the system of determinations that he elaborates in the *Foundation of the Entire Wissenschaftslehre* on the basis of his fundamental principle concerning the self-positing I as a work of transcendental philosophy, treating primarily, as Kant did, conditions for the possibility of experience, but he breaks with the nature of Kant's transcendental idealism more radically than Reinhold did, in claiming that it is not necessary to posit a 'thing in itself' as the source of passive sensible intuitions in order to understand the validity of the application of the fundamental categories in experience (Fichte 2021: 266).[76] This last claim is one Hegel is certainly in favour of, since he is explicitly critical of Kant's idealism precisely because 'the Kantian objectivity of thinking itself is only subjective again, as according to Kant, thoughts . . . are *only our* thoughts

---

75. Whether Hegel's comments about the inescapably problematic nature of the attempt to begin with a fundamental principle fairly apply to Fichte I will not address here. It seems likely to me that a case could be made for treating Fichte's self-positing I as exhibiting something closer to the "self-movement" of Hegel's Concept than the latter seems to acknowledge.

76. I cannot discuss here Fichte's case for replacing this notion with that of a "not-I" posited by the "I" itself.

and distinguished from what the thing is *in itself* by an insurmountable gulf' (*EL* §41Z2). And yet, while Hegel acknowledges that Fichte's 'pure knowledge of the "I" takes away its limited meaning, to have its unsurpassable opposition to an object', he still maintains that Fichte's fundamental principle 'also remains, on closer inspection, a subjective I', and that the subjective character of the first principle thereby imparts its subjective character to the idealist system that Fichte erects on its basis, preventing it from addressing the real 'existence of what is inner in *thinking*', that is of developing a metaphysics that treats both subject and object, or thinking and being, together (*WL* 54–55/5:77–78).[77]

Ultimately, then, for all that Fichte seems to express Hegel's modern problem of beginning perhaps more clearly than any other historical philosopher, Hegel clearly remains dissatisfied with his approach. As I have indicated, this is in part because he views what he sees as the problematically subjective nature of Fichte's fundamental principle as vitiating the idealism that Fichte develops on its basis and, in part, because he thinks that the case that Fichte makes for the absolute, immediate certainty of the principle is questionable (although he may, in fact, extend his criticism to *any* attempt to provide a fundamental principle in the form of a proposition).

Before turning to Hegel's own approach to the topic of beginning and its differences from the manner in which the topic has been addressed in this section, I should also very briefly mention Hegel's erstwhile collaborator Schelling, who, curiously, seems to represent to Hegel a significant step forward in the direction of identifying a genuinely idealist principle and of developing a genuinely idealist metaphysics, the determinations of which are neither merely subjective or objective on its basis but, at the same time, a significant step backward in terms of an adequate methodological concern for the beginning, for the adequate justification of that fundamental principle.[78]

In Schelling's work, Hegel finds an idealist metaphysics the fundamental principle of which is envisioned neither as merely subjective, in the form of the "I", for example, nor as merely objective, as in an appeal to thoughtless nature as the ground of all of its determinations, but which encompasses both such characterisations (hence Hegel's suggestion that Schelling's early idealism in some sense combines the principles of Fichte and Spinoza [*VGP* 820/20:423]). Hegel notes that, perhaps most explicitly during the period of

---

77. Compare, for example, *VGP* 801–2/20:388–89, or *D* 155/2:94, where Hegel again levels the charge of an excessively subjective idealism at Fichte. I will not discuss the responses that could be made on Fichte's behalf here. I presume that he would likely see in Hegel's desire a move away from transcendental philosophy and towards pre-Kantian dogmatism.

78. See *VGP* 799/20:386, where Hegel describes Fichte as responding to what Hegel perceived as the inadequacies of Kant's derivation of the logico-metaphysical determinations at stake, and Schelling as responding to what Hegel perceives as the inadequacies of Kant's idealism.

his "Identity Philosophy", Schelling characterises the fundamental principle of both thought and being as 'the absolute identity of the subjective and the objective, the absolute indifference of real and ideal . . . in this identity of the two there is neither the one nor the other' (*VGP* 825/20:434). Because of this characterisation, Hegel thinks, the determinations that Schelling will derive in the form of a system on the basis of this principle, too, will be neither merely determinations of thought nor merely of entities but of both.[79] And it is worth noting in passing that this principle, as a 'point of indifference of subjectivity and objectivity' (*VGP* 825/20:435), is not expressed straightforwardly in the form of a proposition, further grounds for which, Hegel thinks, would then need to be sought. This is not to say, however, that its expression is ultimately adequate, in Hegel's eyes.

Despite his erstwhile enthusiasm for Schelling's idealism during their time together in Jena, Hegel famously seems to come to think that Schelling's account of the fundamental principle as the "point of indifference of subjectivity and objectivity" is problematically vague and abstract, such that it is difficult to see how the determinations of a system of metaphysics could really be derived from it, appearing to target it in the preface to his *Phenomenology* with his remark about the '*absolute* presented as the night in which, as one says, all cows are black' (*PhG* §16/3:22). He also at times seems dissatisfied with the methods Schelling adopts in order to derive the determinations of his system from its principle (*VGP* 826/20:436), but it is not these criticisms that are most relevant here.[80] What seems really disastrous about Schelling's approach to the modern problem of beginning from Hegel's perspective is that no real attempt is made to show that this proposed fundamental principle must be true. There is no real attempt to adequately address what I called, in Section 2.2, the matter of "the methodological beginning". As Hegel puts the thought:

---

79. I note also, in passing, that Kant's firm line between preparatory critique and metaphysics, already perhaps somewhat blurred in Fichte's *Wissenschaftslehre*, seems to have been fully abandoned in Schelling's work, with its system of metaphysics with two sides, a philosophy of nature and a "transcendental philosophy" which derive from the same principle and mutually imply one another. Schelling's "transcendental philosophy" seems closer to a metaphysics of spirit than to Kantian critique.

80. In his *Lectures on the History of Philosophy*, Hegel is actually rather more charitable to Schelling than the popular picture of the "night in which all cows are black" allows. He suggests that Schelling's metaphysics is not ultimately founded on a problematically abstract conception of "absolute identity", but one which is 'concrete' (*VGP* 825/20:434) and one which, although it begins from something immediate, allows for the possibility that 'it is a process, which has mediation in itself as well' (*VGP* 826/20:436). The real problem, Hegel thinks, is that rather than setting out this metaphysics and its principle logically and thus establishing its validity, Schelling only appeals to intellectual intuition in its favour, which results in misunderstandings. For this reason, Hegel insists that it is crucial to distinguish Schelling's genuine metaphysics from those of his less acute followers who, led astray by the appeal to intellectual intuition, develop a genuinely vacuous, abstract, and unsatisfactory metaphysics (*VGP* 835-36/20:451–54).

The deficiency in the Schellingian philosophy is that the point of the indifference of the subjective and the objective, placed at its start, this identity is absolutely posited, without proving that it is the truth. Often Schelling makes use of the form of Spinoza, and posits axioms. [But] one wants, when one philosophises, to have it proven that such-and-such is the case. (*VGP* 825/20:435)[81]

Schelling's fundamental principle, thinks Hegel, looks completely arbitrary. Schelling, as Hegel acknowledges, in fact appeals to the idea that the fundamental principle is known by way of intellectual intuition, but Hegel is clearly not convinced, remarking in his *Lectures on the History of Philosophy* that such a beginning is merely 'an assertion, an oracle, that one simply has to put up with' (*VGP* 825/20:435), and in "With what must the beginning of the science be made?", as I have already pointed out, he ridicules the notion of beginning from something intellectually intuited as an attempt to be 'exempt from *method* and logic' (*WL* 45–46/5:66).[82] And here it seems to me that Hegel is probably in the right. As Förster (2012:247–49) has argued, even if there is a case to be made for Fichte's rehabilitation of the notion of intellectual intuition in the context of the I's activity of positing itself, it is difficult to see what could license Schelling to appeal to this notion in order to secure direct access to the fundamental nature of reality.[83]

With this brief and in many ways inadequate discussion of Schelling, I will draw my discussion of Hegel's account of the modern problem of beginning to a close. I have tried to show that what Hegel sees as the two key elements of this problem—that it exhibit a methodological concern for beginning the development of a systematic science of metaphysics in a manner that is properly justified and that the correct way to do this is to begin from a fundamental principle which is placed first in the order of the exposition of the system, and from which all of the determinations of thought and being (or logic and metaphysics) can be derived—mean that the modern problem of

---

81. Hegel goes on to add that Schelling's appeal to intellectual intuition just amounts to the demand that one ought to intellectually intuit this principle of absolute indifference of subjectivity and objectivity. The implication, I take it, is that simply telling a sceptical interlocutor, "Just intellectually intuit the truth and you will see that I am right!" is not a convincing argument. This is again to nod in the direction of the necessity of a project like that of Hegel's *Phenomenology*, when it comes to making the case for idealism against a sceptical opponent.

82. See also *PhG* §27/3:31, where Hegel makes much the same point, where it also may well be directed at Schelling. As I noted, during his earlier work with Schelling in Jena, Hegel is much less critical of the notion of intellectual intuition (e.g., *D* 109–11/2:41–43). It seems plausible to me that this shift in perspective is attached to his greater appreciation of the necessity of being able to address sceptical opposition to the philosophical system that he seeks to develop, which I discussed in Section 1.2.2. Thus Schelling, in Hegel's eyes, remains closer to his own earlier tendency to merely assert the legitimacy of a scepticism-proof, speculative position. See also Forster 1989: 181–82, for a brief discussion of Hegel's growing 'impatience with Schelling's dogmatic appeal to intellectual intuition'.

83. As Förster puts it, 'the intellectual intuition adapted from the *Wissenschaftslehre* is of no use in [Schelling's] *Naturphilosophie* since it is not we who create nature [as the "I" posits itself], but nature which creates itself' (Förster 2012: 247).

beginning in fact amounts to a version of the regress problem, coupled with a preference for a foundationalist solution to that problem. I have also tried to show that the modern problem of beginning appears most clearly in the work of certain post-Kantian idealists, perhaps most clearly Reinhold and Fichte, but that despite this, Hegel finds the attempted solutions provided by his forebears, whether the principle of consciousness, the self-positing "I", or the absolute indifference of subjectivity and objectivity, all to be wanting for various reasons.

One might think, accordingly, that Hegel's next task in "With what must the beginning of the science be made?" is to provide an improved solution to this modern problem of beginning: to identify a fundamental principle which can be recognised immediately to be absolutely certain and is thus not vulnerable to any sceptical criticisms and from which the determinations of logic and metaphysics can be adequately derived. In the final section of this chapter, however, I will suggest that this is not quite the case. Rather, I think that Hegel's problem of beginning is, in some important respects, different from the "modern perplexity about the beginning" to which Reinhold, Fichte, and Schelling are responding.

2.4 HEGEL ON FIRST PRINCIPLES AND THE BEGINNING

I think that Hegel clearly accepts the importance of a methodological concern for where the elaboration of such a science of metaphysics begins from, so much so that he remains dissatisfied, as I have attempted to show in this chapter, with the attempts of all of his predecessors on this score. And I think that it often looks as though Hegel is also committed to the idea that, in order to amount to a science, metaphysics must take the form of a system that is derived on the basis of a single, fundamental principle, where this fundamental principle is the absolute ground of determinations which are to be understood, in an idealist fashion, as determinations of thought and of being: as the fundamental principle of a logic which is also a metaphysics, where this principle is what Hegel refers to as "the Concept".[84] So it looks as though Hegel *is* interested in providing a foundationalist solution to the regress problem, as it applies to the attempt to provide an idealist, systematic science of metaphysics. Yet where Reinhold, Fichte, and Schelling all supposed, as Hegel put it, that

---

84. I admit, however, that I have not engaged in any depth with those readings of the Concept which suggest that it should not be understood as a fundamental metaphysical principle. Nor will I engage with those readings here, since, as I will argue, I take Hegel's problem of beginning ultimately to be distinct from the problem of how the determinations of logic and metaphysics are ultimately grounded in his *Logic*, and the former problem is the subject matter of this book.

'the *principle* should also be the beginning, and what is the *Prius* for thought should also be the *first* in the *course* of thinking' (*WL* 46/5:66), I think that Hegel in fact differs from them somewhat on this score.

There is a case to be made, as I have indicated in Section 0.1 and in Section 1.2.1, as well as in the earlier parts of this chapter, for understanding what Hegel calls "the Concept" as the fundamental principle of his systematic philosophy, upon which all of the determinations of logic and metaphysics are ultimately grounded.[85] Thus, to briefly repeat the case, Hegel claims in the preface to the second edition of the *Logic* that, the Concept 'is the foundation of the determinate concepts', that is, of the all the logico-metaphysical categories derived in the work (*WL* 19/5:30). And in Doctrine of the Concept itself, Hegel is just as explicit, saying that "the Concept ... is to be viewed as *absolute foundation*' (*WL* 508/6:245). And although, as I pointed out in the previous section, Hegel is critical of the idea of a fundamental principle expressed as a proposition, since he thinks that this always remains vulnerable to the regress problem,[86] he also claims that a genuine speculative philosophy precisely does *not* express its principle 'in the form of a proposition' (*VGP* 480/19:393); he instead understands the system of the categories he develops to be grounded in the Concept as 'moment[s] of the form as a totality' (*WL* 19/5:29-30), rather than upon a single proposition. Since this totality is not something distinct from the determinate categories that it grounds, Hegel characterises it, as I mentioned earlier, in terms of the 'self-movement' of the content that derives from it (*VGP* 482/19:398), and seems to think that such a self-moving totality of determinations does not invite the question of further, separate grounds, nor of any apparent arbitrariness, in the manner that a putative fundamental proposition did.[87] And the Concept seems to fit well with Hegel's remarks, when setting out the modern problem of beginning, concerning the need for a first principle which is both subjective and objective, since he conceives of it as the source of determinations which are both metaphysical and logical, comparing it to the objective 'substance' of Spinoza but maintaining also that it be conceived as '*subject*', along the lines of Kant's 'unity of the "*I think*"' (*WL* 511–15/6:249–54).[88] To this extent, then, it can

---

85. Readings of Hegel on the Concept that understand it in roughly this sense include, I think, Franks 2005, de Boer 2010, Bowman 2013, and Hanna 2013. I think that it is also at least strongly suggested in Knappik 2016.

86. See also *D* 103/2:36, and *PhG* §24/3:27.

87. It may be helpful to compare the manner in which Hegel conceives of the true infinite not as distinct from the finite but instead as unified with it, as the movement of the determination of finite moments (*WL* 118/5:164).

88. I think that this line of thought is nicely captured by Bowman, who describes Hegel's idealism as 'the position that the whole sphere of categorically constituted, finite objectivity is both *independent* of *finite* cognizers and radically *dependent* on an *infinite* ground that does not itself in turn fall under the categories, but is the activity of which they are manifestations' (Bowman 2013: 115).

appear that Hegel is attempting an improved solution to the modern problem of beginning.

Whether Hegel's idea of grounding a system of logico-metaphysical categories in a principle in the form of a totality that encompasses them and determines them provides a more satisfactory response to the regress problem than the attempt to ground such a system in a fundamental proposition, however, is not the issue here. The issue, clearly, is that this fundamental principle, the Concept, is precisely *not* presented at the *beginning* of Hegel's *Logic*. Indeed, it only makes its appearance in the third book of the *Logic*. If the Concept, *qua* fundamental principle, is the "*Prius* for thought" (and, indeed, being), Hegel does not at all seem to think that it must also come "*first* in the *course* of thinking".[89] The *Logic* begins, instead, merely with the meagre concept of '*Being, pure being*—without any further determination' (*WL* 59/5:82). And Hegel goes on to add that while such an 'abstract immediate is indeed a *first* . . . its foundation is . . . to be sought' (*WL* 508/6:245). This is a crucial difference from the approaches to the modern problem of beginning from Reinhold and Fichte, who sought to begin with a principle that was immediately self-evident.[90]

By way of explanation, Hegel claims that '[w]hat *the nature of the Concept is* can little be given immediately' (*WL* 508/6:245). Despite the fact that all of the categories of the Objective Logic ultimately have the Concept as their 'substantial foundation' (*WL* 19/5:30), their examination amounts, Hegel thinks, to the '*genetic exposition of the Concept*', so that, in a sense, the Concept is derived from the categories which it grounds, at least in the order of the investigation of the *Logic*. It is in this sense that Hegel calls the procedure that he follows in the *Logic*, whereby one category is derived from another, a 'progression [that] is a *retreat* into the *ground*' (*WL* 49/5:70).

If this procedure is valid, Hegel has, in effect, found an alternative way to solve Fichte's Agrippan dilemma for an attempt to identify a fundamental principle, which argued that 'it cannot be *proved* or *defined* if it is to be the absolute first, foundational principle' (Fichte 2021: 200). To be sure, Hegel is not merely defining or asserting the nature of the Concept. It seems, however, that he is precisely trying to *prove* its validity, by deriving it *from* all of the categories which it ultimately grounds. But, in providing this alternative solution to the regress problem, or the problem of identifying a fundamental principle, as it applies to the project of a scientific system of idealist metaphysics, Hegel has effectively created a new problem. He remains committed

---

89. See also Stang 2021: 118, for a defence of this claim.
90. See Franks 2005: 377–79, for a slightly different take on this material. Franks thinks that Hegel's *Logic* does begin with its fundamental principle but only 'an initial and still inadequate expression' of that principle. I cannot discuss the significance of this distinction, nor of Franks' accompanying discussion of Hegel's take on intellectual intuition, here.

to the idea that 'the *thought-determinations* are to be demonstrated in their *necessity* and that they are essentially to be *derived* . . . from thinking itself' (*EL* §42A), but now, at least in the order of the investigation pursued in his *Logic*, this derivation cannot begin from its fundamental principle, since this principle is itself to be proved as one of the results of that derivation. And if it begins from somewhere questionable, or arbitrary, then this may be to put the content of the entire derivation that follows from it, including the case for the validity of Hegel's Concept as fundamental principle, on shaky ground. The beginning itself, then, even if it is not considered in terms of a fundamental principle, must be secured against sceptical objections.[91]

What this means, I think, is that the regress problem, or the problem of identifying a fundamental principle, and the problem of *beginning*, have come apart in Hegel's thought, at least by the time that he writes his *Science of Logic*. If the system of the categories of logic and of metaphysics *and* their fundamental principle are to be derived from "thinking itself", where ought this thinking to begin? This, I think, is the problem of beginning that Hegel attempts to solve in "With what must the beginning of the science be made?" And this is why, after concluding his short history of the problem of beginning with his characterisation of the modern problem of beginning which seeks to identify the beginning with the fundamental principle, Hegel does not announce that he himself will attempt to solve that problem in those terms but instead writes, 'Only how the *logical* beginning appears is to be considered here' *WL* 46/5:66). With that problem addressed at the start of the *Logic*, Hegel will then be free to make his case for the derivation of one logico-metaphysical concept from another and, ultimately, for the derivation of the Concept as their fundamental principle. Analysing and evaluating Hegel's success in these latter tasks goes beyond my goals in this book, but Hegel's presentation of and solution to *his* problem of beginning will be examined in great detail in the remaining three chapters.

2.5 CONCLUSION

This chapter, and the previous one, have both been primarily occupied with laying the groundwork for the examination of Hegel's presentation of the problem of beginning, and of its solution, in "With what must the beginning of the science be made?" The previous chapter reconstructed the importance

---

91. I take Hegel effectively to have the same concern as the one expressed here: 'The fear is that, there being no philosophically neutral way to begin, the selection of a starting point, which will probably mean of both a preferred type of evidence or subject matter and a preferred way of handling that subject matter, will create an unjustified evidence-filter that biases and skews the enterprise' (Cahoone 2013: 4).

of Pyrrhonian Scepticism for Hegel's thought, especially the Agrippan modes, which I suggested give rise to the general dilemmatic form of a number of distinct "Agrippan problems", such as the epistemic regress problem or the problem of the criterion. This chapter has provided some analysis of and expanded upon Hegel's short sketch of the history of the problem of beginning which he inserts into "With what must the beginning of the science be made?", in order to clarify his understanding of the nature of the problem, as well as to prepare the ground for his attempted solution.

I have attempted to show that Hegel distinguishes the problem with which he will engage at the beginning of the *Logic* not only from earlier attempts to identify a "subjective" or an "objective" beginning in the sense of a fundamental metaphysical principle but also from the "modern perplexity about the beginning", which is most clearly present in the works of Reinhold and Fichte in the 1790s, where an attempt is made to derive system of logico-metaphysical categories on the basis of a single, fundamental, self-evident principle. In Hegel's *Logic*, I have suggested, the problem of identifying a fundamental principle and the problem of beginning have come apart. While it is possible that this enables a stronger case for the validity of the fundamental principle, it leaves the question of where the derivation of the determinations of Hegel's logical project ought to begin. The problem that must be overcome in order to solve this latter question is the principal focus of the next chapter, where I will argue that this problem, too, Hegel's problem of beginning, amounts to a distinctive Agrippan problem.

Chapter Three

The Problem of Beginning

3.0 INTRODUCTION

In this chapter, I aim to give a close reading and interpretation both of Hegel's expression of the problem of beginning and of the form of its solution, as he presents them in "With what must the beginning of the science be made?" I will proceed as follows: after a brief, preliminary examination of Hegel's statement of this problem and its solution, I will make a case for understanding this problem as a distinctive Agrippan problem, its dilemmatic form following Sextus' presentation of the Two Modes. This problem, I will suggest, consists in the apparent unavoidability of beginning the derivation of the categories in a science of logic from something immediate, in which case the beginning and what follows from it look merely arbitrary, or from something mediated, in which case the beginning appears to refer back to some supporting argument for its validity, the validity of which itself is then in question, leaving the project again looking problematically arbitrary.

After setting out the nature of the problem in detail, I turn to the solution that Hegel offers in "With what must the beginning of the science be made?" Here I try to accomplish two things: Firstly, I identify the *form* of Hegel's proposed solution to the problem of beginning, which turns on locating a thought-determination which is *both* mediated *and* immediate in such a way as to overcome the problematic arbitrariness which, Hegel thinks, accompanies the attempt to begin with something merely immediate, or merely mediated. Secondly, I suggest that Hegel actually provides two different versions of this solution, sharing the same form. The first, in the *Science of Logic*, appeals to the argument of his *Phenomenology of Spirit* in order to secure the beginning against sceptical objections. The second, in the *Encyclopaedia Logic*, appears to replace this appeal to the *Phenomenology* with one to a project of what Hegel describes as a 'completed scepticism' (*EL* §78A). Considering the plausibility of these two solutions is the task of chapters 4 and 5, respectively. Before concluding this chapter, however, I first spend some time offering some criticisms of alternative interpretations of Hegel's problem of beginning and its solution and follow this by attempting to anticipate and defuse some objections that might be levelled at the interpretation that I provide here.

3.1 THE PROBLEM OF BEGINNING: PRELIMINARY INVESTIGATION

I suggested in the previous chapter (in Section 2.4), that although Hegel seems to endorse a kind of foundationalism when it comes to the matter of how the fundamental categories of thought and of being, treated in his *Logic*, are grounded, the principle which he understands to provide this ultimate ground, the Concept, is one of the *results* of his derivation of those categories, rather than something provided, as self-evident, at the beginning. Still, Hegel is committed to the idea that these categories must be strictly derived, or proved, from thinking itself, in order to provide a genuinely scientific treatment of logic. This raises the question of where this derivation is to begin, and how that beginning itself is justified. Its justification clearly matters, I take it, since, if the beginning of the derivation is fundamentally questionable, then even if Hegel's method of demonstration in the *Logic* is perfectly valid, it is possible that, in beginning with the wrong determination, Hegel has proceeded down the wrong path, leaving the results of his logical project, including his account of the Concept, open to doubt. Unless this concern is resolved, Hegel cannot take himself to have provided a genuinely scientific treatment of logic. This is the concern, I think, motivating Hegel's statement the problem of beginning:

> The beginning of philosophy must be either *something mediated* or *something immediate*, and it is easy to show that it can be neither the one nor the other; so that either way of beginning finds its rebuttal. (*WL* 45/5:65)

Upon a first reading, it seems to me, the exact meaning of this problem is not clear, but what is clear is that a few pages later, a solution has been found: 'The beginning is thus *pure being*' (*WL*: 48/5:69). The remainder of "With what must the beginning of the science be made?", after this solution has been reached, consists primarily of clarificatory material on what is involved in thinking and beginning with this concept of pure being, and of criticisms of some alternative approaches to the matter of beginning, as I indicated in

Section 0.3.4. After this, the main body of the text of Hegel's *Science of Logic* does indeed begin with pure being, with Hegel apparently satisfied that he has justified this beginning in such a way that the derivation of the categories which follows from it can proceed on the basis of a beginning which has overcome the problem in question.

I think it is worth reiterating here that the fact that Hegel's solution to the problem of beginning is to begin with the concept of pure being lends support to the case I made in Section 2.4, to the effect that Hegel's problem of beginning is not an attempt to provide a foundation for the systematic logico-metaphysical project that he develops in this work, thereby securing its claims against any sceptical objection. The concept of "pure being" with which Hegel concludes here is no foundational principle but instead merely something 'abstract', for which 'the foundation is . . . to be sought' (*WL* 508/6:245). Indeed, rather than providing an ultimately satisfactory ground for the system of categories which Hegel sets out in his *Logic*, the concept of pure being, which Hegel describes as 'pure indeterminateness and emptiness' (*WL* 59/5:82), appears to be the least informative concept examined in the work, and Hegel's examination of it quickly results in the derivation of determinateness, or quality, and thus shows that being 'goes over into *determinate being* [*Dasein*]' (*WL* 58/5:82).[1] The problem of beginning, then, must be a distinct problem of its own, having to do only with where a science of logic should begin, not with its ultimate foundation.

Whatever has taken place then, between the statement of the problem of beginning and the statement that a science of logic must begin with pure being, must be taken by Hegel to satisfactorily launch his scientific account of the fundamental categories of thought in a rigorous manner, so that the beginning can play its part in contributing to a logical project which can 'demonstrate the necessity of its content' (*EL* §1), or which is not open to the kind of concern that I mentioned previously: that if the beginning is unjustified or arbitrary, then what follows from it cannot lay claim to the status of a scientific investigation.[2]

---

1. Pippin, in fact, takes the passage which I take to express the problem of beginning to be an anticipatory statement of the inadequacy of the concept of "pure being" and to indicate the move to the concept of determinateness or existence (Pippin 2019: 197). I am confident that the passage expresses a problem, the solution to which, Hegel thinks, is to *begin* with pure being, rather than an anticipation of the dialectic of being, nothing and becoming which follows it, but that is not necessarily to disagree with Pippin's account of this latter material. It is merely to say that I do not think that this specific passage supports his account in the way that he takes it to.

2. The importance I am attaching to this problem of beginning might be thought to be in tension with Hegel's comments warning against a 'self-satisfied "thoroughness"', which obsesses over the beginning of the *Logic* and refuses to engage any further 'until the beginning has been securely proven' (*WL* 21/5:32). A closer look at the context of that passage relieves this worry, however. Firstly, it is clear that Hegel has in mind here critics of his who obsess over the validity of the dialectical opposition between the concepts of "being" and "nothing", not those who challenge the case for beginning

The primary difficulty we face in grasping Hegel's problem of beginning is to understand what Hegel means by asserting first the necessity and then the impossibility of beginning either with something immediate or with something mediated. And yet, even before Hegel's terminology is clarified, the form of the problem is clear. It can be expressed like this:

(P1) One must either begin with something immediate or with something mediated.
(P2) One cannot begin with something immediate.
(P3) One cannot begin with something mediated.
(C) Therefore, beginning is impossible.[3]

I take it that there is nothing unusual about posing a problem in this way before going on to present a solution, usually either by challenging a crucial inference or by rejecting a premise. And this is clearly an impasse Hegel thinks he has a way out of. This is made evident simply by the fact that the book which opens with the statement of this problem does not end straight away once the apparent impossibility of beginning has been stated.

The issue one faces, however, in trying to understand Hegel's strategy for solving this problem, is that he does not do a great deal straight away to make explicit the meaning of the terms utilised in its expression. He says that "it is easy to show" that one cannot begin with something immediate or with something mediated, but he does not make clear why this is the case. If we are to understand Hegel's proposed solution to this problem, we need to do more to understand the problem itself. I attempt to provide a satisfactory explanation of the meaning of Hegel's expression of this problem in the next section.

3.2 THE PROBLEM OF BEGINNING AS AN AGRIPPAN PROBLEM

The manner in which I propose to go about clarifying the nature of the problem is to focus attention on the relevant passages from the remainder of "With what must the beginning of science be made?", especially those following shortly after the expression of the problem itself. In particular, I will

---

with the concept of being. The dialectic of being, nothing, and becoming is not the topic of "With what must the beginning of the science be made?" so this warning does not apply here. Secondly, Hegel is taking issue here with critics who attack the beginning of the *Logic* on the basis of principles which themselves are dogmatically taken for granted. This objection, on Hegel's part, actually *lends* support to the idea that the issue of avoiding dogmatism at the beginning is of vital importance, since it is here that Hegel is attempting not to make the same mistake as these critics.

3. See also Wolff 1996: 240–41, and Hentrup 2019: 151, for similar formulations of Hegel's argument.

concentrate on Hegel's uses of "immediacy" and "mediation" in this context. Admittedly, this material deals with Hegel's solution to the problem, but it also sheds some light on the meaning of the problem itself. Those elements of the material which pertain specifically to the solution I will ignore until Section 3.3. I will also appeal here to Hegel's discussion of the problem of beginning in the *Encyclopaedia Logic* (*EL* §1).

We find in this material that Hegel does explore the two possibilities mentioned in his expression of the problem of beginning. First, Hegel suggests that a 'beginning is *logical* in that it should be made in . . . *pure knowing*. It is thereby *mediated*' (*WL*: 46/5:67). He elaborates: 'logic has . . . the science of spirit in its appearance for its presupposition, which contains and demonstrates the necessity, and thereby the proof of the truth of the standpoint that is pure knowing, and of its mediation' (*WL*: 47/5:67). Leaving aside for now the meaning of the terms "pure knowing" and "the science of spirit in its appearance", I take it that this expresses clearly what is involved in beginning with something mediated: to begin with something mediated is to begin with a result. In other words, it is to begin with something supported by some argument, which it accordingly presupposes. Here "to presuppose", I think, need not imply an illegitimate assumption but the sense in which a conclusion presupposes the argument which supports it, or perhaps is even taken to prove it. The motivation for beginning with something mediated is, therefore, clear. I have already indicated that Hegel believes that a science of logic must "demonstrate the necessity of its content". Applied to the beginning, this appears to imply that we should begin with something which is supported by or presupposes an argument which does exactly this. This interpretation is supported by Hegel's discussion of the problem of beginning in the *Encyclopaedia*, I think, which acknowledges the 'requirement . . . to *prove*' the validity of the content in question (*EL* §1). Insofar as one begins with something "proven", then, one begins with something mediated.

The question now becomes why such a beginning should "find its rebuttal".[4] I think that the answer to this is precisely what we are concerned with *beginning*. Because of this, the validity of the presupposed argument in question cannot be taken for granted. Since it precedes the logical inquiry, it cannot itself be treated as justified within it (*WL* 46/5:67). Hegel makes this clear when he distinguishes logic from all other sciences by claiming that only nonlogical sciences are entitled 'to speak from lemmas, to apply

---

4. di Giovanni translates *Widerlegung* in Hegel's statement of the problem of beginning as "contradiction", but I think that this is misleading. Rosen (2014: 82), for example, claims that what is wrong with beginning either with something mediated or with something immediate is that each is 'self-contradictory', but I think that there is nothing obviously contradictory about, for example, the idea of an immediate beginning. It is just that it appears to be merely arbitrary and can thus be equally immediately rebutted with an alternative.

... presupposed forms of definitions and the like without further ado ... in order to fix their general concepts and fundamental determinations' (*WL* 23/5:35). Logic, on the other hand, is not permitted to presuppose any such content, thinks Hegel.[5] The support offered by whatever "proof" it is that a mediated beginning presupposes is therefore nullified so that the necessity of the beginning in question has not, in fact, been demonstrated after all. This is to render the proposed beginning effectively arbitrary, despite its apparent support. Insofar as it is arbitrary, its necessity has no more been demonstrated than that of any opposing candidate for the beginning. In this sense, it finds its rebuttal.[6] In fact, a sceptical interlocutor might object that they could begin with some other mediated concept which presupposes some entirely different argument, with just as much right. As Hegel express the consequences of this line of thought in the *Encyclopaedia*, 'making or treating as valid *presuppositions* or *assurances* appears invalid' in the context of logic (*EL* §1). This problem for the idea of beginning with something mediated—that such a beginning depends on something presupposed, the validity of which itself is fundamentally questionable—recalls, I think, Sextus' characterisation in the Two Modes of the possibility of apprehending something by means of something else as being unacceptably dogmatic (*PH* I:179).[7]

Secondly, Hegel suggests that,

> Should no presupposition be made, however, and the beginning be taken *immediately*, then it is only determined in that it should be the beginning of logic, of thought for itself. Only the resolve to consider *thinking as such* is present, which can also be viewed as something arbitrary. (*WL*: 48/5:68)

This, I think, clarifies what is involved in beginning with something immediate. In the context of the problem of beginning, at least, "immediacy" implies mak-

---

5. This recalls, I think, his rejection of the possibility of prefacing a science of metaphysics with a preparatory discipline like Kantian critique, which I discussed in Section 2.3.2.

6. This interpretation of what is wrong with beginning with something mediated seems to me to be better than that proposed by those like Rosen, who think that the issue with beginning with something mediated is that it is therefore not, in fact, the beginning. (See Rosen 1992: 40. See also Rosen 2014: 82 and Wolff 1996: 241.) Hegel seems quite alert to the possibility that one might genuinely *begin* with something mediated. His claim is not that this would then not be a beginning but instead that such a beginning is bound to be rebutted, presumably because its support in fact offers no real support at all.

7. It may be that the problematic status of what a mediated beginning presupposes is explained more clearly in terms of Hegel's demand that the beginning of a science of logic be an 'absolute beginning' (*WL* 23/5:35) rather than an explicit worry about an infinite regress of presuppositions. Still, it seems plausible that the unsatisfactory nature of an infinite regress is behind Hegel's insistence that an absolute beginning need be made. This is perhaps especially likely in the case of a repeating regress, if whatever is presupposed by the beginning of the science of logic is expressed using thought-determinations which are only properly treated within the logical science itself. Vieweg (2020: 3), for one, seems to think that Hegel's rejection of a mediated beginning should be understood in terms of the threat of a regress.

ing no presuppositions, or "presuppositionlessness" (*Voraussetzungslosigkeit*).⁸ The motivation for adopting such a beginning is also fairly straightforward. If depending upon presuppositions, as in the case of beginning with something mediated, is to render the beginning problematically dependent upon material which is taken for granted, then, one might think, perhaps it is better to begin without any presuppositions at all, in order to avoid dogmatism.⁹

Why should this approach find its rebuttal? I think that the answer is suggested by Hegel's description of this option itself. Beginning with something immediate may avoid a problematic dependence upon presuppositions that have been dogmatically assumed at the beginning, but to describe a beginning as "presuppositionless" is, in fact, just another way of saying that it is a beginning which has *nothing* supporting it or nothing in its favour. This is why Hegel says that such a beginning "can also be viewed as something arbitrary". Beginning with something immediate, or without any presuppositions, looks *just as arbitrary* as beginning with something mediated, or supported by questionable presuppositions, since it is to begin merely by asserting something, without providing any reasons for anyone to accept it as the correct determination from which to begin. As such, it has nothing to recommend it over any other beginning, and it is, therefore, immediately open to a rebuttal. As Hegel expresses the thought in the introduction to his *Phenomenology*, '*one* bare assurance is exactly as valid as another' (*PhG* §76/3:70). This problem for beginning with something immediate—that it appears fundamentally arbitrary—recalls, I think, Sextus' characterisation in the Two Modes of the possibility of apprehending something by means of itself, as unacceptably dogmatic (*PH* I: 178). In fact, the resemblance is even more striking if one recalls the simplified version of this mode which I discussed in Section 1.1.3, where I suggested that it can be read as a version of the Agrippan mode of hypothesis, which targets something asserted arbitrarily without any supporting reasons. And if one turns to Hegel's *Encyclopaedia* expression of the problem of beginning, one finds that Hegel there suggests that 'a beginning as *something immediate* . . . is itself such a presupposition' (*EL* §1), where Hegel's word "presupposition" (*Voraussetzung*) is, as I have already pointed out, also the term he uses to translate Sextus' "hypothesis".¹⁰

---

8. "Immediacy" clearly does not mean "presuppositionlessness" every time Hegel uses the term. It only has this meaning in the context of the problem of beginning. The concept of "essence", for example, is described as a 'simple immediacy as sublated immediacy' (*WL* 356/6:38), but it clearly presupposes the entire range of qualitative and quantitative concepts treated in the Doctrine of Being from which it is derived.

9. The emphasis on the undogmatic character of the presuppositionless beginning is at the heart of Houlgate's influential account of the beginning of the *Logic*, which I discuss in Section 3.4.1.

10. Compare this account with Forster's claim that 'What [Hegel] does find epistemologically problematic is the . . . making of ungrounded claims *against which opposite claims can be advanced*

I think that one can now see exactly why, in the context of beginning either with something mediated or with something immediate, Hegel says that "it is easy to show that it can be neither one nor the other". The problem of beginning is a problem about *arbitrariness*. If we begin with something mediated, then we rely problematically on presuppositions, the validity of which, Hegel notes, cannot be established '*before* the science' (*WL* 46/5:67), which undermines the attempt to render that beginning non-arbitrary by relying on the support of those presuppositions. If, on the other hand, we begin with something immediate, or presuppositionless, then the beginning is straightforwardly arbitrary. In both cases, it seems that no good answer is available to a sceptical interlocutor who asks, "Why should I not begin with some other determination, some other concept?"

di Giovanni, in his translation of the *Science of Logic*, notes that Hegel's expression of the problem of beginning resembles Fichte's dilemma for establishing a first, absolutely unconditional fundamental principle, which I discussed in Section 2.3.4, where the fundamental principle in question can neither be proved nor defined, just as Hegel's "beginning" can be neither something mediated nor something immediate. I think that di Giovanni is right to point out this resemblance, although, as I argued in Section 2.4 and Section 3.1, I think that Hegel's problem of beginning is ultimately a distinct problem from that of identifying a fundamental principle. Ultimately, however, the resemblance between these two distinct problems is to be explained by appealing to the fact that both share the form of Sextus' expression of the Two Modes, which reject both the possibility of apprehending something merely by means of itself, and of apprehending it by means of something else. This to say, in effect, that both problems share the basic dilemmatic form of an Agrippan problem, which, as I described it in Section 1.1.3, is fundamentally a dilemma between, on the one hand, the arbitrariness of a claim that is made without any support, and on the other, the arbitrariness of a claim whose support can be shown to be fundamentally inadequate.[11]

---

in a similarly ungrounded fashion, which gives rise to the equipollence problem in its fourth trope of Agrippa version' (Forster 1989:110).

11. Hentrup (2019: 151) also understands Hegel's problem of beginning to be modelled after Sextus' Two Modes, as does Xiong (2022), following the accounts in Hentrup 2019 and Dunphy 2020b. Neither Hentrup nor Xiong, I think, explicitly appeal to the distinction and relation between the problem of beginning and the problem of the fundamental principle of Hegel's system, as I have done here. Other readers of Hegel's problem of beginning seem to miss that it expresses a distinct problem of its own and approach it merely as a part of Hegel's broader refutation of Pyrrhonian Scepticism in the name of speculative logic and metaphysics. Röttges, I think, understands the problem this way, as an engagement with Sextus' expression of the Agrippan modes of hypothesis and of the infinite regress specifically (Röttges 1987: 138–44). By contrast, Trisokkas (2012: 331–42) locates Hegel's broader refutation of Pyrrhonian Scepticism in Hegel's Doctrine of the Concept but, I think, does not perceive that there is a distinctive Agrippan problem present at the beginning of the *Logic*.

Why it is that an Agrippan problem should arise in the context of the beginning of Hegel's *Logic*, after he has shifted the matter of demonstrating the validity of the fundamental principle of his logico-metaphysical system to the *results* of the derivation of that system in order to solve the regress problem facing Fichte-style attempts to place the principle at the beginning, can, I think, be briefly reiterated here: if Hegel's attempt to derive the Concept as one of the results of his science of logic, by means of a method of demonstration from concept to concept the progression of which is, at the same time, a "retreat into the ground" is successful, then the foundation of Hegel's logic and his metaphysics does not face the dilemma that Fichte outlined for attempts to legitimise a first principle, since the principle can, in fact, be proven. However, Hegel is still committed to the claims (a) that a properly scientific treatment of logic must proceed by way of strict derivation, and (b) that this derivation begins from his account of the concept of pure being. In the face of these claims, it seems perfectly reasonable for a sceptical interlocutor to object to the beginning of Hegel's account in more or less the same manner as they might to an attempt to legitimise a foundational first principle, that is, by means of the kind of dilemma constitutive of an Agrippan problem. Such a sceptic need only scrutinise the legitimacy of beginning with the concept of pure being: has this concept been derived (is it something mediated)? If so, why should one accept the validity of this derivation, particularly if this concept is supposed to constitute the *beginning* of the science? Or has it instead been simply defined or assumed (is it something immediate)? If so, why should one accept this assumption? This is the Agrippan problem of beginning with which Hegel is grappling in "With what must the beginning of the science be made?", I think.

This problem of beginning can, like other Agrippan problems, be expressed by means of three jointly incompatible propositions, as I illustrated in the case of the epistemic regress problem in Section 1.1.3. In the case of the problem of beginning, it would look like this:

(B1) It is possible that there is some non-arbitrary concept with which to begin a science of logic.
(B2) A concept needs to presuppose something for its support in order to render itself non-arbitrary.
(B3) Anything presupposed at the beginning of a science of logic does not offer genuine support.

As in the case of the regress problem, any two of these propositions can be affirmed at once, but it seems impossible to affirm all three together. This *seems* to point towards three likely kinds of response:

One could deny (B3) and claim that it is legitimate to begin with something mediated that takes certain presuppositions which support it for granted, without the apparently dogmatic nature of the reliance upon those presuppositions rendering the beginning effectively arbitrary. This might seem reasonable, especially if what is presupposed is something that is never or only very rarely questioned, but it is difficult to see how this strategy can escape the determined sceptic who will latch on the fact that nothing has been said to show that one could not instead begin by presupposing something quite different, and thus begin with some quite different concept.[12]

Alternatively, once could deny (B2) and maintain that beginning with something immediate, that presupposes nothing at all, is legitimate after all and not problematically arbitrary. The idea of a presuppositionless beginning certainly has a certain allure to it, for an obvious reason: it seems to avoid the charge of dogmatically relying upon presuppositions. Yet it still seems to me that the sceptic is at this point liable to remind someone denying (B2) that a presuppositionless beginning is, in fact, a beginning with no support at all or nothing which justifies it. There is then nothing at all to appeal to when the sceptic asks why beginning elsewhere or otherwise might not be preferable. It is not obvious how to respond to this threat, and I have tried to show that Hegel seems to be sensitive to it.[13]

This leaves denying (B1), which results either in scepticism or a kind of self-conscious dogmatism, since it involves acknowledging that the beginning of the logical project is inescapably arbitrary. If this prompts one to suspend judgement concerning the results of the logical derivation that follows from Hegel's discussion of the concept of pure being, the result is scepticism. If one instead resolves straightforwardly to endorse its results, despite the arbitrariness of the beginning, then the result is dogmatism.

It does not seem to me that Hegel wants to adopt any of these strategies. But unless Hegel has a successful solution to this particular Agrippan problem, the problem of beginning, then it appears that the starting point of his logical project, and thus the derivation which follows it, will remain vulnerable to this kind of Agrippan sceptical objection. And if it is vulnerable in this manner, the project cannot amount to a "proof" of its results. Hegel's logical project would thus fail to constitute a genuine science, by his own lights.

Having set out the nature of Hegel's problem of beginning in some detail here, and having made the case for treating it as a distinctive Agrippan

---

12. Deleuze seems to think that Hegel adopts this strategy by making use of a certain 'subjective presupposition' which is not itself justified at the beginning of his *Logic* (Deleuze 2004: 164). It is not clear to me, however, what this "subjective presupposition" could amount to, in the context of Hegel's characterisation of the emptiness and indeterminacy of pure being. It is possible that it is a reference to the decision on behalf of an individual to engage in the kind of thinking which characterises logic, but it seems to me that these contingent facts about the philosopher have no bearing on the justificatory status of what is thought. In this, I am following Houlgate (2006: 60-71).

13. I think that Houlgate's interpretation of Hegel's case for beginning a science of *Logic* with pure being amounts to a version of denying (B2). I discuss this interpretation in Section 3.4.1.

problem, the next task, accordingly, is to examine the case that Hegel makes for his solution to the problem of beginning.

3.3 THE SOLUTION TO THE PROBLEM OF BEGINNING

In this section, I will provide a detailed reading of the pages of "With what must the beginning of the science be made?", which follow Hegel's historical sketch of the topic of beginning and his statement of the problem of beginning. My account is divided into two parts. The first part considers the initial steps of Hegel's solution and sketches the basic form of that solution by identifying the criteria a concept must meet if it is to be the beginning of a science of logic in a manner that is not vulnerable to the charge of arbitrariness. In the second part, I acknowledge that Hegel provides two different versions of this solution, in the *Science of Logic* and in the *Encyclopaedia Logic*, although they share the same form. I proceed to spell out the details of both solutions, the comparative prospects of which are then discussed in chapters 4 and 5.

3.3.1 The Form of Hegel's Solution

Hegel's response to the problem of beginning, I think, is not to abandon hope of beginning his deduction of logical categories in a rigorous or scientific manner. Nor is it to settle on one side of the dilemma he has constructed between beginning with something immediate or with something mediated and to attempt to overcome the charge of arbitrariness encountered there. Instead, I think that Hegel proceeds in a series of fairly clear steps,[14] the first of which is to acknowledge that the problem of beginning, as it has been expressed in the previous section, depends on the assumption that the "or" in the phrase "something mediated *or* something immediate" must be understood as an *exclusive* "or", so that the beginning is understood '*either* as a result, in a mediated fashion, *or* as beginning proper, in an immediate fashion' (*WL* 46/5:66, my emphases).[15]

The next step is to argue that this assumption can be jettisoned. Hegel says of immediacy and mediation, 'that both these determinations show themselves to be *unseparated* and *inseparable* and their opposition to be a nullity' (*WL* 46/5:66). He repeats this claim in his *Encyclopaedia* discussion of the beginning, arguing that,

---

14. See Dunphy 2021b: 56–57, for an abbreviated statement of these steps.
15. Hegel frequently criticises approaches that rely dogmatically upon an unexamined exclusive "or" and takes Pyrrhonian Scepticism as well as his own speculative philosophy to target precisely the dogmatism that 'holds fast to the one-sided determinations of the understanding with their exclusion of opposites. This is in general the strict *either-or*' (*EL* §32Z). See also Hentrup 2019: 151.

> The opposition of a self-standing immediacy of content or knowing and an opposing, equally self-standing mediation which is incompatible with the former, is first of all to be set aside, because it is a mere *presupposition* and an arbitrary *assurance* (*EL* §78).

This claim has broader implications in the context of Hegel's philosophy, but here, I want to focus only on the solution to the problem at hand.[16] The rough form of that solution is suggested by Hegel's rejection of the exclusive opposition between the determinations of mediation and immediacy: "It looks as though you must begin *exclusively* either with mediation or immediacy", I take Hegel to be saying, "but if that is the case then beginning is impossible. *If*, however, we give up this presumption concerning the exclusivity of mediation and immediacy and instead examine the possibility of beginning with some thought which can be characterised in terms of *both* of these elements, it may be that we can begin this science of logic in a non-arbitrary, scientifically rigorous manner after all".[17]

Hegel's solution to the problem of beginning, then, consists in locating a beginning for logic which is somehow both immediate *and* mediated or, put differently, a beginning which is presuppositionless *and* which presupposes something for its support. More needs to be said, of course, not only because this sounds like a peculiar or perhaps even paradoxical claim, but also because it is not obvious that taking two unsatisfactory options, as beginning with something mediated and beginning with something immediate have been shown to be, and then combining them will therefore, eliminate what is unsatisfactory about either. If one's problem is a hungry houseguest who is allergic to both gluten and peanuts, the solution is not to offer them peanut butter on toast. I think that Hegel's solution to the problem of beginning turns on arguing that it is the coincidence of immediacy and mediation in the concept with which the science of logic is to begin that enables each of these determinations to negate what was problematically arbitrary in beginning with the other alone. If this is the case, then it would become clear why beginning with something that is both mediated *and* immediate avoids the problematically arbitrary character of beginning only with something mediated, or only with something immediate, and thus solves the problem in question.

---

16. See Vieweg 2020: 14–22, for some discussion of the idea that it is chiefly in the Doctrine of Essence that Hegel develops his broader account of the inseparability of mediation and immediacy and of its significance.

17. This move is characteristic of Hegel's broader approach. For example: 'the idealism of speculative philosophy proves to reach over above the one-sidedness of abstract determinations of the understanding . . . it is essentially *just as much* the one *as also* the other and thereby *neither* the one *nor* the other, i.e., such determinations in their isolation are invalid, and they are valid only as sublated' (*EL* §32Z). This accurately captures his approach to the determinations of mediation and immediacy in the problem of beginning, I think.

If this claim about the benefit of combining the two determinations at the beginning is added to fact that, clearly, Hegel must have a way to make sense of the idea that a concept can be both mediated and immediate, be presuppositionless and presuppose something, at the same time, then Hegel's criteria for a successful solution to the problem of beginning can be expressed as follows: for a beginning to be truly non-arbitrary, it must presuppose something or be mediated by something that renders it non-arbitrary, *but in such a way that this presupposition or mediation does not undermine or clash with the status of the beginning as at the same time presuppositionless or immediate*, and it must be presuppositionless or immediate, *but in such a way that this presuppositionless or immediate status does not undermine or clash with the element of mediation or presuppositions rendering the beginning non-arbitrary*. In being thus mediated, it avoids the immediately arbitrary character of a *merely* presuppositionless beginning. And in being thus immediate, it avoids the arbitrary character of depending upon presuppositions the validity of which is questionable.

Accordingly, the remaining steps of the solution to the problem of beginning, following the statement rejecting the opposition of mediation and immediacy in the *Logic*, amount to an attempt on Hegel's part to identify the concept which meets these criteria, and with which the science can begin in a manner that does not invite a sceptical rebuttal on grounds of arbitrariness. Hegel identifies and describes the two determinations—first the element of mediation in the beginning and then the element of immediacy—and explains how it is that their coincidence yields the first category proper of the *Logic*, which, as I have already stated, is that of pure being.[18]

The questions that must now be answered in order to render Hegel's solution intelligible are as follows: (*i*) What is the element of immediacy in the beginning? (*ii*) What is the element of mediation? (*iii*) How do they coincide in such a way as to eliminate the problems which occur when beginning with either alone? As I indicated in Section 0.3.3, however, there is a difficulty that presents itself when considering the steps that make up this part of Hegel's

---

18. The approach to legitimising beginning with the concept of pure being which I have outlined so far differs somewhat from the interpretation of this material offered by Wolff. Wolff refers to Hegel's statement of the problem of beginning as a 'negative dilemma' and claims that it is then 'transformed' into a 'positive dilemma' which guarantees that logic must begin with pure being, where this latter dilemma functions as a proof by cases: "immediacy or mediation; if immediacy then pure being; if mediation then pure being; therefore pure being" (See Wolff 1996: 240-42). I do not see that this account pays sufficient attention to Hegel's remarks about the importance of giving up the exclusive opposition between mediation and immediacy. If Hegel's solution to the problem of beginning is a proof by cases, rather than a case for the genuine coincidence of mediation and immediacy in the concept of pure being, then it is much harder to see how the problematically arbitrary status of beginning merely with one or the other has been eliminated. Vieweg (2020: 4–5), curiously, seems to follow Wolff's proof by cases reading, even while insisting on the importance of giving up the opposition between mediation and immediacy. I think that the account I offer here makes better sense of this material.

solution to the problem of beginning: he appears to present two versions of his solution, one in the *Science of Logic* and in one the *Encyclopaedia Logic*. Although these two versions share the same basic form in that they turn on rejecting the exclusivity of mediation and immediacy and on providing an account of the concept of pure being according to which that concept can be understood as both mediated and immediate in such a way that each determination eliminates the threat of arbitrariness which accompanies beginning with the other alone, they are not identical. In particular, the identity of the element of mediation to which the solution appeals appears to differ across the two. Accordingly, in the account that follows, I will set out both solutions, calling attention to their shared form but remarking upon the differences in their content.

3.3.2 Two Versions of the Solution to the Problem of Beginning

The previous section closed with three questions. I will begin here with the first two of them. In both the *Science of Logic* and the *Encyclopaedia Logic*, Hegel proceeds to identify the two elements of mediation and immediacy in the beginning and to argue that they coincide in the concept of pure being. What follows is an abridged excerpt of that material from the first text, the greater *Logic*, with the discussion of the element of mediation indicated with a [1], and the discussion of the element of immediacy indicated with a [2]:

> [1] [The beginning] is thereby *mediated* in that *pure knowing* is the ultimate, absolute truth of *consciousness* . . . [T]he *Phenomenology of Spirit* is the science of consciousness, and its exposition . . . Logic has to this extent the science of spirit in its appearance for its presupposition, which contains and demonstrates the necessity, and thereby the proof of the truth of the standpoint that is pure knowing, and of its mediation . . .
>
> Here [pure] being is the beginning, presented as having emerged through a mediation . . . which at the same time is its own sublation; with the presupposition of pure knowing as the result of finite knowing, of consciousness. [2] Should no presupposition be made, however, and the beginning be taken *immediately*, then it is only determined in that it should be the beginning of logic, of thought for itself. Only the resolve to consider *thinking as such* is present, which can also be viewed as something arbitrary . . . thus it may *presuppose nothing*, must not be mediated by anything nor have a ground . . . It must therefore be simply *an* immediacy, or rather only *immediacy* itself. Just as it cannot have any determination against another, so too it can have none in itself, can contain no content, for that would amount to distinction and the relation of different elements to each other, thus a mediation. The beginning is therefore *pure being*. (*WL*: 46–48/5:67–69)

As I explained in Section 3.2, Hegel associates "mediation" in this context with an argument, the content of which is presupposed in order to justify the beginning of the logical project and "immediacy" with the notion of presuppositionlessness. The passage just quoted enables us to identify these two elements. In brief, the element of immediacy, or presuppositionlessness, is identified as "pure knowing", while the element of mediation, or the argument which the beginning is to presuppose, is identified with the critical interrogation of ordinary consciousness which Hegel undertakes in his 1807 *Phenomenology of Spirit*. I will elaborate on these in turn.

By its very nature, it is difficult to say much about the element of immediacy in the beginning.[19] Still, if one interrogates the account provided in "With what must the beginning of the science be made?", it is possible to clarify to some extent what Hegel has in mind. The first striking term used in the description of immediacy in the context of the beginning of the *Logic* is that of purity. The element of immediacy is described as the "result" of a mediation, or the point at which it is called "pure knowing". As Hegel puts it, '[p]ure knowing . . . has sublated every relation to an other and to mediation; it is something without distinctions; this something without distinctions thus ceases to be knowing; only *simple immediacy* is present' (*WL* 47/5:68). This emphasis on purity is perhaps not surprising, since the concept that is to be thought at the beginning is that of "pure being". Hegel suggests that this a concept which is 'without content' (*WL* 49/5:71). He writes, later in "With what must the beginning of science be made?", '[T]he beginning itself is thus to be taken as something unanalysable in its simple, unfilled immediacy, thus *as being*, as total emptiness' (*WL* 52/5:75). This characterisation of the concept which the element of immediacy grasps as "empty" is reiterated in the discussion of pure being proper in the first chapter of the Doctrine of Being, where Hegel uses the term 'empty thinking' to describe thinking the concept of being (*WL* 59/5:83).[20]

This description of "pure knowing" as a kind of "empty thinking" connects it to two other important terms shared by the characterisation of the element of immediacy. The first is that what is at stake in the element of immediacy is the idea of considering "thinking as such", and the second is that this has the character of something "simple". It seems that what Hegel

---

19. Compare *WL* 530/6:274. And, as I have already suggested, one should be cautious about referring to other instances of Hegel's use of the term "immediacy" for clarification, as no other use of the term on Hegel's part appears to signify genuine "presuppositionlessness", since every other concept examined in the *Logic* presupposes, at the very least, the logical development which precedes it. It is clear that the "immediacy" at the beginning of the *Logic* is a special case.

20. It is, of course, precisely this indeterminate emptiness that enables the slippage between the concepts of being and nothing, according to Hegel; a slippage that, when grasped as a unity, gives rise to the first determinate, or qualitative concept examined Hegel's *Logic*, that of *Dasein* (*WL* 80–84/5:111–17). See Houlgate 2006: 284–301, for a good discussion of this material.

has in mind is the idea of a purely reflexive thought, a thought where we simply think thought itself, but without characterising it in any way, or without that thought having any content at all, beyond the simple understanding that thought is occurring.[21] As Hegel puts it more fully, the thought which he identifies as that of the element of immediacy 'is pure indeterminateness and emptiness. There is *nothing* in it to intuit ... There is just as little anything to be thought in it, or it is just as much only this empty thinking' (*WL* 59/5:82–83). It is important to acknowledge here that Hegel's claim is that, although this immediacy is apparently the result of some mediation, in being empty, pure, or simple, it makes no reference to the mediation which demonstrates its necessity, or which it presupposes. It has "sublated every relation to an other and to mediation". It is clearly this that Hegel thinks entitles him to characterise the element of immediacy as "presuppositionless", since the fact that the beginning has sublated every relation to mediation means that it presupposes nothing.

Potentially problematic in the context of Hegel's account of the element of immediacy, however, is the acknowledgment on his part of the possibility of arbitrariness. As he says, the element of immediacy amounts to the resolve "which can also be viewed as something arbitrary" to consider thought as such. This might seem problematic if it is taken to be an admission on Hegel's part that the beginning of the science of logic does in fact have something of an arbitrary character, given that I have argued that Hegel's approach to the problem of beginning is motivated by the attempt to avoid arbitrariness. I think, however, that there are two possible ways to make sense of this passage which avoid this worry. The first is to notice that it sounds as though what is being described as arbitrary is not the thought but the resolve on our part to think. If this is the case, then there is no problem, because *why* one has decided to pursue some line of questioning should have no bearing on the justificatory status of what is thought. If, however, one were not to accept this explanation, and to insist that the element of immediacy itself is being characterised as potentially arbitrary, then I think that this could be read in such a way that it supports my interpretation, rather than undermining it. Hegel says, after all, only that the element of immediacy "can" be considered arbitrary. I would suggest that this "can" indicates the two possibilities for considering the problem of beginning. If one has retained the exclusive

---

21. This interpretation of Hegel's conception the empty, presuppositionless thinking involved in conceiving pure being is largely indebted to the account provided by Houlgate. See, in particular, Houlgate 2006: 29–53, for a detailed elaboration of what is involved in thinking pure being without presuppositions. I follow Houlgate in taking Hegel's claim that the beginning of the *Logic* is presuppositionless seriously. I think that Hegel is genuinely challenging the common assumption that '[*a*]*bsolute* neutrality, or presupposition-less-ness, is unavailable. No inquiry starts from zero' (Cahoone 2013: 4), rather than simply recommending a healthy fallibilistic attitude, as Sedgwick (2012: 156–58), for example, seem to suggest.

opposition between immediacy and mediation and attempts to begin simply with the immediacy of empty thinking, then it will be problematically arbitrary. If, however, one gives up the assumption of that exclusive opposition, and engages in the immediacy of empty thinking on the basis of a mediation which necessitates it and coincides with it, then the charge of arbitrariness will not apply.

At this point, I should identify the element of mediation. This is more straightforward than attempting to grasp the notion of empty thinking, as Hegel is quite explicit. The element of mediation is clearly identified in the passage cited previously with the critical investigation of ordinary or "natural" consciousness carried out in his 1807 *Phenomenology of Spirit*. A lengthy investigation of the contents of the *Phenomenology* cannot be accomplished here, but from the perspective of a concern for the problem of beginning in the *Logic*, it is clear that the *Phenomenology* amounts to an argument, the conclusion of which demonstrates the necessity of that beginning.[22] More specifically, the argument of the *Phenomenology* begins from an account of consciousness which *opposes* itself to the idea that a priori thought might provide us with the fundamental categories with which we think because it insists that one begins 'from empirical, *sensuous* consciousness' (*WL*: 47/5:67). The argument of the *Phenomenology*, regardless of whatever else it might also achieve, provides 'liberation from the opposition of consciousness', by comprehensively showing such an assumption to be false, a liberation which the *Logic* 'presupposes' (*WL*: 29/5:43).[23] By 'going through all forms of the *relationship of consciousness to the object*' (*WL* 28/5:42) and showing each dogmatic conception of this relation to fail, this "science of spirit in its appearance" demonstrates the necessity of pure knowing, by leaving what started as the dogmatic position of ordinary consciousness nothing but the immediate, reflexive relation towards its own thinking as such, constitutive of the thought of pure being.

The text of Hegel's solution to the problem of beginning in "With what must the beginning of the science be made?" thus clearly identifies the

---

22. Hegel earlier makes the same claim: that the 'absolute beginning' of the *Logic* presupposes the work carried out in the *Phenomenology*, and that this work thereby justifies that beginning (*WL*: 28-29/5:42-43).

23. One potentially confusing element of this account is Hegel's use of "presupposition". He refers to the argument of the *Phenomenology*, as I have indicated, as the presupposition of the beginning of the *Logic*, and clearly intends there to be a sense in which this is not problematic: the sense in which a position presupposes the argument which proves its validity (although, as I argued in Section 3.2, Hegel also suggests that such a procedure may be problematic when it comes to the "absolute beginning" of logic). Hegel also, however, tends to refer to the dogmatic conceptions of the relationship between thought and its objects endorsed by natural consciousness which are the target of the *Phenomenology*'s criticism as "presuppositions", in the sense of unjustified assumptions which are to be rejected. The *Phenomenology* is thus a presupposition of the *Logic* insofar as it is an argument, the primary contribution of which is the rejection of dogmatic presuppositions.

element of immediacy in pure being as pure knowing (or empty thinking) and the element of mediation as the result of the argument of his *Phenomenology*. The third question that I asked above was how it is that these two determinations coincide in such a way as to eliminate the problems which occur when beginning with either alone. Before examining the details of the answer to this third question, however, I want to turn briefly to the alternative solution to the problem of beginning that Hegel presents in his *Encyclopaedia Logic*, in order to show that Hegel's answer to the second question I asked previously ("What is the element of mediation?") differs in this account.

The *Encyclopaedia* form of the solution is, I have already suggested, the same. Hegel identifies the elements of mediation and immediacy which coincide in the concept of pure being after challenging the assumption about their mutual exclusivity which structured the problem of beginning. I will again present the material, abridged, and indicate the discussion of mediation with a [1] and of immediacy with a [2]. After suggesting, just as he did in the *Science of Logic*, that the exclusive opposition between mediation and immediacy should be "set aside" because it is itself "a mere presupposition", Hegel continues,

> [1] Just as much are all other presuppositions or prejudices to be given up upon at the entrance to the science, whether they be taken from representation or from thought . . .
> *Scepticism*, as a negative science which has run through all forms of cognition, would offer itself as an introduction in which the nullity of such presuppositions would be demonstrated . . . [2] The demand for such a completed scepticism is the same as the demand that the science should be preceded by *doubt about everything*, i.e., total *presuppositionlessness*. It is really completed in the resolve *to think purely*, by means of the freedom which abstracts from everything and grasps its pure abstraction, the simplicity of thought. (*EL* §78–78A)

Just as in "With what must the beginning of the science be made?", shortly after presenting this material, Hegel begins the first part of his science of logic, the Doctrine of Being, with the concept of pure being (*EL* §86). And I think it is clear that the element of immediacy in the beginning has not changed between the two solutions to the problem of beginning. Here, just as in the *Science of Logic*, the immediacy of the beginning is identified as a simple, or pure thinking, which, having abstracted from all content, is thereby an empty thinking, and this again amounts to "total presuppositionlessness" (*gänzliche Vorraussetzunglosigkeit*).

The identity of the element of mediation, however, is different in this version of Hegel's solution. No mention is made of the argument of the *Phenomenology of Spirit*. Instead, it is suggested that a "negative science" of "completed scepticism" might be presupposed by the beginning of the

Logic.²⁴ As Fulda puts it, Hegel appears to consider two different possible "introductions" to his logical project: a phenomenological introduction and a sceptical introduction.²⁵ Despite this difference in identity, however, I think it is clear that this completed scepticism is conceived of by Hegel as playing much the same role as that played by the *Phenomenology*: of exhaustively going through all dogmatic accounts of cognition and rebutting them so that that thought is left only with the simple immediacy of pure being. Here the beginning of the science of logic would presuppose a completed scepticism which would also have presuppositionlessness as its result, or which would demonstrate the necessity of the empty thinking which characterises the concept of pure being, which might otherwise appear merely arbitrary. What prompted Hegel to consider such a change is at this point unclear, although I will suggest in Section 4.2 that there are a number of problems with the version of the solution to the problem of beginning which relies upon the argument of the *Phenomenology*, which Hegel may well have come to appreciate himself.

There is, however, yet *another* puzzle presented by Hegel's *Encyclopaedia* presentation of the solution to the problem of beginning: Although he clearly considers having a negative science of completed scepticism play the role of the element of mediation in the solution in *EL* §78A, in material I have not presented in the abridged excerpt reproduced just now, Hegel appears ultimately to *reject* this proposal, suggesting that it would be 'not only an unpleasant, but also a superfluous way' to rid thought of dogmatic assumptions at the beginning of a science of logic (*EL* §78A). This appears to indicate a more radical difference from the account provided in the *Science of Logic*: Hegel seems to be concluding in the *Encyclopaedia* that it is, in fact, perfectly acceptable to begin merely with something immediate after all, and thus to break with the form of the solution to the problem of beginning that he had developed in the longer work. I will discuss this additional puzzle at some length in Section 5.1. For now, I will ignore it and restrict my focus to the two solutions that share the same form: treating the concept of pure being in terms of the coincidence of mediation and immediacy but differing as to the identity of the element of mediation: the *Phenomenology of Spirit* in the *Science of Logic*, completed scepticism in the *Encyclopaedia*.

The final part of Hegel's solution, on either formulation, consists in an answer to the third question with which I closed Section 3.3.1. This can be rephrased as follows: How do the elements of mediation and immediacy, or the phenomenological or sceptical criticism of dogmatic ordinary consciousness on the one hand and empty thinking on the other, *coincide* in the concept

---

24. I consider and reject the possibility that this reference to a negative science of completed scepticism might, in fact, be a covert reference to the *Phenomenology* in Section 5.2.
25. See Fulda 1975: 21–54.

of pure being in such a way that they overcome the deficiency of beginning *merely* with something immediate, or *merely* with something mediated? The rough answer to the first part of this question—how the two coincide—has to some extent already have been suggested in the examination of the two elements: if the project either of phenomenology or of scepticism amounts to an argument, then the conclusion of that argument *is* the pure knowing or "simple immediacy" which Hegel calls empty thinking. It is a mediation which results in immediacy. From the perspective of the beginning of the *Logic*, either the *Phenomenology*, or a negative science of completed scepticism, is an argument which is presupposed, and which has presuppositionlessness for its result.

I think that the Hegel's solution is intended to work the same way across both versions. In what follows, however, I will focus my discussion on the version of the solution that Hegel presents in "With what must the beginning of the science be made?", where the argument of his *Phenomenology of Spirit* is identified as the element of mediation in the concept of pure being. This is partly for reasons of clarity, to avoid constantly switching between references to the *Phenomenology* and to a completed scepticism, but also because this version is spelled out in far greater detail by Hegel.

As I have already noted, the *Phenomenology of Spirit* is an investigation of ordinary or 'natural consciousness' (*PhG* §78/3:72), where this refers to a position or a series of common positions on the relationship between thought and the object of thought, which take as their starting point the prejudice that thought must begin from some empirical or sensuous content, given to it from outside of itself. Insofar as Hegel, in his *Logic*, is attempting to provide an a priori deduction of the basic categories of thought, or a scientific examination of thought by thought itself,[26] he therefore encounters this prejudice of natural consciousness's as a position fundamentally opposed to his own. In this sense, he says, 'the standpoint of consciousness . . . counts as the *other* of science' (*PhG* §26/3:30).

The argument of the *Phenomenology* is, accordingly, a critical investigation of the variations of natural consciousness, aimed at validating the self-examination of thought which characterises the procedure of the *Logic*. It is, however, an *immanent* critical investigation, in that the criterion according to which such positions are evaluated is that of consistency between the standard which a given position of natural consciousness affirms as the standard of truth, and individual first-order knowledge claims about objects in the world.[27] This means that Hegel need not illegitimately presuppose the validity

---

26. '[H]ere *thinking* is to be made the object of thinking' (*EL* §17).
27. A detailed discussion of the immanent critical approach of the *Phenomenology* and the manner in which a given iteration of natural consciousness revises its criteria for knowing, and thus itself, is provided in Westphal 1988. I have more to say about this topic in Section 4.2.3.

of the position he adopts in his *Logic* when evaluating natural consciousness in the *Phenomenology*. As he puts it, 'the concept and the object, the standard and that which is to be examined, are present in consciousness itself... what remains to us for our part is only purely looking on' (*PhG* §85/3:77). The argument of the *Phenomenology* traces the modifications that the positions of natural consciousness must make to themselves in the face of the discovery of internal inconsistencies, with the ultimate result, according to Hegel at least, that the prejudices of natural consciousness are replaced with a position in which thought is able to conduct its self-examination along the lines of the investigation of his *Science of Logic*. I showed earlier that Hegel takes it that the argument of the *Phenomenology* 'demonstrates the necessity, and thereby the proof of the truth of the standpoint that is pure knowing' (*WL* 47/5:67). At the end of the *Phenomenology*, Hegel refers to the position he has arrived at there as "absolute knowing", or 'the simple unity of knowing' (*PhG* § 796), noting that what this form of thought produces is 'comprehending conceptual knowing [*begreifende Wissen*] ... is science' (*PhG* §798/3:582–83). If this mention of "science" is taken, as seems reasonable, to be a reference to Hegel's logical project, then one might suppose that the *Phenomenology*'s "absolute knowing" is identical to the *Logic*'s "pure knowing".[28] Accordingly, the conclusion of the argument of the *Phenomenology* appears to coincide with the beginning of the *Logic*.

This alleged coincidence of the conclusion of the *Phenomenology* and the beginning of the *Logic* prompts the question of the compatibility of the two works, or of how it is that Hegel is able to say both that the beginning of the *Logic* is presuppositionless, and that it presupposes the work of the *Phenomenology*. Notably, it is through the examination of this question, rather than the problem of beginning itself, that William Maker approaches the beginning of the *Logic*, in his *Philosophy Without Foundations*. He asks, 'How then are we to understand the *Phenomenology* as the presupposition for presuppositionless science, as the necessary mediation which brings us to the point of an immediate beginning?' (Maker 1994: 76). Although this approach differs somewhat from the one adopted here, I take it that Maker, too, is engaging with Hegel's problem of beginning. Furthermore, it seems to me that Maker's work on the relationship between the *Phenomenology* and the *Logic*, and his attempt to render the two compatible, is useful in considering how the coincidence of the conclusion of the examination of consciousness and empty thinking might be thought to overcome the inadequacy of beginning merely with something mediated or merely with something immediate.

The problem concerning the compatibility of the conclusion of the *Phenomenology* with the beginning of the *Logic* can be put in the following way:

---

28. See also *PhG* § 796/3:581.

the conclusion of the *Phenomenology*, despite being the result of all of the developments occurring over the course of the examination of consciousness in that work, and despite needing to necessitate the beginning of the *Logic*, seems as though it cannot actually amount to anything that could be considered as a substantive presupposition from the perspective of the beginning of the *Logic*. Were it to amount to such a presupposition, it would be incompatible with, rather than coincide with, the presuppositionless immediacy of the beginning of that work. This would be to render Hegel's solution to the problem of beginning unworkable. And the matter does look potentially rather awkward, since the conclusion of the *Phenomenology* is the culmination of a work which has made a number of claims about matters epistemological, ethical, political, religious, metaphysical, and seems to result, as Stephen Houlgate puts it, in 'a determinate concept of being as universal reason' (Houlgate 2006: 162). If such a conclusion were to be presupposed at the beginning of the *Logic*, it seems as though it would be clearly incompatible with the characterisation of that beginning as empty, immediate, and presuppositionless (and, indeed, in terms of "indeterminate being"). It is precisely here that Maker's account of the relation between the *Phenomenology* and the beginning of the *Logic* looks appealing. I provide a more detailed and ultimately critical engagement with Maker's interpretation in Sections 4.1 and 4.2, but here a brief sketch of its nature should suffice.

The key elements of Maker's account of the *Phenomenology* are as follows: (1) the *Phenomenology* is a critique of the dogmatic assumptions of ordinary consciousness, and (2) this critique must be understood *radically negatively*. (1) is uncontroversial. There are many interpretative disagreements concerning the *Phenomenology*, but I do not think that anyone disputes the claim that Hegel's original focus in that text is what he calls "ordinary" or "natural consciousness", that he takes it that "the standpoint of consciousness . . . counts as the *other* of science" or is opposed to the idealist philosophical position that he himself will develop, and that what is therefore required is that natural consciousness be subjected to a critique, or, in fact, subjects *itself*, or its own dogmatically held knowledge-claims and criteria for evaluating them, to a critique, the result of which will eventually be the replacement of the dogmatic presuppositions of natural consciousness with a philosophical or scientific perspective, or the '*education* of consciousness itself into science' (*PhG* §78/3:73).

Unusual in Maker's understanding of this project is (2): the idea that the critique of natural consciousness 'must be understood *negatively*' (Maker 1994: 71). This is to suggest that, despite appearances, the development of the dogmatic position of natural consciousness into that of speculative philosophy is not carried out in that work as the replacement of one model of cognition with another, or one set of presuppositions with another, but *only* as the total elimination of the dogmatic presuppositions of natural consciousness, so that the conclusion of the *Phenomenology* amounts to no more than the total absence of the presuppositions characteristic of natural consciousness which were encountered along the way. This is what Maker calls the 'radically negative outcome' of the *Phenomenology* (Maker 1994: 93). As he puts it, 'the task of the *Phenomenology* as introduction to science is the *critical* task of showing that . . . consciousness, as a determinate and presupposed structure, comes to eliminate itself' (Maker 1994: 78).

The virtue of this interpretation in this context is clear, I think: If the *Phenomenology* does indeed have this purely negative trajectory, so that its conclusion is the total absence of dogmatic presuppositions, then this conclusion coincides with the empty thinking of the beginning of the *Logic*, while if the conclusion were instead some substantive doctrine about the nature of "spirit" or some set of metaphysical, epistemological, or methodological scientific principles, this coincidence would be impossible.[29]

At this point, I have introduced a suggestion as to how the conclusion of the *Phenomenology* and the beginning of the *Logic* might be thought to coincide successfully. I think that this allows one, in turn, to make sense of Hegel's solution to the problem of beginning. The problem was that beginning merely with something immediate, or presuppositionless, looked unjustified because it was to begin simply by asserting something, without supporting it in any way, while beginning with something mediated, or on the basis of something presupposed, looked unjustified because, from the perspective of the beginning, what was presupposed appeared merely to have been taken for granted and, therefore, offered no true support. I suggest that Hegel's solution should be understood in terms of the model of the coincidence of the conclusion of the *Phenomenology* and the beginning of the *Logic* that I have outlined earlier in this chapter. The mediation in question is the argument of the *Phenomenology*, which, setting out from the presuppositions of natural consciousness and concluding in the total absence of any presuppositions, necessitates the empty thinking of the beginning of the *Logic*, identified as the immediacy in question. In this sense, the beginning is both mediated and immediate.

On this basis, one can describe pure being, the beginning of the *Logic*, as mediated, or as a beginning the necessity of which has been demonstrated by what it presupposes, because this demonstration is the argument of the

---

29. Maker's interpretation has received further support from various other commentators. See, for example, Winfield 2013: 21 and 377–78, or Comay and Ruda 2018: 148, n.17. By contrast, see Houlgate 2006: 162, where he suggests that the conclusion to the *Phenomenology* is far more substantive than Maker's radically negative account allows, and that, therefore, between the *Phenomenology* and the *Logic*, some 'act of abstraction' must occur, in which the majority of the conclusions of the *Phenomenology* are set aside.

Phenomenology. This renders the beginning immune to the sceptical charge Hegel levelled at beginning with something merely immediate or presuppositionless, since this beginning is not just an arbitrary assertion: it is supported by the argument that demonstrates its necessity and thus does not straight away find its sceptical rebuttal. And if that argument concludes negatively, in the collapse of the dogmatically held presuppositions of natural consciousness and thus the coincidence, rather than incompatibility, of the conclusion of the *Phenomenology* with the beginning of the *Logic*, then the mediated status of the beginning does not undermine the immediate status of the beginning.

At the same time, one can describe pure being as immediate, or presuppositionless, because the empty thinking characteristic of the beginning does not retain any content from the argument which it presupposes. This renders the beginning immune to the charge Hegel levelled at beginning merely with something mediated, or on the basis of something presupposed, as this beginning cannot be said to be taking for granted some substantive result of the prior investigation: Because it is merely empty thinking, it is taking nothing for granted. Thus it again does not find its sceptical rebuttal. And again, because of the coincidence, rather than incompatibility, of the conclusion of the *Phenomenology* and the beginning of the *Logic*, this presuppositionlessness, or the immediate status of the beginning, does not undermine the mediated status of the beginning.[30]

Accordingly, I think that Hegel understands the coincidence of mediation and immediacy in the concept of pure being to enable this beginning to avoid the sceptical charges of arbitrariness that were levelled at beginning merely with something mediated, or merely with something immediate. As such, beginning a science of logic with pure being, understood according to the model presented previously, has this advantage over any other possible beginning: It is not problematically arbitrary to begin with pure being in a manner that invites immediate sceptical rebuttal. It thus solves the problem of beginning as it was explicated in Section 3.2.

In fact, one can notice that this solution, set out at length here, has the following character: it replaces an opposition between two exclusive determinations which appeared to prevent Hegel's logical project from going anywhere. Instead, one determination—mediation—negates itself and results in its opposite—immediacy. The unity of these two determinations, the concept of pure being, solves the problem of their opposition. This solution conforms to Hegel's *Encyclopaedia* characterisation of the '*moments* of every *logical reality* . . . every concept or every truth' (*EL* §79A), which I discussed in

---

30. One might more flippantly characterise Hegel's solution to the problem of beginning, as I have presented it here, in terms of eating one's presupposition cake and having it too.

Section 1.2.1.[31] Although Hegel's dialectical or speculative model of demonstration is not the object of the investigation here, this conformity on behalf of the solution developed earlier to Hegel's account of logical demonstration suggests that, by his lights, the solution of the problem of beginning represents an instance where an *'immanent connection and necessity* enters into the content of the science' (*EL* §81). This reiterates that its role is one of contributing to the task securing the scientific status of Hegel's logical project.

The version of this solution that Hegel entertains in the *Encyclopaedia* is less thoroughly developed than the one that appeals to the *Phenomenology*, not least because, as I noted, Hegel appears ultimately not to endorse it in that later text. I think, however, that he understands it as functioning in precisely the same way as the solution presented in this chapter. The characterisation of the "pure thinking" of the beginning of the logical science in the *Encyclopaedia* version is clearly identical to the element of immediacy as it is presented in "With what must the beginning of the science be made?", as I have already shown. The exact nature of the negative science of completed scepticism which replaces the *Phenomenology* in the role of mediation appears rather undetermined,[32] but this at least has the immediate advantage that it does not face the same challenge which faces readers of the *Phenomenology* from the perspective of the beginning of the *Logic*: that it is not obvious that the wide-ranging and complex argument of the *Phenomenology* can have a conclusion which is compatible with the empty presuppositionlessness of the *Logic*. The only explicit information Hegel provides in *EL* §78A about this completed scepticism is that it could 'run through all form of cognition' and demonstrate the 'nullity' of all of their presuppositions and that this amounts to '*doubt about everything*', which is to say that a completed scepticism would have 'total *presuppositionlessness*' as its conclusion. For all that this version of the solution is not fleshed out in the *Encyclopaedia*, then, the manner in which it enables the coincidence of mediation and immediacy in the concept of pure being, and thereby solves Hegel's problem of beginning by avoiding the arbitrariness which accompanies beginning with either determination alone, is, if anything, made more explicit than in the case of the version from the *Science of Logic*. Further discussion of the specificities of this version of Hegel's solution must wait until chapter 5.

Having now set out the nature of Hegel's problem of beginning and of its solution, as well as the two different presentations of that solution that Hegel provides, the chief remaining task of this book is to evaluate the prospects of

---

31. See *EL* §§79–81, for Hegel's account of these moments. It should be clear that the problem of beginning as I have presented it here corresponds to this account. See Wolff 1996 for further discussion of the relation these moments bear to the beginning of the *Logic*.

32. I attempt to develop Hegel's characterisation of completed scepticism by appeal to his discussion of Pyrrhonian Scepticism in Section 5.2.1.

these two solutions. Before carrying out that evaluation in the remaining two chapters, however, I will draw this chapter itself to a close by critically considering some alternative accounts of the material on Hegel's problem of beginning and its solution which I have discussed here, as well as by attempting to anticipate and rebut some objections that might be levelled at my account.

3.4 ALTERNATIVES CRITICISED AND OBJECTIONS ANTICIPATED

The account of Hegel's problem of beginning and its solution that I have presented in this chapter engages with material that has received a not insignificant amount of attention in the literature on the *Science of Logic*. It is, therefore, worthwhile spending a little time here setting out how my interpretation differs from some prominent alternative readings of the text and trying to make the case that the account here is to be preferred. After doing so, I will attempt to anticipate and address a number of objections that might be directed towards the interpretation of Hegel's problem of beginning and its solution presented here, principally those which might be made by appealing to other remarks that Hegel makes in "With what must the beginning of the science be made?" Both of these tasks thus afford the opportunity to discuss material from that essay which has not featured in the account I have presented so far.

3.4.1 Alternatives Criticised

Hegel's problem of beginning, as I presented it in Section 3.2, takes the form of a dilemma: one either begins with something mediated or with something immediate, and either way the sceptic will rebut the case on grounds of arbitrariness. I went on to suggest three responses, none of which, I claimed, were Hegel's: to simply give in to the sceptic, or to double down either on beginning with something mediated or with something immediate and to argue that the charge of arbitrariness can be overcome. No one, I think, reads Hegel as submitting to scepticism, but I think that there are some readers who might plausibly be understood to be arguing that Hegel doubles down on one side of the dilemma.[33] It is to such accounts that I turn first in this section.

In the context of close readings of the beginning of the *Logic*, I do not think that there are many explicit instances of readers taking Hegel to defend

---

[33]. For such readers, I suppose that the argument of "With what must the beginning of the science be made?" must be read in the following way: "It *seems* as though beginning either with something mediated or with something immediate will be rebutted", Hegel says in expressing the problem of beginning, before going to argue: "But *actually*, I can show that one of these options is not so problematically arbitrary after all". Such a reading would strike me as rather forced.

only the validity of beginning with something mediated, since this involves reading so heavily against the grain of Hegel's repeated characterisations of pure being in terms of its immediacy and presuppositionlessness. One notable attempt to read the beginning of Hegel's *Logic* in such a fashion was presented, some time ago, by Evander McGilvary. In fact, McGilvary goes so far as to say of the claim that the beginning of Hegel's *Logic* is presuppositionless that 'no such pretension is made' because the *Logic* presupposes the argument of the *Phenomenology* (McGilvary 1897: 497–98). It is clear, however, that Hegel *does* characterise the beginning of the *Logic*, as I have shown earlier, in terms of "total presuppositionlessness". McGilvary is clearly right to notice that Hegel *also* claims that his *Logic* presupposes the argument of his *Phenomenology*, but this does not license the straightforward rejection of claims to the effect that logic is to be presuppositionless. It rather demands a reading of the text which attempts to render these two claims compatible, as in the case of the interpretation provided by Maker, which I introduced in Section 3.3.2. McGilvary's position is that '[t]he presupposition of the *Logic* is the *Phenomenology*, and the presupposition of the *Phenomenology* is immediate, sensuous consciousness' (McGilvary 1897: 499), but not only does this reading simply ignore the dilemma that Hegel expresses as the problem of beginning altogether (and thus fail to explain why Hegel says that it is easy to show that beginning with something mediated will find its rebuttal), but it also appears to suggest that logic is to take its ultimate orientation from empirical experience; this is a claim that Hegel explicitly rejects (*WL*: 47/5:67).[34] Such a reading which has Hegel beginning from something merely mediated—the deliverances of empirical experience, by way of their treatment in the *Phenomenology of Spirit*—does not make good sense of Hegel's text, I think.[35]

But if readings of Hegel which take him to begin logic merely with something mediated are clearly unpopular, the same cannot be said for readings

---

34. The fact that McGilvary (1897: 499) insists so clearly that 'sensuous consciousness is an unquestionable point of departure', even in the context of the beginning of the *Logic*, raises the question of whether other readers who suppose that Hegel's *Logic* is not a genuine a priori science of thought, but rather draws upon empirical material to assemble the concepts that are its subject matter, even though it then treats that subject matter abstractly, would also suppose that Hegel's *Logic*, therefore, begins merely with something mediated (I am thinking primarily of readings of Hegel that emphasise perceived commonalities with pragmatism. Examples would include Emundts 2014 and Brandom 2019). Without being presented with explicit readings of "With what must the beginning of the science be made?" along these lines, it is difficult to say.

35. I have not presented the most sympathetic possible rendition of McGilvary's reading here but rather emphasised those elements of his account which insist that logic begin with something mediated. He does go on to acknowledge, however, that the concept of pure being with which the *Logic* begins is 'apparently, without presupposition', even though it presupposes the absolute knowing which is the conclusion of the *Phenomenology* (McGilvary 1897: 512–13). In these remarks, though, McGilvary sounds as though he is moving away from the one-sided emphasis on beginning with something mediated in the direction of the kind of treatment of the beginning of the *Logic* that I have outlined earlier in the chapter.

which take him to begin merely with something immediate. An influential and compelling reading of the beginning of Hegel's *Logic* along these lines, I think, is the one developed by Houlgate, most notably in his 2006 work, *The Opening of Hegel's* Logic.[36] Houlgate, I think, does not offer an explicit discussion of the passage in which Hegel expresses what I am referring to as the problem of beginning in its dilemmatic form, and the primary focus of his interpretation is on the validity of beginning with something immediate and presuppositionless. Thus the primary challenge that Houlgate sees Hegel attempting to meet at the beginning of his *Logic* is the following one:

> If we are to examine thought without presupposing that is has any particular structure, operates with any particular concepts, or is governed by any particular rules, what are we to understand thought to be? (Houlgate, 2006: 31)

Houlgate's position is that answering this question with the concept of pure being is enough to provide an adequate beginning for Hegel's logical project. While he is happy to acknowledge that the argument of the *Phenomenology* might help one in attaining the position whereby one engages in the kind of empty thinking characteristic of the beginning of the *Logic*, he does not think that this argument is necessary to the validity of the beginning of the *Logic*, or that without its support, the *Logic* is problematically arbitrary. Instead, he emphasises that,

> Hegel points out that there is a direct route into speculative logic. All one needs to do is freely suspend and abstract from all determinate presuppositions about thought and being and render explicit whatever is entailed by the indeterminate thought (of indeterminate being) that results from this act of abstraction. (Houlgate, 2005: 49–50)

If this is the case, however, then I think that it is rather less clear what it would be that makes it "easy to see" that beginning with something immediate finds its rebuttal, as Hegel explicitly states. On the contrary, Houlgate's Hegel seems precisely to think that beginning with something immediate invites no rebuttal; the challenge consists only in identifying this immediate thinking as that of pure being. This defence of a simply immediate or presuppositionless beginning turns, I think, on the idea that such a beginning is superior to beginning with some other concept precisely because it presupposes less and is, therefore, not open to the charge of uncritical dogmatism in the way that any

---

36. But also in the first volume of his 2021 commentary on the entire Doctrine of Being: *Hegel on Being*. This work appeared too late during the composition of this book for it to be possible for me to provide any sustained engagement with it here, unfortunately, but my impression is that Houlgate's approach to the matter of beginning with pure being has not substantially changed.

other beginning would be.[37] But this seems to me not to answer the challenge posed to the value of presuppositionlessness in Hegel's problem of beginning: that *mere* presuppositionlessness is indistinguishable from an unsupported, arbitrary position. To overcome this objection, the presuppositionlessness in question must be necessitated by something which it presupposes and not simply be the result of a decision to think abstractly, as Houlgate would have it.[38] This is not to disagree with Houlgate that the "resolve to think purely" could result in thinking the concept of pure being,[39] but it seems to me that there is a world of difference between a thinking of pure being which has been *necessitated* by the elimination of dogmatic alternatives through phenomenological or sceptical criticism and a thinking which is the result merely of the thinker's decision to "abstract from everything", precisely because, as Hegel says, the *mere* resolve to think pure being "can also be viewed as something arbitrary".[40] Only the former option, it seems to me, can guarantee that the beginning of the *Logic* can avoid sceptical objections on grounds of arbitrariness, and only the former option looks as though it adequately responds to the demand that a scientific philosophy "demonstrate the necessity of its content".

I therefore remain convinced that only a reading of "With what must the beginning of the science be made?" that acknowledges both the Agrippan problem that Hegel presents there and the idiosyncratic nature of his solution—which turns on treating the concept of pure being as both mediated and immediate in such a way that it avoids the threat of arbitrariness that looms over either side of the dilemma taken alone—can make full sense of the argument of that essay. But I am not alone in reading the essay this way. A recent account by Miles Hentrup also remarks upon the similarity of Hegel's problem of beginning to Sextus' presentation of the Two Modes and also finds that the key to Hegel's solution is to jettison the mutual exclusivity of mediation and immediacy and recognise that the beginning must be understood as both mediated and immediate (Hentrup 2019: 151–53).

---

37. See, for example, Houlgate 2006: 30–2.
38. It should be pointed out, to save confusion, that Houlgate does defend the possibility of certain 'presuppositions of presuppositionless thought' (Houlgate 2006: 54), such as the willingness of a philosopher to engage in the type of thinking present at the beginning of the *Logic*, or historical trends towards self-criticism in philosophy. I am entirely in agreement with him here, but this material is intended by Houlgate to defend the genuine possibility of presuppositionless thought from Hegel's critics. It is *not* intended, I think, to justify the presuppositionlessness with which the *Logic* begins, where this justification is taken as necessary to the success of that beginning, or to amount to a defence of the kind of solution to the problem of beginning that I am attributing to Hegel here.
39. Nor indeed with his elucidation and defence of the empty thinking involved in grasping this concept, which I think is compelling and which I have followed in Section 3.3.2.
40. Compare McGilvary 1897: 512: 'Such a contingent resolve is itself a presupposition, and a very insecure presupposition upon which to found an absolute science'. It seems to me that McGilvary is in the right here.

There is a crucial difference between Hentrup's account of Hegel's solution, however, and the one I have presented here. According to Hentrup, pure being is to be understood as mediated not because it is the negative result of the phenomenological or sceptical elimination of all dogmatic presuppositions but rather because, after beginning immediately, pure being *goes on to mediate itself*. As Hentrup understands the matter, 'The *Logic* begins . . . with something immediate in precisely that spurious and one-sided sense of excluding all mediation' (Hentrup 2019: 153), but this beginning is then revised over the course of the argument of the *Science of Logic*, in which all of the concepts examined mediate themselves and give rise to further concepts, until this course culminates in Hegel's account of the absolute idea, which itself once again gives rise, Hegel suggests, 'to the simple unity that is its beginning; the pure immediacy of being' (*WL* 752/6:572). As Hentrup puts it:

> Because pure being proves to be grounded upon—that is, mediated by—the absolute idea, its initial claim to immediacy turns out to be a mere presupposition, supplanted by the subsequent demonstration of its absolute self-mediation. (Hentrup 2019: 155)[41]

It should be acknowledged that Hentrup is absolutely right to note that Hegel claims that, despite the fact that '*pure being,* this absolute immediate, is just as much absolutely mediated' (*WL* 50/5:72), from the perspective of considering this concept as the beginning of the *Logic*, it should be treated merely as 'indeterminate immediacy' (*WL* 59/5:82). This is compatible, however, either with the claim that pure being is a pure immediacy because it is the result of some mediation with a "radically negative outcome", or with the claim that the beginning is made precisely in the problematic, one-sided sense of immediacy, which then comes to mediate itself, so such remarks do not decide the case between Hentrup's interpretation and my own. On the account I have presented earlier, it is crucial the pure being be understood as both mediated and immediate if it is avoid the charge of arbitrariness and solve the problem of beginning, but this is not to deny that the result of this solution is precisely the abstract, empty, "immediate" concept of pure being, which itself immediately goes over into more determinate concepts and is, in that sense, mediated as the logical science progresses.

Hentrup is also right to call attention to the fact that Hegel does remark upon the circular structure of his logical project in "With what must the beginning of the science be made?", writing that '[t]hrough this advance the beginning thus loses that one-sidedness which it has in this determination, to be simply something immediate and abstract; it becomes something mediated,

---

41. This account exhibits some commonalities with the reasons Hegel gives for rejecting the need for a sceptical introduction to logic in *EL* §78A, which I discuss in Section 5.1.

and the line of the scientific forward movement thereby makes itself *into a circle*' (*WL* 49/5:71). This sounds as though it strongly supports the interpretation of Hegel's solution to the problem of beginning that Hentrup is putting forward. Yet, for textual reasons and for reasons of having to do with the nature of Hegel's argument, I do not think that this suggestion—to the effect that the pure being can be understood to be both mediated and immediate and thus to solve the problem of beginning because, although it begins as something merely immediate, the progression which it begins turns in a circle and returns to its beginning, rendering it also thereby mediated—can truly be the solution to the problem of beginning that Hegel has in mind.

Firstly, the textual reasons: As I have shown earlier, after Hegel presents the problem of beginning in "With what must the beginning of the science be made?" and specifies that the key to its solution lies in rejecting the mutual exclusivity of mediation and immediacy, Hegel explicitly states that the beginning of the *Logic* is mediated insofar as it 'has . . . the science of spirit in its appearance for its presupposition, which contains and demonstrates the necessity, and thereby the proof of the truth of the standpoint that is pure knowing' (*WL*: 47/5:67). This explicit appeal to the argument of the *Phenomenology*, which Hentrup does not address, appears to suggest that, if Hegel in fact goes on to also appeal to the circularity of the logical science in order to render the beginning mediated, then this is at most an additional, supplementary case, following the one which he presents first, and which takes the mediation in question to *precede* the beginning of the *Logic* in the form of a project of phenomenological criticism of dogmatic presuppositions. And, in fact, I do not think that it can even amount to that. After Hegel sets out the sense in which the beginning can be both mediated and immediate by appealing to the way in which the result of the argument of the *Phenomenology* can coincide with the empty thinking of the beginning of the *Logic*, he concludes: 'The beginning is therefore *pure being*' (*WL* 48/5:69). Immediately afterwards, he writes:

> After this simple exposition of that which first belongs to . . . the logical beginning, the following, further reflections can be added; however, they cannot serve as elucidation and confirmation of the exposition, this is finished on its own account, but are rather prompted by representations and reflections which can get in our way beforehand. (*WL* 48/5:69)

I think that this is perfectly clear. Hegel takes himself at this point to have presented his solution to the problem of beginning, and thereby explained why logic must begin with pure being. The remainder of the essay is precisely *not* dedicated to elucidating and confirming that solution, but rather it is, as I suggested in Sections 0.3.4 and 0.3.5, to offering some anticipatory, clarificatory remarks concerning the relation of the beginning of the *Logic* to the remainder of the project, and to combatting prejudices which might obstruct understanding of the beginning of the project, as well as to criticising a few alternative candidates for beginning, such as Fichte's "I" (which I discussed in Section 2.3.4). Here is the key point: all of these remarks to which Hentrup appeals, concerning the circularity of the science of logic, the manner in which the absolute idea returns to the immediacy of being, the way in which the immediacy of being is itself mediated as the argument of the *Logic* progresses, occur *after* the passage which I have just cited. Whatever their exact function, then, they simply do not belong to Hegel's solution to the problem of beginning.[42]

In terms of Hegel's argument, too, I do not think that an appeal to the manner in which the progression of the logical science turns in a circle and thus turns out to mediate its own beginning can ultimately provide the solution to Hegel's problem of beginning. Hentrup's account here seems similar to various others which appeal to the *Logic*'s circularity in order to justify its beginning. David Carlson, for example, understands the passage in which Hegel sets out what I have identified as the problem of beginning as Hegel insisting upon a *choice* between mediation and immediacy. As he puts it, Hegel 'chooses immediacy' and then 'justifies the choice because what is here presupposed is (much later) proven . . . His philosophy will take us in a circle. If the beginning is also the end, then the beginning is justified' (Carlson 2007: 26–27).[43]

I think that there are two ways that one might interpret the idea that Hegel relies upon the circular nature of the *Logic* to secure the beginning. The worse way to understand this idea would be to suppose that Hegel genuinely thinks that it is legitimate to have the beginning depend for its justification upon that which it itself is to play a key role in justifying. This would be to make the argument of the *Logic* viciously circular. Happily, I do not think that anyone seriously defends this idea. The better way to conceive the role of circularity here is to suppose that Hegel is asking the sceptical reader to proceed in the *Logic* in a provisional manner, temporarily putting aside any concerns about the arbitrariness of the beginning and accepting it as a hypothesis, only to have those concerns eventually soothed by the way in which the end of the project ultimately returns to and secures the beginning, thereby rendering it no longer arbitrary. This, I think, is suggested by Carlson's characterisation

---

42. I think that this issue also affects the account of the beginning of the *Logic* provided in Xiong 2022. Xiong, following Hentrup 2019 and Dunphy 2020b and 2021a, agrees that the beginning of the *Logic* must be both mediated and immediate but suggests that the element of mediation is neither the argument of the *Phenomenology* nor the progression of the logical science subsequent to its beginning, but rather appeals to a separate argument for the 'alternativelessness' of beginning with pure being (Xiong 2022: 100–4). This account also relies upon remarks that, it seems to me, according to Hegel, do not properly belong to his solution to the problem of beginning. Unfortunately, I cannot provide a lengthier engagement with Xiong's interpretation here.

43. See also Rosen 1992: 39–49, or Kreines 2015: 241–45.

of the beginning presented earlier, as well as Hentrup's suggestion that Hegel does, in fact, begin with pure being as a "spurious and one-sided" immediacy and then later corrects the problematic nature of this beginning by deriving it at the end of the *Logic*. It seems to me that this is a slightly awkward reading of Hegel's text, since he is clear that it is "easy to show" that one cannot begin with something merely immediate since it will straight away be rebutted, yet such a reading then appears to force Hegel, however provisionally, to begin in precisely such a problematic fashion. But that is not enough, perhaps, to rule out the very possibility of proceeding this way.

Unfortunately for this interpretation, however, I think that the text of the "With what must the beginning of the science be made?" makes it clear that Hegel himself rejects precisely this kind of approach to securing the beginning, for he states,

> The said beginning is neither something arbitrary and only temporarily assumed, nor an arbitrary appearance and an entreated-for presupposition, from which it is however subsequently shown that one has done the right thing in making it the beginning. (*WL* 50/5:71)

Hegel makes much the same point in his *Encyclopaedia*, rejecting the 'insufficiency' of beginning from a hypothesis (*EL* §10A).[44] Despite a degree of prima facie plausibility, then, appealing to the circularity of the *Logic* cannot be the right way to think about Hegel's solution to the problem of beginning. I cannot discuss Hegel's wariness of this procedure at length here, but it seems to relate to his demand that logic proceed as a strictly demonstrative science.[45] Hegel characterises the attempt to begin with a hypothesis by saying that one would have to proceed 'one knows not how, until somehow, further on, it turns out that one has reached the *original truth* on such a path' (*EL* §10A). Hegel's sceptical tone suggests to me that he views such a procedure as rather a haphazard one, and certainly as falling short of strict demonstration or proof demanded by a science of logic.[46]

---

44. In both the *Science of Logic* and in the *Encyclopaedia*, Hegel targets Reinhold as a proponent of beginning from a hypothesis. The works Hegel has in mind belong to the period of Reinhold's "rational realism", after his break from Fichte. Hegel, in fact, claims, as early as his *Differenzschrift*, in the context of his reading of Reinhold, that 'by means of something hypothetical or problematic absolute nothing is grounded' (*D* 181/2:123).

45. One might also compare Hegel's attitude here to Sextus' rejection of appealing to hypotheses in general and to attempting to legitimise them by appealing to what follows from them, in particular at *AL* II: 367–78.

46. Curiously, at *WL* 750–51/6:570, Hegel appears to soften his attitude towards beginning with a hypothesis somewhat. I think that this is best explained as a remark to the effect that, if one begins with pure being, one can at least arrive at the results that Hegel claims to derive in his *Logic*, even if one has not, strictly speaking, proved them from a beginning which is not arbitrary. I cannot see that he anywhere retracts the criticisms that he levels at beginning with a hypothesis in "With what must the beginning of the science be made?" and in *EL* §10A.

I conclude that interpretations of the beginning of Hegel's *Logic* which take the crucial element of mediation to occur only *after* the beginning, or which appeal to the circularity of the science to justify the beginning, cannot capture the nature of Hegel's solution to the problem of beginning. Still, the passages from "With what must the beginning of the science be made?" to which such accounts appeal are clearly important, even if they are not part of the solution to the problem of beginning. It is, therefore, worth briefly indicating what I think that Hegel is getting at when he makes these remarks, if they are not part of his treatment of the problem of beginning, in order to diagnose where I think accounts like the ones presented by Hentrup and by Carlson go wrong. A helpful passage is the following one:

> The essential thing for the science [of logic] is not so much that the beginning be a pure immediacy, but rather that the whole science is a circle, in which the first becomes the last and the last also the first. (*WL* 49/5:71)

Here, I think, Hegel is talking not about what is essential for the *beginning* of a science of logic but instead what is essential for that science as whole. And what is essential for that science, Hegel says, is *not so much* the issue of its beginning but that its exposition take, in some sense, a circular form. I think that the most natural way to read this passage, in its context at the beginning of Hegel's *Logic*, is as saying that while the issue of the beginning of such a science is of some importance and must be addressed, *more* significant to Hegel's logical project in its entirety is that it have this circular structure.

This insistence upon circularity is not something unique to Hegel's presentation of a philosophical system.[47] The most significant precursor here, is Fichte, who demands that his *Wissenschaftlehre* exhibit a circular structure when he writes that:

> A foundational principle has been exhausted when a complete system has been erected upon it, that is, when the principle in question necessarily leads to *all* the propositions that are asserted [within this system] and when *all* these propositions necessarily lead back to that foundational principle. (Fichte 2021: 172)

As I noted in Section 2.3.4, Fichte claims that this kind of circular procedure amounts to a proof of the completeness, or systematicity, of the science. I think that the same applies to Hegel's remarks about circularity: The central function of the circular structure of Hegel's *Logic* is to facilitate a completeness proof in the context of the science: a demonstration that *all* of the fundamental concepts of thought have been derived, examined, and systematically

---

47. Kant, for example, claims that 'Reason is driven . . . to find peace only in the completion of its circle in a self-subsisting systematic whole' (*KRV* A797/B825).

related to one another, without leaving a remainder or exception which could serve as a focal point for a sceptical objection to the results of the science. If Hegel is to claim that he has presented a demonstrative, systematic account of the determinations of thought, then it is crucial that a sceptical interlocutor not be able to point to some fundamental concept which has gone untreated in the account, the relations of which to the other concepts which Hegel has treated is left unclear.[48] Were this possibility to be left open, then the introduction of such a missing element might demand the reworking of the relations that Hegel takes himself to have established between various fundamental concepts, or even threaten some of his more notable conclusions concerning logic, for example, the claim that conceptual oppositions can be encompassed within further, more adequate concepts. Presumably, all that it would take would be the presence of a concept not amenable to this dialectical treatment to cast doubt upon Hegel's results. Hegel, it would seem, agrees with Kant when the latter says of his own treatment of pure reason that 'it is never trustworthy unless it is *entirely complete* down to the least elements' (*P* 4:263).[49] This is why Hegel insists that, in a science of logic, each of the various determinate concepts must be understood as 'a moment of the form as a totality' (*WL* 19/5:30).

Hegel's way of arriving at such a self-sufficient totality is (a) to have the account proceed, as he insists that it does, by way of strict derivation, a priori, from concept to concept, and (b), since strict derivation alone is not sufficient for completion, have the account also demonstrate that no further concepts are to be derived, by having the conclusion of the account give rise to its beginning again.[50] The result of such a procedure, in Hegel's eyes, is a complete, systematic, demonstrative science of logic. If this interpretation is correct, then it is not surprising that Hegel puts so much weight on the circular structure of his treatment of logic, even in "With what must the beginning of the science be made?": This circular structure has implications not merely for the beginning of Hegel's logical project but also for that project as a whole.[51]

---

48. There will be many empirically informed concepts not treated in a science of logic, of course, some of which will be crucial to the metaphysics of Hegel's *Realphilosophie*, but the claim is that the account of a priori concepts in the *Logic* must be complete.

49. Fichte, for his part (2021: 173–75), appears not to completely rule out the possibility that one might, in the future, encounter some principle which was not treated within the circle of the system and which would prompt its revision.

50. I take it that this suggestion accords with Hegel's remarks at *WL* 752/6:572, to the effect that, in having the absolute idea return to the concept of pure being at the beginning of the *Logic*, the science of logic has become comprehensive and developed into systematic science.

51. I would like to reiterate, however, that I think Hegel does still insist on allocating *some* importance to solving the problem of beginning, even if it does not compare to the significance of the systematic completeness of the logical science as a whole. I am open to the possibility that the full significance of the results of Hegel's *Logic* can only be grasped on the basis of a reading that, after reaching its end, returns to the beginning and reads it again in the light of its circular structure (Nuzzo [2011] makes this suggestion, I think), but such a reading is only possible if the first reading can treat

The mistake I believe that Carlson, Hentrup, and various others are making is to confuse this issue with that of solving the problem of beginning. They are taking the insistence upon the circular structure of the work, which Hegel thinks is essential to the results of the science as a whole, not specifically to the issue of beginning, and supposing that this is also his solution to the problem of beginning.[52] Admittedly, though, Hegel himself does not separate these two issues as clearly as one might hope since he describes the circularity of the *Logic* precisely in terms of the coincidence of its end with its beginning.

Having now spent some time criticising some notable alternative accounts of the beginning of Hegel's *Logic*, I turn now to a consideration of some objections that might be levelled at my own account, as I have developed it in this chapter.

3.4.2 Objections Anticipated

In the final part of this chapter, I will attempt to anticipate potential objections to my presentation of Hegel's engagement with the problem of beginning. The first objection would be to dispute the claim that the concept of pure being occurs as the coincidence of the elements of mediation and immediacy because Hegel states, on more than one occasion, that pure being is not mediated. So, for example, he writes, in the context of the account of pure being, that, 'the first beginning cannot be anything mediated' (*EL* §86). It is also true that the account of pure being in the Doctrine of Being proper, which follows the essay, "With what must the beginning of science be made?", makes mention only of the immediacy of pure being. This does not, however, detract from the fact that, in that essay, Hegel has described pure being 'as having emerged through a mediation' (*WL*: 47/5:68). It is not sufficient to point to those occasions where Hegel describes being as purely immediate in order to dismiss the claim that it is also mediated, when Hegel's solution to the problem of beginning, as I have presented it earlier, turns precisely on identifying a mediation which is compatible with the pure immediacy of being.

---

the material, as Hegel wants to, as a matter of scientific demonstration, without supposing that it begins from somewhere problematically arbitrary. Solving the problem of beginning remains therefore necessary to Hegel's project, I think.

52. I would say much the same for those elements of Hentrup's account which appeal to the fact that the system of concepts which begins with pure being are ultimately grounded in the Concept, or in its final and most concrete expression in the *Logic* as the absolute idea: It does seem important to Hegel to show that his logical system is ultimately grounded on a satisfactory foundation, but if the problem of beginning and the problem of identifying that foundation come apart in Hegel's work, as I have suggested in Sections 2.4 and 3.1, then the tendency of the course of Hegel's logic away from its abstract beginning and toward its concrete foundation can belong to solving the latter problem, not the former, and it would be a mistake to confuse the two issues.

The way to understand Hegel's subsequent emphasis only on the immediacy of pure being, *after* he has presented his solution to the problem of beginning, then, is to accept that this concept is both mediated and immediate but to remember that once this has been accepted, in considering the concept of pure being on its own terms, we attend only to its simple immediacy. Hegel makes this clear when he writes, as I noted earlier, that '*pure being,* this absolute immediate, is just as much absolutely mediated. But it must just as essentially be taken only in the one-sidedness of being purely immediate, *precisely because* it is here the beginning' (*WL* 52/5:72). This remark fits with my presentation of Hegel's solution of the problem of beginning, I think. The beginning must be presuppositionless in such a way that, although it requires some presupposition to render it non-arbitrary, its presuppositionless character undoes the problematic nature of a reliance upon presuppositions. Thus, when considering pure being, we should expect it no longer to refer back to the mediation which it presupposes, and to be considered as a simple immediacy. This explains Hegel's occasional insistence that pure being not be considered as including mediation, without thereby conflicting with the solution to the problem of beginning as I have presented it here.

A further objection to the idea that the concept of pure being solves the problem of beginning insofar as it is both mediated and immediate might be made by claiming that Hegel disallows such a possibility when he rejects the idea that the beginning could consist in a 'relation of different elements, [which] thereby contains *mediation* within itself' (*WL*: 52/5:75). He adds,

> [T]hat with which the beginning is to be made . . . cannot be the sort of thing that contains a relation *within its self*. For such a thing presupposes a mediation and a going over from a first to an other within itself . . . But the beginning itself should not already be a first *and* an other; such a thing, that is in itself a first *and* an other, already contains a progression. (*WL* 52/5:75)

It might be thought that here Hegel is ruling out the idea that pure being could be the coincidence of mediation and immediacy, especially if, as I have suggested, that coincidence consists in the *result* of the mediation being identified with the element of immediacy, since this sounds dangerously close to insisting that pure being contains a first and an other. But, as I have argued in this chapter, grasping pure being as an empty thinking which coincides with the result of his phenomenological project is precisely what Hegel has defended in his presentation of the solution to the problem of beginning, which occurs only a few pages earlier in the text than this passage. He cannot, therefore, conceive of this coincidence in terms of a first and an other. I think that it is helpful to put this problematic passage in context. When Hegel makes this remark, he is explicitly entertaining the notion of beginning *not* with pure being but instead with the notion of "beginning" itself. He is prompted to entertain this notion in order to dispense with the objection that perhaps even pure being presupposes too much at the beginning and that, therefore, beginning with 'beginning itself' might be preferable (*WL* 51/5:73). The general thrust of Hegel's response here is to claim that such a presupposed '*representation*' of beginning in fact presupposes rather more than pure being does, in that it contains the idea of becoming,[53] and that therefore to begin with pure being, if it is conceived properly, as 'total emptiness', better satisfies the demand for presuppositionlessness after all (*WL* 52/5:75).[54] The passage itself, therefore, does not target the idea that pure being might be arrived at as the result of the purging of dogmatic presuppositions by way of phenomenological or sceptical criticism.

How is it, then, that the characterisation of pure being as both mediated and immediate does not *also* imply that the concept has a connection within itself, that it is "first and other"? I think that the answer to this question must lie in the nature of the *genuine coincidence* of the elements of mediation and immediacy in the concept of pure being, facilitated by the fact that the conclusion of the mediation in question is an entirely negative or empty one, such that it can immediately coincide with the empty thinking of pure being, rather than amounting to a distinct, prior step, a first to an other. The concept of pure being, Hegel has argued, is to be thought of as an immediacy which no longer exhibits any relation to the mediation which gave rise to it. If it were to be suggested that this concept still cannot admit of a description in terms of both mediation and immediacy, given its "purity," I would respond that Hegel will later claim of the concepts examined in the *Logic* that '*every* concept [is a] unity of opposed moments' (*WL* 158/5:217). On pain of contradiction, this must also be true of the concept of pure being, which suggests that its purity is compatible with describing it as the unity of mediation and immediacy after all, without thereby transforming it into a first and an other. And strikingly, it seems to be Pyrrhonian Scepticism that Hegel credits here with this discovery, claiming that 'Ancient Scepticism did not spare itself the bother of pointing out the contradiction or the antinomy in all the concepts that it found in the sciences' (*WL* 158/5:217). Thus, just

---

53. See *WL* 51/5:73: 'The beginning is not pure nothing, but rather a nothing from which something should proceed; being is thus also already contained in the beginning. The beginning thus contains both, being and nothing; is the unity of being and nothing'. This is precisely how Hegel describes becoming (*WL* 59/5:83).

54. The account of the beginning of the *Logic* provided by Gentry (2021: 41–42), for example, risks, it seems to me, taking this discussion of beginning with the unity of being and nothing as an elucidation of what is involved in beginning with pure being, rather than a way of showing that beginning with "pure beginning" is to begin already with too complex a representation. I cannot consider this matter further here, however.

as Hegel's reading of Sextus' account of the Two Modes shaped his expression of the problem of beginning, so, too, does his reading of Pyrrhonism as conducting an exhaustive inquiry which exhibits the antinomial nature of all finite concepts and points in the direction of their possible unification allow one to make sense of the manner in which Hegel understands the elements of mediation and immediacy to coincide in the concept of pure being in his solution to that problem.

3.5 CONCLUSION

In this chapter, I have presented Hegel's problem of beginning, with which he opens the essay, "With what must the beginning of the science be made?", as a distinct Agrippan problem which targets the attempt to begin a science of logic with the examination of some concept in a non-arbitrary way. I have argued the dilemma Hegel presents between beginning with something mediated and with something immediate shares its form with Sextus' account of the Two Modes, and that Hegel's preferred response to this problem is neither to double down on beginning with something mediated, nor with something immediate. Nor again is it to concede to the Sceptic. Instead, Hegel attempts to identify a concept with which he can begin a science of logic which is both mediated *and* immediate, specifically in such a way that the coincidence of these two elements eliminates what was problematically arbitrary about beginning with either one alone. I proceeded to argue that, while the immediacy with which Hegel is concerned is that of "empty thinking" or "pure knowing" across his mature works, he appears to give two different accounts of the element of mediation. In his *Science of Logic*, he identifies it as the argument of his *Phenomenology of Spirit*, while in his *Encyclopaedia*, he identifies it with a "negative science" of "completed scepticism". Despite this difference, I have argued that his solution is conceived as operating in the same manner across both versions: The element of mediation functions as a thorough critique of all dogmatic presuppositions which has, as its purely negative result, the mere absence of all such presuppositions. It thus coincides with the empty thinking of pure being in such a way that it necessitates that empty thinking, without remaining itself as a substantial presupposition which, from the perspective of the beginning of a science of logic, would itself appear questionable. Thus, according to Hegel, the coincidence of the elements of mediation and of immediacy here avoids the arbitrariness which accompanies merely beginning with something immediate as an arbitrary assertion, and that which accompanies merely beginning on the basis of some presuppositions which have not themselves been validated within the logical science.

The task remaining for the final two chapters of this book is to critically consider the two versions of Hegel's solution to the problem of beginning that I have outlined here and to attempt to evaluate the extent to which they can successfully solve that problem, as Hegel has conceived it. I begin in chapter 4 with the coincidence of the results of phenomenology and presuppositionlessness.

Chapter Four

Mediation I – Phenomenology

4.0 INTRODUCTION

In the previous chapter, I presented Hegel's problem of beginning as a problem concerning the *arbitrariness* that, according to Hegel, vitiates any attempt to begin an a priori science of logic either with something merely mediated or with something merely immediate. In the account of the nature of Hegel's solution to the problem that followed (Sections 3.3.1–3.3.2), after indicating that this solution turns on identifying a concept ("pure being") with which to begin that combines both mediation and immediacy in such a way as to avoid the problematically arbitrary character of beginning with either alone, I suggested that properly understanding Hegel's solution depended upon the answers to three questions: (*i*) What is the element of immediacy in the beginning? (*ii*) What is the element of mediation? (*iii*) How do they coincide in such a way as to eliminate the problems which occur when beginning with either alone? I went on to identify two distinct versions of Hegel's solution, in the greater *Science of Logic* and in the *Encyclopaedia Logic*, differentiated by the answer to question (*ii*). In the *Encyclopaedia Logic*, I suggested, the element of mediation which results in and coincides with the "empty thinking" of the beginning of logic was identified as a "negative science" of "completed scepticism". In the *Science of Logic*, it was identified as the argument of Hegel's 1807 *Phenomenology of Spirit*.

The remaining task is to consider in detail how each of these solutions answers the third of the three questions above: How does the result of the element of mediation, on either account, coincide with the empty thinking of the beginning of logic, and indeed, how convincingly, or successfully? To answer this question is to evaluate the success of Hegel's solutions by his own lights. In the next chapter, I will consider the *Encyclopaedia* version of Hegel's solution, which relies upon the "negative science" of "completed scepticism", but in this chapter, I am concerned to evaluate the version of the conclusion which relies upon the argument of Hegel's *Phenomenology*. That is to say, I am concerned with the compatibility of the conclusion of the argument of the *Phenomenology* with the beginning of the *Logic*, as it appears from the perspective of the solution to the problem of beginning outlined in "With what must the beginning of the science be made?" The general thrust of that essay, as I explained in the previous chapter, was that the pure thinking of the beginning of logic presupposed or was mediated by the argument of the *Phenomenology* and thus relied upon it for its justification or proof, although in such a way as to not leave the beginning of logic saddled with a substantive presupposition that would be incompatible with its "presuppositionless" character. And although the matter is not disputed, a number of Hegel's remarks elsewhere in his *Logic* do suggest that the position taken up at the start of that work depends crucially for its justification upon the work carried out in his earlier *Phenomenology of Spirit*. Hegel writes, for example,

> In the *Phenomenology of Spirit* I have presented consciousness in its progression from the first immediate opposition of itself and the object up to absolute knowing. This path goes through all forms of the *relation of consciousness to the object* and has the *concept of science* as its result. This concept thus needs no justification here . . . because it received it there . . . a definition of science or, more precisely, of logic, has its *proof* only in the necessity of its origination . . . The concept of pure science and its deduction is thus presupposed in the present work insofar as the Phenomenology of Spirit is nothing other than the deduction of it. (*WL* 28/5:42–43)

Although the picture of the relationship between the argument of the *Phenomenology* and the beginning of the *Logic* suggested by such remarks, and by the contents of "With what must the beginning of science be made?", appears to be reasonably clear, a brief examination of the secondary literature on the topic makes it clear that the exact nature of this relation is actually rather a vexed topic. Although I will touch on a number of difficulties concerning this relation in this chapter, I will keep the focus squarely upon what is demanded of that relation by a successful solution to Hegel's problem of beginning. I thus offer a thematically very narrow engagement with Hegel's *Phenomenology* in general and its relation with his *Logic* in particular. Accordingly, multiple aspects of that extraordinarily rich text and of its relation to Hegel's other works receive no attention at all here.

I should also note here that the idea that the beginning of the *Logic* relies upon the argument of the *Phenomenology* for its justification, as Hegel claims, is a significant one. It means that the argument of the *Phenomenology* must be valid in the entirety, across each step and each of its criticisms of the various forms of consciousness that it examines since this is what is required in order to get from the "first immediate opposition" of consciousness and object all the way to the "absolute knowing", which coincides with the beginning of the *Logic*. Interrogating the various steps in the argument of the *Phenomenology* cannot be accomplished here by any means, so I will continue in this chapter on the basis of the significant assumption that the argument of the *Phenomenology* is valid all the way through and that it does indeed demonstrate the necessity of its result.[1]

This chapter has two principal parts. In the first part, I will examine in broad terms some competing accounts of the relation between the *Phenomenology* and the *Logic*. I will argue that, from the perspective of a concern for Hegel's problem of beginning, the interpretation of this relation notably defended by Maker, which I briefly introduced in Section 3.3.2, appears most promising. In the second, longer part, I present three objections to the plausibility of Maker's account of the relation between the argument of the *Phenomenology* and the beginning of the *Logic*. These objections lead me to suggest that the result of the argument of the *Phenomenology*, even according to what I take to be the strongest interpretation (from the perspective of the beginning of the *Logic*), is not, in fact, compatible with the presuppositionlessness of the empty thinking of the beginning of the *Logic*. I will thus conclude this chapter with the suggestion that the first version of Hegel's solution to the problem of beginning fails. It should be clear, however, that although the objections I develop here lead me to conclude that the version of Hegel's solution which depends on the argument of the *Phenomenology* fails, this is an issue only for his solution to the problem of beginning. I make no criticisms here of the coherence or validity of the argument of Hegel's *Phenomenology* itself.

4.1 THE *PHENOMENOLOGY* AND THE BEGINNING OF THE *LOGIC*

It is well-known that the *Phenomenology* was envisioned as the introduction to Hegel's system,[2] and the brief engagement with that text in the previous chapter furnishes one of the senses in which it functions as an introduction: The *Phenomenology*, it would seem, is an introduction to the system in a justificatory sense. As the mediation of what Hegel refers to as "natural consciousness"—our dogmatic or everyday understanding of how thought

---

1. See Förster 2012: 375–77, for some concise remarks in favour of Hegel's argument in the *Phenomenology*.
2. Hegel refers to the work specifically as the 'introduction' to his system in *EL* §25A, and for the advertisement he published for the *Phenomenology* in 1807, he writes that the work 'examines the *preparation* for science' (*PhG*: 468–69/3:593).

relates to the world—the *Phenomenology* of *Spirit* leads one to the standpoint referred to at the end of the *Phenomenology* as "absolute knowing," or at the beginning of the *Logic* as "*pure knowing*", the standpoint of "science" or philosophy proper, whence thought's pure, reflexive consideration of itself can begin. This identification of the absolute knowing of the *Phenomenology* with the pure knowing of the *Logic*[3] is at the heart of the version of Hegel's solution to the problem of beginning presented here, since it is the sublation of the former, understood as the element of mediation, into its negation, the latter, understood as the element of immediacy, and thus into their unity in Hegel's concept of "pure being", which guarantees the coincidence and compatibility of those two opposing elements and allows the beginning to avoid the arbitrariness of something mediated or something immediate taken alone. This is to say that the *Phenomenology* plays a justificatory role without which the beginning of the *Logic* appears problematically arbitrary. It is not enough, however, simply to assert the validity of this justificatory role, or of the sublating process by which it functions. It must be examined and found to be coherent and persuasive.

Here is a problematic, although possibly not unfamiliar sketch, of how the *Phenomenology*'s fulfilment of its justificatory role might be thought to proceed: Hegel, having decided on a standpoint or model for scientific or philosophical thought which crucially involves in some sense the identification of knower and known, thought and being, or subject and substance,[4] notes that this model differs from the model of cognition common to everyday thought, in which the knower is identified with a thinking subject on the one hand, and what is known is identified with an existing object, quite distinct in kind from the thinking subject, on the other.[5] According to the latter model, the activity of knowing would primarily be occupied with the challenges of crossing the divide between subject and object. As such, he proceeds, by way of a method of immanent criticism, to demonstrate that this dogmatic model of cognition—that of natural consciousness—is inconsistent, and that its various inconsistencies, properly examined, transform it dialectically, by way of

---

3. For all that they coincide at the end of the *Phenomenology* and beginning of the *Logic*, there may be a case to be made for distinguishing absolute knowing and pure knowing. *PhG* §808/3:590–91, of the *Phenomenology* suggest that absolute knowing refers to knowing across the breadth of Hegel's philosophical system, while pure knowing can arguably be taken to refer only to the empty thinking at the beginning of the *Logic*, or perhaps to logic in general (See Pippin 2019: 5, for an account of "pure thinking", which he takes to apply to Hegel's logic in general). On this interpretation, absolute knowing is no longer "pure" in this sense, either when it achieves some determinacy, early in the *Logic*, or when it begins to engage with empirical matters in the *Realphilosophie*. I shall not investigate this further here. What matters for my purposes in this essay is that the absolute knowing of the conclusion of the *Phenomenology* coincides with the pure knowing at the beginning of the *Logic*.

4. See *PhG* §17/3:22–23.

5. Hegel describes this model, that of natural consciousness, as one in which consciousness 'knows objective things as opposed to itself and itself as opposed to them' (*PhG* §26/3:30).

a long and tortuous series of determinate negations,[6] into the very model of scientific or philosophical cognition that it was originally thought to oppose. At this point, having attained a properly justified model for thought, the activity of the *Logic* can begin.

This sketch is problematic for two reasons: Firstly, if Hegel has decided in advance on a standpoint or model of cognition for the *Logic* and the *Phenomenology* is dedicated to its justification, this conflicts with his comments in the introduction to the *Logic* to the effect that the method and form of logical inquiry cannot be set out in advance of its exposition (*WL* 23/5:35). Secondly, it would also be to make guaranteeing the idealist position of Hegel's philosophy (however precisely it is understood) into a substantive presupposition of the *Logic*, which looks as though it would be incompatible with the demand that the beginning of the *Logic* be presuppositionless. Variants of this account exist in the contemporary literature on Hegel's *Phenomenology*: With his construal of the *Phenomenology* as resolving a sceptical equipollence problem between pre-established models of cognition, for example, it seems to me that Forster's conception of the justificatory role played by the *Phenomenology* comes close to this sketch.[7]

And even if one retreats from phrasing the investigation of the *Phenomenology* as a method for deciding in favour of one of two pre-established models (a phrasing to which, in fairness, Hegel's preface to the *Phenomenology* does lend itself at times),[8] the sketch remains problematic in that it

---

6. I will say more about the notions of immanent criticism and determinate negation in Sections 4.2.2–4.2.3. For now, I note that Hegel characterises the method of criticism in the *Phenomenology* as one whereby 'it is not necessary for us to bring standards with us and to apply *our* ideas and thoughts in the investigation' because, 'consciousness gives its own standard to itself, and the investigation will thereby be a comparison of its standard with itself' (*PhG* §84/3:76–77). I will also acknowledge Hegel's characterisation of the unsatisfactory nature of a critical investigation which proceeds negatively but not *merely* negatively. In this vein, he criticises the scepticism which, in opposing mutually inconsistent views, 'sees only ever *pure nothing* in the result and abstracts from the fact that this nothing is determinately the nothing *of that from which it results*'. Instead the negative, critical procedure that Hegel identifies as occurring in the investigation of the *Phenomenology* is characterised as attending to the fact that '[n]othing is only in fact the true result when taken as the nothing of that from which it comes; it is thereby itself *something determinate* and has a *content* (*PhG* §79/3:74). The method Hegel is criticising here is clearly the abstractly negative one of the Pyrrhonists, which I discussed in Section 1.2.1.

7. See Forster 1998: 159–60 and 167–74, and Forster 1989: 104–6 and Ch.9. In both works, he presents the task of the *Phenomenology* as that of resolving a sceptical equipollence problem of deciding between two models of cognition which are held up for examination in advance. I am concerned that this model conflicts with the idea that either the *Phenomenology* or the *Logic* are properly presuppositionless in their approaches to their respective subject matters.

8. See, in particular *PhG* §26/3:29–30. In this discussion of philosophical science's approach to natural consciousness, it certainly sounds as though one is dealing with two pre-established models. The only way to make sense of this in an unproblematic manner, it seems to me, is to recognize that the preface is written on the basis of having completed the work of the *Phenomenology*, so Hegel is already writing from his scientific perspective, and conceiving here of its opposition to the position of natural consciousness retrospectively. This does not require him to be holding to a model of scientific cognition in advance while undertaking his examination of natural consciousness in the main body of the work.

seems to characterise the position attained at the end of the *Phenomenology* as a substantive idealist philosophical standpoint, described in terms of the identity of subject and substance, developed dialectically from the various formulations of consciousness and spirit which preceded it.[9] Aside from the fact that, as I have already noted, Hegel is of the opinion that the concept of a science of logic or the method of scientific investigation is to be developed within and on the basis of the logical investigation itself and not to be given beforehand, the presence of a substantive idealist philosophical standpoint or model of cognition at the beginning of the *Logic* still looks incompatible with Hegel's declarations concerning the "presuppositionless" nature of the beginning of that investigation. A philosophical account of the nature of cognition developed over the course of the *Phenomenology of Spirit*, if it is taken as given at the beginning of the *Logic*, would seem to constitute a substantive presupposition that goes far beyond merely "empty thinking".

A more explicit way of expressing the problem encountered in the previous sketch is this: In order for the element of mediation to be able to coincide with the element of immediacy at the beginning of the *Logic* so as to render it non-arbitrary without robbing it of its immediate or presuppositionless status, the mediated element, despite being the result of the entirety of the development of the *Phenomenology of Spirit* and despite needing to be able to necessitate the pure knowing with which the *Logic* begins, seems as though it cannot amount to anything which would constitute a substantive presupposition from the perspective of the *Logic*, either in terms of the form or content of the inquiry. Were it to amount to such a presupposition it would seem to risk clashing, rather than coinciding, with the element of immediacy. In other words, it would fail the test of compatibility required by the form of Hegel's solution to the problem of beginning.

Resolving this problem is at the heart of understanding how the *Phenomenology* can fulfil its role of justifying the beginning of the *Logic* by functioning as the element of mediation in that beginning, and of how it is that the elements of mediation and immediacy are thought to coincide at the beginning of the *Logic*. An elegant solution and, to my mind, perhaps the best possible candidate for making sense of the *Phenomenology* as the necessary justificatory introduction to the *Logic* is the account put forward by Maker in his *Philosophy Without Foundations*, which I briefly discussed in Section 3.3.2.[10]

---

9. I take it that something like this is the position taken by, among various others, Bristow (2007: 102), and perhaps Stewart (2000: 455–68).

10. The question of whether the *Phenomenology* is a *necessary* introduction to the *Logic*, or whether it might be possible in certain circumstances to do without it without thereby compromising the security of the logical investigation, is ongoing in the literature on Hegel. Maker, among others, clearly believes the *Phenomenology* to be necessary. Houlgate, for example, does not. He believes that its justificatory function is only required by those unable or unwilling to simply abstract from all determinate content and commence pure knowing (see, for example, Houlgate 2005: 50). My own

The key to Maker's interpretation lies in explicating a sense in which the *Phenomenology* really is the necessary presupposition to the *Logic* and, therefore, in some sense, justifies it but in a special manner which still allows us to characterize the *Logic* as presuppositionless. It is in this context that he writes: 'I aim to show that Hegel proposed to introduce the standpoint of autonomous reason and philosophical science through a radical and consummately destructive *critique* of foundational epistemology' (Maker 1994:13). Later, he argues that Hegel's project is that of securing the scientific character of philosophy by way of 'a systematically deconstructive critique of foundationalism' (Maker 1994: 50). These two phrases—"a destructive critique of foundational epistemology" and "a systematically deconstructive critique of foundationalism"—indicate the specific manner by which Maker's account purports to resolve the problem being considered here. This is because the two phrases just quoted are nothing other than Maker's characterisation of the project of the *Phenomenology* itself. "Foundational epistemology" is the term Maker uses to describe the dogmatic model according to which natural consciousness attempts to justify its knowledge claims—in other words, the very thing being undone by way of the immanent criticism of the *Phenomenology*.

Without getting into an extended discussion of Maker's at times idiosyncratic characterisation of "foundationalism" and of the "antifoundationalism" that he believes Hegel to espouse, one can see that what is distinctive about Maker's presentation of the "destructive" project of the *Phenomenology* is that it is a radically *negative* one, as I emphasised in the previous chapter. This point is important enough to be worth repeating. As Maker sees it, 'both the *Phenomenology* as introduction, and absolute knowing as the deduced concept, must be understood *negatively*' (Maker 1994: 71).

In the sketch I presented earlier, two possibilities were suggested and rejected—that Hegel begins with two opposing standpoints and criticises one, thereby justifying the other, requiring him to have presupposed the form of philosophical or scientific inquiry in advance, or that Hegel begins only with the standpoint characteristic of and provided by natural consciousness, and from that develops a substantive philosophical standpoint characteristic of philosophical science, or absolute knowing. Both of these possibilities, I suggested, looked incompatible with the demand for a presuppositionless beginning for logic. Maker's suggestion, however, is that Hegel begins the *Phenomenology* with the standpoint characteristic of and provided by natural consciousness, but instead of ending up with a substantive alternative model, he ends up simply with the *total collapse* of the model of natural

---

position should be clear: In the context of the version of Hegel's solution to the problem of beginning under consideration in this chapter, I think that he considers the *Phenomenology* necessary to the legitimacy of the beginning of the *Logic*; without it, the immediacy of the beginning of the *Logic* is problematically arbitrary.

consciousness and its associated content. Maker calls this the 'radically negative outcome' of the *Phenomenology* (Maker 1994: 93). According to him, what is signified by "absolute knowing" is really just the result of the *elimination* of the presuppositions of natural consciousness. As he puts it, 'the task of the *Phenomenology* as introduction to science is the *critical* task of showing that . . . consciousness, as a determinate and presupposed structure, comes to eliminate itself' (Maker 1994: 78). The presupposition of the *Logic*, then, according to this interpretation, is not a developed model of cognition or an idealist standpoint of philosophical science. Instead, the presupposition of the *Logic* is simply the complete elimination[11] of all of the presuppositions of natural consciousness.

As I suggested in the previous chapter, it is on this basis that, by way of Maker's interpretation, one might connect the mediation of the *Phenomenology* to the immediacy of empty thinking: The mediation in question justifies the beginning of the *Logic* by deducing it from the collapse of natural consciousness, but the result of that mediation is indeterminate and immediate; it necessitates a situation in which thought can only think itself without any determinations already in place. This is to say that the *Phenomenology* justifies the beginning of the *Logic* because the end result of the former just *is* the beginning of the latter. In this very specific manner, it would seem that the elements of mediation and immediacy can coincide unproblematically. To repeat Hegel's expression of this point, absolute or '[p]ure knowing . . . has sublated every relation to an other and to mediation; it is something without distinctions; this something without distinctions thus ceases to be knowing; only *simple immediacy* is present' (*WL* 47/5:68). At this point, Hegel seems to think, the concept of "pure being," being both necessitated by the phenomenological investigation which it presupposes, and at the same time radically presuppositionless, allows his logical project to get underway in a rigorous or scientific manner because it is no longer open to the charges of arbitrariness which might otherwise vitiate the beginning of such a project.

Maker's take on the relation between the conclusion of the *Phenomenology* and the beginning of the *Logic*, then, looks as though it provides a good answer to the third question essential to understanding Hegel's solution to

---

11. The elimination is, in fact, an "auto-elimination" because the *Phenomenology* is an exercise in immanent criticism, as I mentioned before. The criticisms of natural consciousness are not made by the phenomenologist, by examining them from the standpoint of a competing perspective and finding natural consciousness wanting, but instead by examining the claims of a given form of natural consciousness and finding that they are incompatible with the criterion of truth proposed by that very form of natural consciousness itself. The following revisions both to the nature of the claims being made and to the criteria by which to measure those claims are thereby generated by natural consciousness itself, and not by the phenomenologist. Hegel outlines this method in *PhG* §§84–87/3:76–80. Insofar as Maker believes that the ultimate result of these revisions is the elimination of natural consciousness itself, it is, therefore, an auto-elimination.

the problem of beginning: the question of how the elements of mediation and immediacy could coincide at the beginning of the *Logic*.[12] The suggestion is that if the two could coincide, then the charges of either straightforward arbitrariness or of a reliance upon illegitimate presuppositions set out in Section 3.2 could be avoided, putting the beginning of the *Logic* on firmer ground. According to some accounts of the relation between the argument of the *Phenomenology* and the beginning of the *Logic*, I have suggested, it is difficult to see how the conclusion of the former's critical investigation of natural consciousness could be compatible with the presuppositionless, empty thinking of the latter, although this is precisely what is required in order to render the solution workable. But if, with Maker, one understands the conclusion of the *Phenomenology* in radically negative terms, as amounting to no more than the dissolution of the presuppositions of natural consciousness, it looks as though one can understand the *Phenomenology* as justifying the beginning of the *Logic* while at the same not amounting to a substantive presupposition which would be incompatible with the presuppositionless character of that beginning. In the remainder of this chapter, however, I will provide a number of reasons for thinking that, despite its ingenuity, Maker's solution fails to provide a coherent picture of how the *Phenomenology* could function as the element of mediation at the beginning of the *Logic*.

4.2 SOME PROBLEMS

I shall argue here that Maker's proposal ultimately fails to render the idea that the *Phenomenology* can play the justificatory role demanded by the form of Hegel's solution to his problem of beginning a convincing one.[13] Since his radically negative interpretation seemed to be the best way to make sense of the idea that the argument of the *Phenomenology* could play the role of the element of mediation in Hegel's account of beginning in the *Logic*, I will thus conclude that the *Phenomenology* cannot successfully play the role that it seemed Hegel's solution to the problem of beginning requires it to and, therefore, that the version of that solution presented in "With what must the

---

12. As I acknowledged in the previous chapter, Maker does not approach this topic specifically through the lens of the problem of beginning but of the relationship between the *Phenomenology* and the beginning of the *Logic*, but I take it that this is another way of getting at the same issue.

13. Bill Maker tragically died while I was composing this book, but on those occasions I was able to meet him and discuss what would become the content of this chapter, he was extremely generous and supportive, despite the fact that the thrust of my argument was critical of his account. I hope he would have recognised how much the account of the alternative solution to Hegel's problem of beginning which I defend in Chapter 5 of this book still owes to his work on the relationship between the *Phenomenology* and the beginning of the *Logic*.

beginning of the science be made?" fails, imperilling the security of the beginning of the *Logic*.

In what follows, I provide three principal reasons for thinking that the *Phenomenology* cannot play such a justificatory role in relation to the beginning of the *Logic*.[14] In so doing, I am taking Hegel's insistence that the beginning of the *Logic* be presuppositionless, both in terms of content and in terms of the form of its inquiry, seriously, and then finding that various elements of the argument of the *Phenomenology* suggest that its result is incompatible with that demand for presuppositionlessness.[15] In brief, these reasons are as follows:

1. The presence of "already-scientific content" in the *Phenomenology* renders its conclusion incompatible with the presuppositionless beginning of the *Logic*.
2. The *determinately* negative procedure of the *Phenomenology* renders its conclusion incompatible with the presuppositionless beginning of the *Logic*.
3. The project of the *Phenomenology* is one of securing what Hegel conceives of as the standpoint of science: one that does not fall prey to the "problem of the criterion" in the specific way that he takes the position of natural consciousness to. Achieving this goal is incompatible with the presuppositionless beginning of the *Logic*.

I shall treat these in turn.

4.2.1 Already-Scientific Content

In the preliminaries to his *Encyclopaedia Logic*, Hegel writes,

> In my *Phenomenology of Spirit* . . . the course was taken which began from the first, simplest appearance of spirit, from *immediate consciousness*, and developed the dialectic of the same up to the standpoint of philosophical science, the necessity of which is demonstrated by means of this progression. But in this,

---

14. No suggestion is made here to the effect that these exhaust the reasons one might have for thinking that the argument of the *Phenomenology* is incompatible with the beginning of the *Logic*. There are certainly additional possibilities which I have not considered here. One might, for example, following Feuerbach perhaps, reject Hegel's initial characterisation of natural consciousness in terms of "sensuous certainty", and thus maintain that the argument of the *Phenomenology* involves a presupposition on Hegel's part rather than that of consciousness, one that is not eliminated in the remainder of the argument of the text. I note here that if such an investigation were to be considered successful, this might speak in favour of the account of "completed scepticism", which I discuss in Section 5.2.1, since this might arguably be thought to engage with natural consciousness on its own terms, rather than assuming that it should be treated at first in terms of sensuous certainty.

15. And, indeed, Hegel famously wishes to collapse this form/content distinction regarding the work of logic. He writes, for example, that 'the method which I follow in this system of logic . . . is not something distinct from its object and content' (*WL* 33/5:50).

it was not possible remain at the formal aspect of mere consciousness; for the standpoint of philosophical science is at the same time in itself the most contentful and the most concrete ... The development of the *content*, of the objects of the specific parts of the philosophical science thereby falls within that development of consciousness which appeared limited to the formal aspect ... The presentation thus becomes more entangled, and what belongs to the concrete parts falls to some extent already within the introduction. (*EL* §25A)

This passage reaffirms the idea that the *Phenomenology* is an introduction intended to justify the position with which the *Logic* begins. But it also complicates the picture, by admitting that it was impossible to provide a straightforward examination of natural consciousness which concluded by establishing the position adopted at the beginning of the *Logic* in merely formal terms because the emergence philosophical or scientific content turned out to be necessary to the narrative and conclusion of the *Phenomenology* itself. I will suggest here that the presence of this "already-scientific content" within the argument of the *Phenomenology* is incompatible with the presuppositionless beginning of the *Logic*.

The passage in question could be taken to amount to a still more serious admission on Hegel's behalf: that because the *Phenomenology* is intended to justify his philosophical system but turns out itself to rely upon material from within that system, he is guilty of viciously circular reasoning. Forster, however, presents what seems to me to be a compelling way to defuse this concern. He points out that the *Phenomenology* is not merely a project of discrediting the presuppositions of natural consciousness in favour of the standpoint of philosophical science but is at the same the narrative of natural consciousness' own sublation, so that it *becomes* scientific thought over the course of the text.[16] And, indeed, Hegel writes in "With what must the beginning of science be made?" that the mediation of natural consciousness 'is its own sublation' (*WL* 47/5:68). Accordingly, as Forster points out, the progression of the *Phenomenology* is both negative and positive. It is negative in that the position(s) of natural consciousness gives way or are negated according to their own inconsistencies but positive in that this '*abolition*' of natural consciousness is simultaneously its dialectical development into the standpoint of philosophical science (Forster 1998: 283–84). Forster's point is that it is not a *problem* for Hegel that scientific content is appearing as the *Phenomenology* progresses. Quite the opposite: It would be deeply strange, if not problematic itself, if this were *not* to occur. The closer consciousness gets to the position of philosophical science, the more one should encounter philosophical content in the position of consciousness. This agrees, as Forster

---

16. See Forster 1998: Ch.7. See Orsini 2021 for a good recent discussion of this topic.

is aware, with Hegel's own comments concerning the *Phenomenology* as the 'becoming of *science*' in the preface to that work (*PhG* §27/3:31).

I believe that Forster's account of the *Phenomenology* as the sublation of natural consciousness makes good sense of Hegel's remarks in §25A of the *Encyclopaedia* and may well help Hegel avoid the charge of circular reasoning if it is made in this context. However, there remains the question of how to square this picture of the *Phenomenology* as the development of ever more scientific content with the demand that the beginning of the *Logic* which it is to justify be at the same time presuppositionless.

It is easy to provide examples of what Hegel is referring to when he suggests that philosophical or scientific content occurs within the narrative of the *Phenomenology*. By the end of that work, Hegel has elaborated a number of reasonably substantive philosophical claims about spirit, touching on, among other things, morality, culture, history, and religion. All of these topics are treated again, often in similar fashion, in his *Philosophy of Spirit*. Perhaps most importantly of all, Hegel has made the claim, in the "Absolute Knowing" chapter of the *Phenomenology*, that natural consciousness finally gives way to a form of knowing which fulfils the promise Hegel made in the preface to that work: 'to grasp and express the true, not just as *substance*, but just as much as *subject*' (*PhG* §17/3:23).[17] This is a philosophical statement of idealism, regardless of how precisely one understands the nature of Hegel's idealism, or the nature of his metaphysics more generally.

The problem posed by the presence of this already-scientific content should be clear. If the *Phenomenology* includes the development of this content, which by Hegel's own admission it does, then its conclusion includes the establishment of this content and is *not* just the elimination of the presuppositions of natural consciousness that Maker suggests that it might be. While Maker's picture allows for greater coherence between the conclusion of the *Phenomenology* and the beginning of the *Logic* (and thus helps Hegel to solve the problem of beginning), it is not faithful to the content of the conclusion of the *Phenomenology* as Hegel presents it. Indeed, as Houlgate points out, rather than merely the abstract, empty thinking of pure being, the principal and substantive conclusion of the *Phenomenology* is a fully determinate notion of spirit (Houlgate 2006: 161–62).[18] This does not mean that we cannot

---

17. See *PhG* §803/3:586–87, for Hegel's expression of the fulfilment of that promise.
18. Houlgate also takes this point to contradict Maker's account, adding, 'I believe that between the end of the *Phenomenology* and the beginning of the *Logic* there must occur an act of abstraction in which we specifically set aside the determinate conception of being and spirit reached at the close of the *Phenomenology*' (Houlgate 2006: 162). Houlgate can believe this because he does not think that the beginning of the *Logic* necessarily requires anything to play the justificatory role of securing its beginning, but as I explained in Section 3.4.1, I believe that this leaves him problematically embracing the immediacy horn of Hegel's dilemma, rather than finding a solution to the problem of beginning that can virtuously combine mediation and immediacy in its first concept.

also understand the *Phenomenology* to be in the business of undermining the presuppositions of natural consciousness (indeed, Houlgate compares it to Descartes' first Meditation for just that reason),[19] but it does provide obvious difficulties for Maker's radically negative account of the text.[20]

The presence of already-scientific content in the conclusion to the *Phenomenology*, then, is incompatible with the demand that the beginning of the *Logic* be presuppositionless.[21] I shall now turn to a second and related reason for thinking that the conclusion to the argument of the *Phenomenology* is incompatible with, and therefore cannot justify, Hegel's position at the beginning of the *Logic*.

4.2.2 Determinate Negation

The second reason for thinking, contrary to the implications of Maker's radically negative account, that the conclusion to the *Phenomenology* is incompatible with the beginning of the *Logic* is arguably the most straightforward. It is simply that Hegel's account of the procedure of the *Phenomenology*, as one of "determinate negation", is *explicitly* not one of mere or "abstract" negativity, which is to say that it is not an account which lends itself only to the elimination of the dogmatic presuppositions of natural consciousness. It is worth quoting from Hegel's account of the nature of the phenomenological investigation of natural consciousness at length here:

---

19. See Houlgate 2013: 8.
20. If Maker were to be prepared to allow for the presence of other elements beside the radically negative epistemological work he emphasises in the *Phenomenology*, then it seems to me that he would have his work cut out in explaining how these other elements, which are surely inextricably bound up with the epistemological material which is his focus, do not contaminate the radical negativity so vital to his interpretation. I think that he would have to make Hegel's comment that the development of scientific content 'must proceed behind the back of consciousness' (*EL* §25A) do a great deal more heavy lifting than it appears able to. I think that it is reasonable to understand Hegel here to mean that the development of this scientific content should not be recognised as such by the natural consciousness undergoing the developmental journey of the *Phenomenology* but not that this content does not still play an integral part of that development, which it seems Maker would need him to mean in order for this content not to be bound up with the negation of the presuppositions of natural consciousness in such a way as to force the result of the *Phenomenology* to clash with the idea that a presuppositionless beginning for logic could occur on its basis.
21. This problem appears to be connected to the famous expansion of the structure of the *Phenomenology* which occurred during its composition. It may well be that Hegel's original plan for the *Phenomenology* did not include the incorporation of already-scientific material (this coheres with the tone of §25A of the *Encyclopaedia*). Perhaps, if the *Phenomenology* had only ever been the 'science of the *experience of consciousness*' promised in its introduction (*PhG* §88/3:80), and if the "Reason" chapter had concluded the work, as Förster (2012: 352–67) has suggest it was originally intended to, with a section entitled "Science", then this problem would not have arisen. I cannot address this possibility here, and the account I would offer would be merely speculative in any case. The fact is that that is not the version of the *Phenomenology* that Hegel chose to produce, and so this problem is very much one that occurs between Hegel's philosophical works as they were published.

[T]he presentation of non-truthful consciousness in its untruth is not a merely *negative* movement. Such a one-sided view . . . is namely the scepticism that sees only ever *pure nothing* in the result and abstracts from the fact that this nothing is determinately the nothing *of that from which it results*. Nothing is only in fact the true result when taken as the nothing of that from which it comes; it is thereby itself *something determinate* and has a *content*. Scepticism, which ends with the abstraction of nothingness or emptiness, can go no further from this, but rather must wait and see whether something new will present itself, and what, in order to throw it into the same empty abyss. By contrast, when the result is grasped as it is in truth, as *determinate* negation, then a new form has thereby immediately arisen and in the negation the transition has been made, whereby the progression results by itself through the complete series of the shapes. (*PhG* §79/3:74)

It seems to me that Maker's interpretation of the procedure of the *Phenomenology* would reduce the negative procedure of the *Phenomenology* to what Hegel here calls "scepticism", by which he seems to mean something which would stall the progress of the investigation of consciousness altogether, rather than encourage consciousness towards further development (as I suggested in Section 1.2.1, I think that it is the abstractly negative procedure of the Pyrrhonian Sceptics that results only in suspension of judgement about whatever is being investigated that Hegel has in mind here). Instead, however, I think it is clear that the determinate negation which occurs in the immanent criticism of any given shape of consciousness in the *Phenomenology* is not *merely*, or abstractly, negative; it is at the same time productive in that it causes a new shape of consciousness to appear, which can then be examined in turn. More than that, it also clearly carries the negated content of the previous shape with it, as it would not be the shape that it is were it not the result of the previous one. As Hegel says, explicitly bearing the example of the *Phenomenology of Spirit* in mind, the new shape is 'higher, richer than the preceding one; for it has become richer by being the negation or opposite of the preceding one, it thus contains it, and also more than it, and is the unity of itself and its opposite' (*WL* 33/5:49). This account of a dialectical or determinately negative progression is clearly not one in which the positions of natural consciousness are simply discarded or eliminated along the way.

I should point out that Maker acknowledges the presence of determinate negation in the *Phenomenology* (Maker 1994: 131) and does not seem to understand it to be in conflict with the idea of what he calls the "radically negative outcome" of that work. In fact, he claims, albeit rather briefly, that his account agrees with Hegel's remarks concerning determinate negation (Maker 1994: 79). To my mind, given the account of determinate negation earlier, it does the opposite. The only way I can see in which we could render Maker's account coherent with that of the determinately negative progression of the *Phenomenology* is to suppose the entire course of the *Phenomenology* to be one, giant instance of determinate negation, with absolute knowing as its negative outcome—a negative outcome that, considered in another light, shows itself to be positive just *as* the beginning of the *Logic*.[22] Maker's comments on the matter perhaps suggest such an account,[23] but I think that this is to ignore the fact that the process of determinate negation occurs over and over again throughout the *Phenomenology*, not just once at its end. Its conclusion thus already contains the positive content that results from the determinate negation of the various forms of consciousness examined throughout the text.

The problem, simply, is that the nature of determinate negation is such that, by the time the *Phenomenology* concludes in absolute knowing, the shape of consciousness or of spirit in question is not the radically empty one demanded by Maker, the journey having been one only of the elimination of all of the presuppositions of natural consciousness, but one in which we have a rich account of spirit's self-comprehension, in which absolute knowing 'is the *truth* of all modes of consciousness' (*WL* 29/5:43).[24] Accordingly, although I have got there slightly differently here, this is, in fact, the same problem as the one indicated in the previous section: The contentful nature of absolute knowing renders it incompatible with demand that the beginning of the *Logic* be presuppositionless.[25]

At this point, I will present my third and final reason for thinking that the *Phenomenology of Spirit* cannot successfully play the role of the element of mediation in the beginning of the *Logic*.

---

22. Winfield's account also suggests this interpretation (see Winfield 2011: 380–81). I am not convinced that he has provided an adequate explanation, however, of the move from an explicitly determinate conception of spirit reached at the end of the *Phenomenology*, to the indeterminacy of pure thinking present at the beginning of the *Logic*. He suggests that the latter "emerges" from the former, but without a fuller account of the nature of this emergence, the relationship between the end of the *Phenomenology* and the beginning of the *Logic* continues to look problematic.

23. See Maker 1994: 92.

24. One might make this conclusion clearer with the following argument: Determinate negation is precisely *not* the abstract negation that only results in pure nothing, which Hegel criticised in the introduction to the *Phenomenology* (*PhG* §79/3:74). But pure nothing, according to Hegel, is 'the same as what pure *being* is' (*WL* 59/5:83). Therefore, if the determinate negation of the *Phenomenology* does not result in pure nothing, then it does not result in pure being.

25. Trisokkas (2012: 89) argues that what he calls the 'rich content' of absolute knowing—the various determinately negated knowledge claims about spirit which it contains—were only held to be true on the basis of their demonstration according to the criteria set up by the various forms of natural consciousness. He thinks that, from the cognitive standpoint of science to which one is committed at the end of the *Phenomenology*, one is no longer entitled to assert the truth of the rich content. I cannot investigate this claim adequately here, but I note that, if one accepts it, it may count against the idea that the *content* of absolute knowing renders it incompatible with the beginning of the *Logic*, but I take it that it does not count against the claim I make in the next section, which is that the establishment of the cognitive standpoint of science itself is incompatible with the presuppositionless beginning of the *Logic*.

4.2.3 Securing the Standpoint of Science

The *Phenomenology*, famously, is intended for 'the task of leading the individual out from his uneducated standpoint to knowing' (*PhG* §28/3:31). In carrying out this task, according to Hegel in the *Logic*, the *Phenomenology* 'contains and demonstrates the necessity, and thereby the proof of the truth of the standpoint that is pure knowing' (*WL* 46/5:67). Arguably, the primary task of the *Phenomenology*, then, is that of securing the standpoint of science, or securing the scientific model of cognition. This model, I have noted, is a purely reflexive one whereby thought has itself for its object.[26] In the language of the chapter on "absolute knowing," Hegel describes this reflexive standpoint by saying that, whereas for earlier shapes of consciousness what was known was '*content*, or the form of representing an *other*, [it] is here the *self's* own *doing* . . . It is spirit knowing itself in the shape of spirit' (*PhG* §§797–98/3:582). This account of self-knowing spirit is the fulfilment of the discussion of standpoint of science in the preface to the *Phenomenology*, where it was described as the "*other*" to the standpoint of natural consciousness, the latter being the standpoint according to which the thinking subject 'knows objective things as opposed to itself and itself as opposed to them' (*PhG* §26/3:30). This is to repeat the point that the narrative of the *Phenomenology* amounts to the move from one proposed standpoint (natural consciousness), whereby what is cognised is separate from and opposed to the one doing the cognising, through criticisms of variants of this standpoint, to the establishment of another standpoint (science), whereby cognition understands its object *not* to be separate from and opposed to it.

As I remarked earlier, the *Phenomenology* gets from the standpoint of natural consciousness to the standpoint of science by way of an extended project of immanent criticism of the former. This immanent investigation of natural consciousness, both of its various claims and of its criteria for evaluating claims turns out to involve a discussion of the classical problem of the criterion (or "standard").[27] Moreover, the resolution of that problem as it occurs for natural consciousness in the *Phenomenology* is at the heart of the immanent criticism of natural consciousness by which Hegel arrives at and demonstrates the validity of the standpoint of science, from which philosophy takes place. Here, I will examine the consequences of the way in which Hegel overcomes the problem of the criterion as it occurs for natural consciousness for the compatibility or incompatibility of the conclusion of the *Phenomenology* with the beginning of the *Logic*.

---

26. See also *EL* §17: '[H]ere *thinking* has to be made the object of thinking'.
27. See *PH* II:18–20, for the classical expression of the problem.

It is not my intention here to advance a new interpretation of Hegel's attempted solution to the problem of the criterion, nor to evaluate that solution as presented by others. Because of this, I will not be spending more time than is necessary in reconstructing Hegel's approach to this problem. My principal goal is to argue that, insofar as that solution involves asserting the truth of a distinctive model of cognition, or indeed a distinctive, idealist philosophical standpoint, commitment to the truth of this assertion is incompatible with the idea of a presuppositionless beginning for thought in the *Logic*.

That Hegel is exploring a variant of the problem of the criterion in the *Phenomenology of Spirit*, and that he sets out his strategy for resolving the problem in the introduction to that work, is commonly accepted.[28] Little work is required to demonstrate this claim, but first, I should briefly recap the nature of the problem, which I briefly discussed in Section 1.1.3. According to Chisholm's influential formulation, the problem of the criterion arises when we consider two separate questions:

(A) '*What* do we know? What is the extent of our knowledge?'
(B) 'How are we to decide whether we know? What are the *criteria* of knowledge?' (Chisholm 1973: 12)

The problem, of course, is that answering (A) seems to require knowledge of (B): one appeals to criteria for knowledge in distinguishing instances of knowledge from non-knowledge. And answering (B) seems to require knowledge of (A): one appeals to particular instances of knowledge in order to validate a proposed criterion. It should be apparent that this quickly prompts the threat either of arbitrarily asserting either a particular instance of knowledge or a particular criterion without justification, or the threat of an infinite regress of first-order knowledge claims and criteria or the threat of reasoning in a vicious circle. The problem of the criterion is, thus, as I have already acknowledged, an Agrippan problem.

That Hegel is engaging with these two questions in the *Phenomenology* is made clear in the introduction to that work. He gives a reasonably explicit statement of the problem:

[T]he examination consists in setting up an assumed standard, and in the resulting equality or inequality of that which is to be examined with the standard lies the decision as to whether what is examined is correct or incorrect; the standard ... is thereby assumed as the *essence* or as the *in-itself*. But here, where science first appears, neither science itself nor anything else has justified itself as

---

28. See, for example, Dancy's popular *Introduction to Contemporary Epistemology*, where the discussion of the problem of the criterion is introduced by way of an appeal to Hegel's *Phenomenology* (Dancy 1985: 227–30).

the essence or as the in-itself; and without such a justification it seems that no examination can take place. (*PhG* §81/3:75–76)

This expression of the problem poses a difficulty for Hegel, because on this basis, it is not obvious how he can go about examining the various knowledge claims made from the standpoint of natural consciousness or, indeed, the standpoint itself. He cannot merely assert that his scientific standpoint is a legitimate criterion or standard against which to judge natural consciousness and its various knowledge claims,[29] but he cannot judge these without a standard or criterion against which to measure.

This challenge motivates the adoption of the method of immanent criticism. Hegel is saved from having to assert the priority of an answer either to Chisholm's A-question or Chisholm's B-question in the investigation of natural consciousness because natural consciousness itself provides both first-order knowledge claims *and* criteria against which to test them. Thus Hegel writes, "[C]oncept and object, the standard and what is to be examined, are present in consciousness itself' (*PhG* §85/3:77). The questions associated with the problem of the criterion—"*What* do we know?" and "How are we to decide whether we know?"—now fall to natural consciousness itself. What is at stake for natural consciousness, rather than being strictly a worry about priority, is whether its standards for truth and its first-order knowledge claims agree with one another or are adequate to one another. Put differently, at stake is the coherence of natural consciousness as a cognitive standpoint. The job of Hegel's phenomenologist then is 'purely looking on' (*PhG* §85/3:77) as natural consciousness examines itself. If the examination turns up a mismatch or an incoherence between natural consciousness' standard and its first-order knowledge claims, then this iteration of natural consciousness has been found wanting on its own terms, and Hegel can dispense with it without having illegitimately imposed a standard upon it from outside in order to do so. This approach also lets Hegel avoid the charge of dogmatically loading the investigation of natural consciousness in advance.

The most detailed and sophisticated account of the manner in which natural consciousness tests itself in the face of the problem of the criterion is that offered by Westphal, originally in his 1988 essay, "Hegel's Solution to the Dilemma of the Criterion". I cannot provide such a detailed account here, but I will outline what seem to me to be the key points of Hegel's description of the way in which natural consciousness tests itself.

Hegel writes that, 'consciousness is, on the one hand, consciousness of the object, on the other hand, consciousness of its own self; consciousness

---

29. As I noted in Section 1.2.2, this realisation in the *Phenomenology* represents an advance upon Hegel's earlier tendency to simply assert the validity of his philosophical standpoint and hold that no sceptical objection could gain any purchase on it.

of that which, to it, is the true, and consciousness of its knowing of it' (*PhG* §85/3:77). This is merely to assert that natural consciousness is the source both of first-order knowledge claims *and* of criteria for evaluating those claims and is therefore itself responsible for their comparison. He then goes on to say that,

> The examination is based on this difference, which is present. If the two do not correspond to one another in this comparison, then it seems that consciousness has to alter its knowing, in order to make it accord with the object; but in the alteration of the knowing the object itself is in fact also altered, to consciousness. (*PhG* §85/3:78)

Thus, natural consciousness examines instances of what it takes to be knowledge and checks them against its criteria for what counts as knowledge. If it should prove that what turns out to be involved in knowing some object exceeds or differs from natural consciousness' dogmatically asserted criteria for knowledge, the latter must be revised, in order to be able to evaluate instances of the kind of knowledge now confronting it.[30] So for example, the form of natural consciousness Hegel calls "sensuous-certainty" at first understands the objects that it knows in opposition to itself to be a 'pure this, or *the singular*' (*PhG* §91/3:83). That is to say it knows only radically simple objects, without any qualities or determinateness. Accordingly, its conception of or criterion of truth amounts to the idea of an '*immediate* pure relation' (*PhG* §91/3:83).

However, it soon turns out that this standard for knowledge is inadequate. Hegel's example takes as its candidate object of knowledge "now", and the claim examined is '*the now is night*' (*PhG* §95/3:84), which, if it *is* in fact night, seems to be something that can be asserted simply and immediately as true. If it is considered during daylight, however, this claim, despite being uttered in just the same simple, immediate manner, turns out to be false. Because of this, as Hegel suggested in the passage from §85/3:78, sensuous-certainty must revise its criterion of knowledge, in order to adequately categorise claims of the kind "now is night". The ultimate result is that knowing comes to be understood according to criteria that allow it to make sense of 'universal', rather than merely singular, immediate knowledge claims, to grasp that assertions of the kind "now is night" concerns an object—"now"—which

---

30. Admittedly, this formulation supposes that, in the case in question, it has been conclusively demonstrated that the object of knowledge demands knowledge claims which operate according to a different criterion to the one originally presupposed, so that merely revising the first-order knowledge claims themselves is not satisfactory. Presumably there will also be instances of this kind for a given shape of consciousness where merely modifying first-order knowledge claims is satisfactory, but these modifications are not of the kind that is pertinent to the argumentative progression of the *Phenomenology*. In the example of the claim "*The 'now' is night*" that follows, for example, it should be clear that revising the first-order knowledge claim while at the same maintaining that knowledge is the immediate grasping of a singular, simple object is not possible.

refers to a plurality of instances, some of which are night and some of which are not (*PhG* §107/3:89).

But, as Hegel suggested, revising the criterion of truth has also led to a revised conception of *what objects are like*. Just as the criterion of knowledge no longer concerns merely "immediate pure relation" but the grasping of an instance of a universal, the conception of objects natural consciousness is working with is no longer that of a simple "this" but a '*thing of many properties*' (*PhG* §85/3:77), since "now", for example, can apply to a variety of different times. But as sensuous-certainty no longer holds either to the conception it had of objects or to the conception it had of the criterion of knowledge relevant to knowing those objects, it is, in fact, no longer the form of natural consciousness—sensuous-certainty—that it originally was. It has given way to a new form of natural consciousness that Hegel calls "perception." At this point, the self-examination of natural consciousness begins all over again.

Hegel's observation that when natural consciousness alters its account of knowing, the object alters for it as well, has an important implication. It implies that the revision of one's conception of knowing will have consequences for one's commitments at the level of metaphysics. This makes sense: If one makes some claim about what is involved in knowing objects, one at least *implies* some claim about what objects are like (that they are the sort of thing amenable to this kind of knowing). Westphal phrases this contention of Hegel's in the following manner: 'Now any epistemic principle implies certain constraints on what the objects of knowledge could be. Therefore the adoption of an epistemic principle brings with it a concomitant ontological principle' (Westphal 1988: 176). This point will be important when it comes to considering the relation between the conclusion of the *Phenomenology* and the beginning of the *Logic* that follows.

This brief and incomplete rendering of the testing of sensuous-certainty indicates that the narrative of the *Phenomenology* is one of continuing revision, not just of first-order knowledge claims but also just as much of proposed criteria of knowledge and, therefore, of the models of cognition which set up these criteria. The way in which the mismatch between criteria and knowledge claims not only demonstrates the invalidity of or negates a particular iteration of the standpoint of natural consciousness but also revises it so that a new iteration is produced which retains the lessons of the previous one, amounts to a demonstration of the notion of determinate negation, discussed previously, as it operates in the *Phenomenology*. The validity or invalidity of any of the determinate negations which make up the argument of the *Phenomenology* fall well beyond the possible boundaries of this investigation, but for the sake of argument, as I acknowledged previously, I will assume that the immanently critical cases made in the *Phenomenology* against any given iteration of natural consciousness are valid.

The end result of the *Phenomenology*'s lengthy chain of determinate negations of both knowledge claims and criteria of knowledge is the attainment of a position in which knowing and its object finally agree with one another, but this turns out to be the position in which the division of the object '*for* consciousness' and the positing of the object as it is '*in itself*' (*PhG* §85/3:78), or between cognition and what is cognised, which prompted the questioning and revision both of the accuracy of first-order knowledge claims and of the criteria by which they are evaluated—the division characteristic of the standpoint(s) of natural consciousness, that is—has been overcome. This position, reached in "absolute knowing," amounts to Hegel's standpoint of science, the validity of which, as the only remaining alternative, is now supposed to be secure.

As I mentioned earlier, this standpoint amounts to an expression of some kind of idealism: It is a standpoint which recognizes the identity of knowing and what is known, or thought and being. In the introduction to the *Logic*, Hegel writes that, 'as the course of the *Phenomenology* showed, it is only in absolute knowing that the separation of the *object* from the *certainty of itself* has been completely resolved.' He goes on to add that, according to this scientific standpoint, '*the being which is in and for itself is the known concept, the concept as such is the being which is in and for itself*' (*WL* 29/5:43). This statement of idealism seems to follow from the establishment of the standpoint of science, and it also accords with the notion expressed previously, that, in Westphal's words, "the adoption of an epistemic principle brings with it a concomitant ontological principle." Here, it looks as though the adoption of a particular philosophical standpoint on the nature of cognition (the epistemic principle) brings with it a basic commitment to idealism (the ontological principle). For the purposes of my argument here, the manner in which one understands Hegel's commitment to idealism, or his metaphysics more generally, does not matter much. All that is required is that we accept that Hegel concludes the *Phenomenology* by establishing a philosophical standpoint that includes a metaphysical commitment to idealism, however understood.[31]

At this point, I have provided a sketch of the manner in which the *Phenomenology of Spirit* is supposed to justify Hegel's position at the beginning of the *Logic*. It does so by securing the idealist standpoint on the basis of which the logical inquiry operates, or whereby logic, as the science of the fundamental conceptual structure of thought, is at the same time metaphysics, or the science of the fundamental structure of being, by showing all standpoints according to which the two are distinguished to be ultimately

---

31. As McGilvary (1897: 518) puts it, 'Logic, as a fruitful science, begins at the point in our philosophical career where we have come to see that knowledge and its object are not opposed, but are one with each other'.

incoherent.[32] If this account can be read as proceeding simply by dispensing with the standpoint(s) of natural consciousness, there may still be the possibility of interpreting Hegel's approach to the problem of the criterion in the *Phenomenology* in terms amenable to Maker's suggestion that the work has a "radically negative outcome". The question on which to focus is this: is the establishment of the idealist standpoint of Hegel's philosophical science something which can be legitimately presupposed without coming into conflict with the idea of a presuppositionless beginning or not? This is different from the principal concern of the previous two sections. There the concern was that the assertion of various first-order knowledge claims about spirit established by the end of the *Phenomenology* ruled out the reading of absolute knowing as "radically negative" and, in so doing, rendered the conclusion of the *Phenomenology* incompatible with the presuppositionless beginning of the *Logic* because of the *content* of those first-order claims. Here the concern is whether or not the philosophical standpoint secured by the end of the *Phenomenology*, according to which first-order claims are to be considered, *itself* is incompatible with the presuppositionless beginning of the *Logic*.

I think that it is helpful for the purposes of answering this question to bring up a contrast that Houlgate makes use of in his discussion of the beginning of the *Logic*—that between what he calls 'the presuppositions of presuppositionless thought' (Houlgate 2006: 54) and what he calls '*founding* presuppositions' (Houlgate 2006: 60). The former are those presuppositions or conditions which Houlgate thinks can be in place, perhaps in a sense even be necessary, to the beginning of the *Logic*, without compromising its presuppositionless status. These include things such as the desire on the part of the philosopher to enter into a properly presuppositionless logical inquiry, those contingent historical and social factors which make it possible to dedicate one's time to such a project, perhaps even the development of a philosophical tradition which prizes autonomy and antidogmatism in thinking. One could alternatively call them "enabling presuppositions". These are permitted, Houlgate thinks, because they do not 'determine in advance the course that . . . philosophy will take' (Houlgate 2006: 61). This is because, however necessary it is to the logical or scientific project that there be willing and able philosophers to pursue it, for example, this itself should not affect the content or method of the inquiry. The inquiry can, therefore, still be accurately categorised as presuppositionless. A founding presupposition, on the other hand, is the kind of presupposition that *does* affect the content or the method of the inquiry, which constrains the horizons of the inquiry in some

---

32. See Pippin 1989: 250, for example, for the suggestion that the *Phenomenology*'s criticism of the standpoints of natural consciousness renders a "transcendental scepticism", according to which the concern is raised that things in themselves might be fundamentally other than our ways of conceiving them, 'epistemically idle'.

manner (by stipulating in advance some logical, metaphysical, or methodological principle, for example) and therefore contradicts the inquiry's claim to be presuppositionless. The central question here, then, is whether Hegel's solution to the problem of the criterion in the context of natural consciousness and thus the establishment of the standpoint of philosophical science is to be understood as a legitimate "enabling presupposition" or whether it is an illegitimate substantive or "founding presupposition".

What follows is an argument designed to show that Hegel's solution to the problem of the criterion—the isolation of the standpoint of science in absolute knowing and the elimination of its various rivals, subsumed under the name of natural consciousness—is indeed incompatible with the presuppositionless beginning of the *Logic*, precisely because it does constitute what Houlgate would call a founding presupposition—one which problematically determines in advance the logical inquiry which is to follow:

1. The *Logic* is (in some sense) a presuppositionless project of both logic and of metaphysics. (*Premise*: Hegel calls the project 'the logical science, which amounts to genuine metaphysics' [*WL* 9/5:16] and clearly endorses the idea that 'science should be preceded by . . . total *presuppositionlessness*'; *EL* §78A.)
2. Because it is intended to be presuppositionless, it can presuppose no logical *or* metaphysical principles, as such principles cannot be established before (or from without) the logical inquiry itself. (*From 1*: When he states that the 'general concepts and fundamental determinations' of logic cannot be presupposed, 'for they amount to a part of its content itself and first have to be justified within it' [*WL* 23/5:35], one can be sure that Hegel is ruling out the possibility of pre-established metaphysical principles here just as much as he is ruling out the possibility of pre-established logical principles, since he thinks that the two sciences coincide.)
3. The *Phenomenology*'s establishment of the standpoint of science involves establishing an epistemic principle. (*Premise*: Here I refer to the principle embodied in "absolute knowing": that genuine knowing is a reflexive activity of thought upon itself. Absolute knowing stipulates that true knowledge occurs only when knowledge becomes identical with its object, or, as Hegel says, '[i]t is spirit knowing itself in the shape of spirit' [*PhG* §§797–98/3:582].)
4. Epistemic principles of this kind imply concomitant ontological principles, which is to say, metaphysical principles.[33] (*Premise*: This was

---

33. The relation between ontology and the traditional disciplines of special metaphysics within the metaphysical project of the *Science of Logic* does not matter here. What matters is merely that ontology is general metaphysics.

clarified in the account of the procedure of the *Phenomenology* previously mentioned—an account of knowledge implies an account of the sort of thing that is there to be known: 'in the alteration of the knowing the object itself is in fact also altered, to consciousness' [*PhG* §85/3:78]).

5. *Therefore* the *Phenomenology*, to the extent that it resolves the problem of the criterion in absolute knowing, establishes a metaphysical principle. (*From 3 and 4*: Again, without stipulating exactly how this is to be understood here, this metaphysical principle is the assertion of the identity of knowledge and object, or thought and being. This is to repeat the claim that the *Phenomenology*, in constituting an argument for the standpoint that it does, also constitutes an argument for a kind of idealism.)

6. *Therefore* the beginning of the *Logic* cannot presuppose the standpoint of absolute knowing with which the *Phenomenology* concludes. (*From 2 and 5*: This is because, in also constituting a metaphysical principle—an assertion of a kind of idealism—the establishment of the standpoint of philosophical science becomes a "founding presupposition". This is the case firstly because all metaphysical principles must be established within the science of logic if it is to be presuppositionless, and secondly, because it constrains the horizons of the metaphysical inquiry of the *Logic* in advance, by stipulating that, whatever else it should turn out to be over the course of the *Logic*, "what is" is fundamentally thought, or fundamentally conceptual in some sense. The claim that the *Logic* is presuppositionless is incompatible with the claim that it presupposes in advance that reality as it is in itself might not be at least in part extra-conceptual, or conceptually inaccessible).[34]

---

34. Trisokkas claims that,

Thought [i.e., what Hegel will call the standpoint of science] and consciousness are *cognitive standpoints*, general frameworks for the inquiry into truth, *not truth-claims*. When Hegel posits the identity of thought and being, he does not characterise an object or an aspect of *what there is*; rather he postulates the most general character of a certain framework for inquiry into the truth of what there is (Trisokkas 2012: 76).

If Trisokkas is right here, it would appear to pose a problem for my account, for it seems to undermine the claim that Hegel's solution to the problem of the criterion amounts to a substantive presupposition from the perspective of the beginning of the *Logic*. If Trisokkas is right, nothing is being asserted as true (an ontological principle or otherwise) at the end of the *Phenomenology*. That would make it far easier to render it compatible with the beginning of the *Logic*. But it seems to me that Trisokkas is not right here; assertions of the truth of a cognitive standpoint or a criterion of truth might not be first-order knowledge claims, but they are knowledge claims nevertheless, merely, as Westphal puts it, 'second-order knowledge claims about what knowledge is and how to distinguish it from error' (Westphal 1988: 174). Trisokkas seems to deny this, but he does not seem to me to have a good reason or argument in favour of doing so. Furthermore, it leads him to make the following, rather surprising claim: '[T]he identity of knowing and being can be immediately said to be true [on the basis of the argument of the *Phenomenology*]. Yet it is only a trivial truth, since it does not encompass the rich content of this element' (Trisokkas 2012: 93). Even if one supposes that Trisokkas is right that the conclusion of the *Phenomenology* does not entail the truth of the "rich content" of absolute knowing,

This argument amounts to my final reason for thinking that the conclusion of the *Phenomenology* cannot unproblematically be presupposed by the beginning of the *Logic* and, thus, that the former is unsuited to play the role of the element of mediation in the latter's presuppositionless beginning. And yet this does seem to be exactly the difficulty that Hegel gets himself into, by claiming that the *Logic* has, as 'a *presupposition*' the result of the *Phenomenology*, that 'in it the opposition of consciousness of a *being existing* subjectively *for itself* and a second such *being*, something objective, is overcome, and in it being is known as pure concept and the pure concept is known as true being' (*WL* 38–39/5:57). On the basis of claims of this kind, it seems that Hegel's solution to his problem of beginning as he presents it in the *Science of Logic*, with its reliance upon the argument of the *Phenomenology of Spirit* as the element of mediation in the beginning, must fail.

4.3 CONCLUSION

I have attempted in this chapter to interrogate the possibility that the investigation of natural consciousness in the 1807 *Phenomenology of Spirit* might successfully play the role of the element of mediation Hegel relies upon to justify the beginning of the *Logic* without, at the same time, undermining its claim to being presuppositionless. Ultimately, I have given a number of reasons for thinking that the *Phenomenology* cannot play this role. This suggests that, as the matter currently stands, Hegel has not acquired the security against charges of arbitrariness which might vitiate his logical project that he desired, and thus that the version of the solution to the problem of beginning which he presents in "With what must the beginning of the science be made?", which relies upon the argument of the *Phenomenology of Spirit*, fails. It fails for at least three reasons, as I have shown:

1. The argument of the *Phenomenology* includes the development of already-scientific content, which renders its conclusion incompatible with the presuppositionless beginning of the *Logic*.
2. The argument of the *Phenomenology* proceeds by way of determinate negation, which guarantees that its conclusion be contentful, which makes it incompatible with the presuppositionless beginning of the *Logic*.

---

it still seems straightforwardly false to claim that the identity of thought (or knowing) and being is a *trivial* truth, or that it does not determine in advance logical and ontological conclusions which are to follow from it. For one thing, it would seem very clearly to place the following constraint on the development of Hegel's metaphysics: that *reality can have no extra-conceptual dimension*. I remain convinced that this constitutes a substantive presupposition and is incompatible with the idea that the *Logic* has a presuppositionless beginning.

3. The argument of the *Phenomenology* is an attempt to secure the idealist standpoint of Hegel's philosophical science. This involves a significant metaphysical result which is not compatible with the presuppositionless beginning of the *Logic*.

If a version of the solution to the problem of beginning is to be successful then, it must avoid all three of these problems which beset the version which relied upon Hegel's *Phenomenology* to play the role of the element of mediation in the beginning. In the final chapter, I interrogate the alternative version of Hegel's solution to the problem of beginning, which, I claimed, he entertains in the *Encyclopaedia Logic*. I argue there that, appropriately fleshed out and clarified, this alternative solution appears to fare rather better than the version examined in this chapter, at least when it comes to the three problems presented in this chapter.

Chapter 5

Mediation II – Completed Scepticism

5.0 INTRODUCTION

In chapter 3, I identified the form of Hegel's solution to the problem of beginning which he sets out in "With what must the beginning of the science be made?" This turned, I claimed, on arguing that the concept of "pure being" could be understood as both mediated and immediate in such a way as to negate the problematic arbitrariness of beginning merely with something immediate (which looked straightforwardly arbitrary) or merely with something mediated (which invited further sceptical questions about the legitimacy of the presuppositions of the beginning), since, if it is understood as both mediated and immediate, then it is at least possible to make a case for seeing the beginning as having been necessitated by what it presupposes but, at the same time as being presuppositionless, since it contains no reference to its mediation, the result of which has completely coincided with the beginning's immediacy. I also identified, in Section 3.3.2, two versions of that solution: one from the *Science of Logic* in which the argument of Hegel's 1807 *Phenomenology of Spirit* played the role of the element of mediation which necessitated and ultimately coincided with the empty thinking of the beginning of logic, and another from the *Encyclopaedia Logic* in which that role was played by a "negative science" of "completed scepticism".

In chapter 4, I argued that the version of the solution which depended upon Hegel's *Phenomenology of Spirit* fails. I suggested that, in order to make sense of the idea that the conclusion of the *Phenomenology* coincides with the beginning of the *Logic* in the way that the form of Hegel's solution to the problem of beginning requires it to, it is necessary to adopt something like Maker's "radically negative" reading of the argument of the *Phenomenology*. Upon closer examination, however, Hegel's *Phenomenology* does not support such an interpretation, and therefore, its conclusion cannot properly coincide with the empty thinking of pure being. The remaining task is to consider the alternative version of the solution, from the *Encyclopaedia*. That is what I attempt to do in this final chapter. Two obstacles, however, immediately present themselves. The first, as I noted when introducing this material in chapter 3, is that Hegel himself, after briefly raising the possibility of such an alternative version of his solution, declares the idea of a "completed scepticism" to indicate "not only an unpleasant, but also a superfluous way" to rid thought of all dogmatic presuppositions and thus necessitate the empty thinking of the beginning of logic. The second is the possibility that when Hegel talks about such a "completed scepticism" (*vollbrachte Skeptizismus*), he is not really considering an alternative version of his solution at all but instead the same one as the one he set out in "With what must the beginning of the science be made?", since this "completed scepticism" might be understood as a veiled reference to the argument of the his 1807 *Phenomenology* itself, which he describes in that text as a 'self-completing scepticism [*sich vollbringender Skeptizismus*]' (*PhG* §78/3:72). Both of these obstacles must be overcome before the idea of an alternative version of Hegel's solution which depends on a completed scepticism can be given its due.

Accordingly, in the first part of this chapter, I will examine Hegel's reasons for rejecting the necessity of such a "negative science" as being "superfluous" and will argue that he errs in this aspect of his discussion of the matter of beginning in his *Encyclopaedia Logic*. At the start of the second part of the chapter, I will explain why I do not think that the "completed scepticism" of *EL* §78 is intended as a reference to the "self-completing scepticism" of the *Phenomenology*. Then, in the interest of fleshing out this alternative, to which Hegel appears not to devote a great deal of explicit attention, I will argue that, rather than the project of his 1807 *Phenomenology*, it is his engagement with Pyrrhonian Scepticism that Hegel has in mind when he discusses the negative science of completed scepticism in the *Encyclopaedia Logic*. Identifying this negative science with Hegel's account of Pyrrhonism offers more in the way of resources for reconstructing what Hegel had in mind when entertaining this possibility. The remainder of the chapter is then concerned with seeing to what extent Hegel's misgivings about the appeal to Pyrrhonian Scepticism in this context can be assuaged, as well as seeing how this alternative version of the solution to the problem of beginning fares in relation to the problems which beset the first version, which I set out in the previous chapter. I will conclude that this version of Hegel's solution seems better placed to succeed in solving the problem of beginning than the previous version before offering a few remarks on what has been achieved if Hegel's solution to the problem of beginning is successful, and what implications this has for a reading of the *Science of Logic*.

5.1 A THIRD SOLUTION?

By way of a reminder, here is the material in which I take Hegel to set out the second version of his solution to the problem of beginning:

> The *opposition* between a self-standing immediacy of content or knowing and an opposing, equally self-standing mediation, which are incompatible with one another, is thus first of all to be set aside, because it is a mere *presupposition* and an arbitrary *assurance*. Just as much are all other presuppositions or prejudices to be given up upon at the entrance to the science, whether they be taken from representation or from thought . . .
> *Scepticism*, as a negative science which has run through all form of cognition, would offer itself an introduction in which the nullity of such presuppositions would be demonstrated . . . The demand for such a completed scepticism is the same as the demand that the science should be preceded by *doubt about everything*, i.e., total *presuppositionlessness*. It is really completed in the resolve *to think purely*, by means of the freedom which abstracts from everything and grasps its pure abstraction, the simplicity of thought. (*EL* §78–78A)

Just as in the account provided in "With what must the beginning of the science be made?", the beginning of the *Logic* is considered in terms of immediacy—"the simplicity of thought"—but here Hegel considers whether the mediation which necessitates the beginning of logic by demonstrating the arbitrariness or "nullity" of the dogmatic presuppositions of ordinary thinking might, rather than by phenomenology, be a carried out by a "negative science" which would, like the project of his *Phenomenology*, eliminate *all* such presuppositions, resulting in "total *presuppositionlessness*".[1] He calls this negative science "completed scepticism". And already, I think it is worth noting that, in characterising this completed scepticism as a "negative science", it might sound as though here Hegel has in mind something closer to the "radically negative outcome" that Maker sought in the *Phenomenology*: a negative science that, in resulting in total presuppositionlessness, amounts to a presupposition for logic which eliminates itself.

However, as I noted in Section 3.3.2, as soon as Hegel introduces the idea of an introduction other than his *Phenomenology* in *EL* §78—this negative science of completed scepticism—he appears to row back on the idea. Despite the fact that in "With what must the beginning of the science be made?" the form of his solution to the problem of beginning required that pure being be conceived as the *unity* of mediation and immediacy in order

---

1. Hegel's language here also recalls his earlier attempts in Jena, before the composition of the *Phenomenology*, to introduce speculative metaphysics with a negative introduction he then referred to as "Logic", which would exhibit the limitations of merely finite thinking. I cannot explore this connection here, however.

for the beginning not to be rebutted by a sceptic on grounds of arbitrariness, in the *Encyclopaedia*, Hegel no longer appears to think that it is so crucially important to distinguish the concept of pure being from a mere arbitrary assumption by deriving it. Instead of insisting on such a mediation, as he did before, Hegel writes that 'it would be not only an unpleasant but also a superfluous path' and suggests instead simply that 'the resolve *to think purely*' and freely abstract from all content is sufficient to commence his science of logic with the concept of pure being (*EL* §78A).[2] It might appear, then, that in fact a third approach to the problem of beginning is being proposed here: one that relies neither upon the *Phenomenology of Spirit* nor a negative science of completed scepticism, but which claims to legitimise the beginning of Hegel's *Logic* purely in terms of the resolve to think purely.[3]

From the perspective of the problem of beginning as it was expressed in "With what must the beginning of the science be made?", even if one allows Hegel the claim that the result of abstracting from all presuppositions, indeed, from all the content of thought, would amount to the concept of pure being, this would still seem to leave him in a position whereby declaring that a science of logic should begin with this concept looks troublingly indistinguishable from beginning with a mere assertion. The question that must be answered in the face of this adjustment, on Hegel's part, is that of why he no longer thinks it necessary to provide some justification for beginning as he does, or why, instead of demonstrating that the concept of pure being occurs as the result of the thorough elimination of all dogmatic presuppositions, he suggests that it is adequate simply to abstract from those presuppositions. Abstracting from various possibilities, after all, is not the same as eliminating them.

The answer Hegel gives as to why he thinks that a scepticism that would "go through all the forms of cognition" and "would demonstrate the nullity" of their presuppositions amounts to a superfluous task is that 'the dialectic

---

2. If Hegel is genuinely asserting here that it is adequate to begin a science of logic merely with immediacy, as it seems that he is, then he is not just rejecting the idea of a negative science of completed scepticism but also the form of the solution to the problem of beginning which he developed in "With what must the beginning of the science be made?" itself. He would be doubling down on the immediacy horn of the dilemma rather than arguing that being must combine both immediacy and mediation. Hegel's position here is thus much closer to the one attributed to him by Houlgate, which I discussed in Section 3.4.1. If this is the case, it might also be taken to suggest a change in Hegel's appraisal of the role or importance of the *Phenomenology of Spirit* as the introduction to his system, a topic which I cannot explore here. See Forster 1998: Chs.18–19, for a good discussion of this topic.

3. *EL* §78A is not the only passage in the *Encyclopaedia* suggesting this "third" approach to the topic of beginning. The text of *EL* §17 also seems to support it, for example. Heidemann (2011: 92), for one, takes Hegel to be committing himself in the *Encyclopaedia* to what I am here calling this "third" solution, although he does not seem to find Hegel's case for it convincing, since he takes it that Hegel 'does not clarify the theoretical status of the "resolve"' to which he appeals (Heidemann 2011: 97). I think that Heidemann is right not to be convinced here.

itself is an essential moment of the affirmative science' (*EL* §78A).[4] I take it that what Hegel is saying is that the argumentative procedure by which the derivation of his logical categories proceeds, *within* the science of logic, is one that involves illustrating oppositions between concepts, oppositions of the kind that, in other circumstances, would give rise to a sceptical conclusion of the kind being suggested here as the element of mediation in the beginning of that science. A little later, he is even more explicit, asserting that the philosophical project of his logic 'contains the sceptical in itself as a moment' (*EL* §81Z2). If this is the case, then introducing the beginning of logic with a completed scepticism and thereafter developing the logical science itself would involve accomplishing the same thing twice. Carrying out such a preliminary sceptical elimination of dogmatic assumptions is superfluous if the same task is to be achieved within the science of logic itself.[5]

So, in his sketch of the procedure of his logical investigation, which I addressed briefly in Section 1.2.1, Hegel claims that, if one considers two opposing or incompatible concepts ordinarily, this '*dialectical* moment . . . constitutes *scepticism*, it contains mere negation as a result' (*EL* §81–81A): The two concepts in question are seen to be incompatible and, in the absence of a compelling case for accepting the validity of one over the other, there is nothing to do but suspend judgement. In the case of the procedure of his logic, however, Hegel thinks that there is an alternative outcome, since he claims to exploit the possibility of 'grasping the unity of the determinations in their opposition to one another, the *affirmative* that is contained in their dissolution and their going over [into one another]'. This he refers to as the '*speculative* or *positive-rational*' side of the reasoning according to which he proceeds (*EL* §82). As I noted in the earlier discussion of the relation between Pyrrhonian Sceptical inquiry and the method of Hegel's Objective Logic, as well as providing a scientific derivation of the fundamental categories of thought, Hegel's project is, at the same time, intended as a critique of any understanding of such categories which does not recognise the possibility of the speculative resolution of their oppositions in more adequate concepts and, ultimately, in the structure of the Concept. As it proceeds, then, it also

---

4. Hegel also complains that such a sceptical project would have to engage with such dogmatic presuppositions only unscientifically, or merely as it encounters them, in an empirical fashion. I will address this in Section 5.2.1, but whether or not this is the case, if it turns out that the task of negating these presuppositions is a necessary one, a complaint about its methodology does not excuse one from the task itself.

5. I think that the background to this remark of Hegel's is the similarity both in method and in terms of what is accomplished that Hegel sees between Pyrrhonian Sceptical inquiry and his own Objective Logic, which I discussed in Section 1.2.1. As I have already noted, Hegel claims in his *Logic* that '[a]ncient Scepticism did not spare itself the bother of pointing out the contradiction or the antinomy in all the concepts that it found in the sciences' (*WL* 158/5:217). I take it that this passage provides further evidence for the identification of the "completed scepticism" of *EL* §78A with Pyrrhonian Scepticism, which I defend later in this chapter.

illustrates the deficiencies in the ordinary or dogmatic grasp of such concepts. Because his "positive" treatment of logic also accomplishes this "negative" task, Hegel is arguing, it is superfluous to insist on an additional negative science of scepticism in order to carry out the negative task before the beginning of the science of logic.[6]

Much more could be said about Hegel's dialectical or speculative logical procedure, but I propose, for the sake of this investigation of the problem of beginning, to simply accept that the argument of his Objective Logic is entirely valid and that his logical project does indeed contain within itself, additionally, a thoroughgoing critique of dogmatic assumptions about the fundamental categories of thought. The problem, it seems to me, that remains for Hegel's treatment of the matter of beginning in *EL* §78 is that, in appealing to the critical or even "sceptical" feature of the speculative procedure of Hegel's logical investigation in order to reject the necessity of mediating or deriving the presuppositionless beginning of that investigation, Hegel has slipped back to his earlier tendency, which I discussed in Section 1.2.2, to simply assert the validity of a notion of speculative reason that encompasses and supersedes sceptical argumentation, without doing the work necessary to persuade the sceptical reader of the validity of such a notion.[7] As I suggested in the discussion in chapter 1, it seems as though one of the primary motivations behind the composition of the *Phenomenology* was Hegel's recognition that it was not sufficient to merely assert the legitimacy of this notion of dialectical-speculative reasoning and to expect a sceptic to go along with the idea, since '*one* bare assurance is exactly as valid as another' (*PhG* §76/3:70). The determinately negative progression of the argument of the *Phenomenology* at least appeared to offer something in the way of an illustration of this kind of reasoning, on grounds accessible and persuasive to the position of natural consciousness. In this case, however, it seems that Hegel has provided a sceptical reader of his *Encyclopaedia* neither with an argument for doubting any of their dogmatic presuppositions or ordinary conceptions of logical categories, nor with an argument for the validity of beginning a science of logic with concept of pure being, nor with an argument in favour of the validity of the kind of speculative inferences with which he will accomplish the task of criticising and superseding one-sided conceptions of logical categories within the Objective Logic. This "third solution", then, looks to me like a significant

---

6. See also *EL* §23Z3. See also Fulda 1975: 35–39, for a similar interpretation of the supposed "superfluity" of a sceptical introduction. This chapter is indebted to Fulda's account of a "sceptical" introduction to the science of logic, although it goes further, I believe, that he did in connecting this notion to a specifically Pyrrhonian Scepticism and in developing the advantages of such a Sceptical introduction, compared to those of the *Phenomenology*.

7. It is worth noting that, in the greater *Logic*, the material that spells out the dialectical procedure of the investigation occurs as one of its conclusions, in the section on the absolute idea (*WL* 736–51/6:550–71).

weakening of the case that Hegel makes for the "scientificity" of his treatment in logic in general and for the correctness of beginning logic with pure being in particular.

It may well be then that the Objective Logic also accomplishes a complete sceptical rebuttal of dogmatic presuppositions about the categories of thought, but it does this only on the basis of having first made the case for beginning logic with the concept of pure being, and a case for the legitimacy of this beginning must first be made if a sceptical interlocutor is to follow Hegel into his dialectical or speculative treatment of the determinations of thought. This requires a solution to the problem of beginning, and if it turns out that that solution requires a preliminary project of completed scepticism, then such a task is not a superfluous one, even if its results will later be duplicated and surpassed within the Objective Logic. Hegel's "third solution", accordingly, should be abandoned. He should instead not have been so quick to dismiss the idea of introducing logic with a negative science of completed scepticism.

One thing that this discussion brings to light is that there seems to be a curious back-and-forth in Hegel's writings when it comes to the solution to the problem of beginning. In the first, 1812 edition of "With what must the beginning of the science be made?", he presents the solution to the problem of beginning which I discussed in Sections 3.3.1 and 3.3.2, which turns on finding a way to combine the mediation and immediacy horns of the dilemma in the concept of pure being. Subsequently, in all three editions of the *Encyclopaedia*—1817, 1827, and 1830—Hegel exhibits the tendency I have discussed here to merely assert that it is legitimate to begin with the pure immediacy of being, on the inadequate grounds that a sceptical critique of dogmatic presuppositions will also be carried out within the science of logic itself. Then, in 1832, the second edition of "With what must the beginning of the science be made?", despite various other revisions, retains the earlier solution to the problem of beginning which requires the unity of mediation and immediacy in pure being. I would like to think that, in revising the first book of his *Science of Logic*, Hegel was reminded of the importance of an adequate solution to the problem of beginning and thus returned to his earlier approach to the topic, but this is ultimately speculation on my part.[8]

One thing that should be acknowledged, however, in rejecting the legitimacy of this "third solution", is that merely resolving to begin with pure immediacy only appears problematic from the perspective of an attempt to take seriously and solve the problem of beginning. If one is primarily interested in presenting the contents of Hegel's treatment of logic (as one might expect

---

8. The return to the reliance on the *Phenomenology* might then cohere with Hegel's well-known, unaccomplished intention to publish a second edition of that work.

from an *Encyclopaedia* edition of that material intended for use in class), then it remains the case that abstracting from the content of all thought presumably does result in the empty thinking of pure being, just as the sceptical criticism of all dogmatic presuppositions might. The difference is just that only the latter would *necessitate* that empty thinking, which is required for a solution to the problem of beginning. If one is content, however, to merely find a way to *arrive* at the concept of pure being, without having showed that this is necessarily where one *must* begin a science of logic, then Hegel's suggestion in *EL* §78A that one can simply "resolve to think purely" will also get the job done. There is then nothing to prevent a reader keeping an open mind and going along with the argument of Hegel's logical science, seeing how concepts imply and are derived from one another, and so on, albeit in a hypothetical fashion according to which something like the following is the case: "*If* it is correct that one ought to abandon one's everyday conceptions and begin with pure being, *then* these results, assuming that the argument of the *Science of Logic* stands up to scrutiny, follow". A great deal can therefore be accomplished on the basis of the approach to the beginning suggested in the *Encyclopaedia*. The only problem is that, as I pointed out in Section 3.4.1, Hegel does not think that such a hypothetical approach is adequate for a genuinely scientific treatment of logic, which must prove the necessity of its results. The hypothetical status of the investigation, however, can only be avoided by providing a genuine solution to the problem of beginning.[9] Since I have suggested that the version of that solution which relies upon the *Phenomenology* fails, it is therefore reasonable to further consider the version that depends upon a completed scepticism instead.

5.2 COMPLETED SCEPTICISM

The other obstacle to a proper consideration of the version of the solution to the problem of beginning that depends on completed scepticism as the element of mediation is the possibility that this is, in fact, no alternative at all but rather that Hegel's characterisation of this "completed scepticism" is intended as a reference to his *Phenomenology of Spirit*. In that case, Hegel would merely be referring to the solution which I discussed and rejected already in chapter 4. It is clear, I think, why one might suspect that Hegel is referring to the *Phenomenology* here. He is explicit in describing the *Phenomenology* as a science—the 'science of the *experience of consciousness*' (*PhG*

---

9. Accordingly, one might read Hegel's appeal to the efficacy of the "resolve to think purely" in a similar vein to his softer remarks on the idea of beginning with a hypothesis in *WL* 750–51/6:570, which I discussed in Section 3.4.1.

§88/3:80)—and, as I showed in Section 4.2.2, it is a science that proceeds by way of (determinate) negation, so it would not seem a stretch to describe it as a "negative science". The task of the completed scepticism that Hegel discusses in *EL* §78A is that of running through "all forms of cognition" and exhibiting the "nullity" of their presuppositions, but this sounds a great deal like the project of the *Phenomenology*, which Hegel understands to 'go through all forms of the *relation of consciousness to the object*' (*WL* 28/5:42) and, by way of its criticisms of their assumptions, reduces them to doubt, if not to 'despair' (*PhG* §78/3:72). And finally, as I have already noted, Hegel's appeal here to a "completed scepticism" (*vollbrachte Skeptizismus*) sounds very similar to his characterisation of the procedure of the *Phenomenology* as one of "self-completing scepticism" (*sich vollbringender Skeptizismus*). My impression is that the assumption that Hegel is referring in *EL* §78A to the argument of the *Phenomenology* is not an unusual one among readers of Hegel today, although I have not often seen it defended in writing.[10]

I do not think, however, that Hegel is referring to the argument of the *Phenomenology* in *EL* §78A. If he were to be, I would see no reason for him not to be more explicit in doing so. One would at least expect that, when expanding on this passage in his lectures on logic, he would make the connection clearer. But if one turns to Karl Hegel's transcription of the 1831 *Lectures on Logic*, Hegel makes no mention of the *Phenomenology* at all in connection to this passage. Instead, he appeals briefly to Descartes, in order to emphasise the idea of beginning by doubting everything, before saying the following:

> [T]he old Scepticism had as its result: the complete quiet of the mind, *ataraxia*; Scepticism proved of everything that it was not secure, and thus that one should not commit one's mind to it, for everything is just as much not what it is, as it is what it is . . . Scepticism stops with the abstraction of nothing: One can make an introduction to philosophy in this manner, in that one can show of everything that it contains a contradiction in itself. (*VL* 71–72/84)

In this passage, including its characteristic discussion of the conclusions of scepticism in surprisingly metaphysical terms and the suggestion that scepticism demonstrates the existence of contradictions,[11] Hegel is clearly talking not about the *Phenomenology* but instead about (his understanding

---

10. Vieweg (2007: 33) comes close, suggesting that 'the self-completing scepticism and thereby the result of the *Phenomenology* remains of fundamental importance in §78' of the *Encyclopaedia*, and that the results of the *Phenomenology* are 'compressed' into the discussion of the beginning of logic there. By contrast, Fulda (1975: 21–54), as I have already noted, clearly distinguishes the idea of a sceptical introduction to logic from that of a phenomenological one. He is too quick, however, in my opinion, to follow Hegel in rejecting the "unscientific" procedure of scepticism in favour of the "scientific" approach of the *Phenomenology*, the suitability of which for the solution to the problem of beginning I have already criticised in the previous chapter.

11. I discussed these peculiar aspects of Hegel's reading of Pyrrhonism in Section 1.2.1.

of) Pyrrhonian Scepticism as an introduction in which the "nullity" of all dogmatic presuppositions would be exhibited, resulting in a complete suspension of judgement about the contents of ordinary thought and necessitating the empty thinking of the beginning of logic.[12] It is therefore Pyrrhonism which Hegel is describing as a "negative science", since it too proceeds primarily by negation, although, as I noted in Section 1.2.1, it is the "abstract" negation of arguing that opposing claims are equally convincing and suspending judgement, rather than the determinate negation of the *Phenomenology*.[13] And precisely because Pyrrhonism operates by way of abstract negation, rather than the determinate negation of the *Phenomenology*, for all that Pyrrhonian Sceptical inquiry might be "completed", it is not a "*self-completing* scepticism". Hegel could describe the argument of the *Phenomenology* as "self-completing" because he took the negation of each of natural consciousness' presuppositions to result, determinately, in something positive—a new shape of natural consciousness—which would then offer itself for (immanent) criticism in turn. By contrast, Hegel takes the abstract negation of the Sceptics, as he indicates earlier, to conclude with the nothingness of suspension of judgement. Such a scepticism is not "self-completing" because, after abstractly negating a dogmatic presupposition, it 'must wait and see whether something new will present itself, and what, in order to throw it into the same empty abyss' (*PhG* §79/3:74).[14] This aspect of how Pyrrhonian Sceptical inquiry would have to be "completed" is presumably responsible for Hegel's remarks in *EL* §78A to the effect that, as a candidate for the element of mediation in the beginning, Scepticism amounts to an "unpleasant" way of achieving this goal, which 'would have to find the finite forms [of thought] only empirically and unscientifically, and to take them up as given'.[15] Addressing this concern, accordingly, belongs to the task of considering the viability of the *Encyclopaedia* version of the solution to the problem of beginning, but for now, I wish only to emphasise that there is a clear difference between the

---

12. The passage I have quoted from the *Lectures on Logic* echoes Hegel's discussion of Descartes and Scepticism at *VGP* 657/20:127. There Hegel is more explicit in distinguishing Descartes from the Pyrrhonists, by pointing out that what, for the latter, was the result of their inquiry, is for the former the beginning of his own. In this Hegel sees Descartes, I think, as a step in the right direction—one which he himself can take further by having philosophy begin from the total presuppositionlessness to which a completed scepticism would give rise.

13. Hegel also describes Pyrrhonism as operating with a 'negative dialectic' (*VGP* 481/19:397).

14. Compare: 'Philosophy however does not remain at the merely negative result of the dialectic, as is the case with Scepticism' (*EL* §81Z2).

15. Staehler (2017: 24–25) raises the topic of how it is that Hegel is able to describe Scepticism both as a "science" and as "unscientific" in *EL* §78. I suppose simply that, in the case of the former, Hegel is using *Wissenschaft* in the general sense of a rigorously pursued discipline, whereas when he complains that a completed scepticism would proceed in an *unwissenschaftlich* manner, he has in mind the dialectical or speculative procedure that, he thinks, characterises a genuinely scientific philosophy.

self-completing scepticism of phenomenology and the idea of a completed Pyrrhonian Sceptical inquiry, for Hegel.

Identifying the *Encyclopaedia*'s negative science of completed scepticism with Pyrrhonism is obviously helpful when it comes to fleshing out this idea, which Hegel appears to entertain and abandon so quickly, since, as I have already shown, his various engagements with Pyrrhonian Scepticism are far more extensive. I turn now, accordingly, to further substantiating the identification of Hegel's negative science of completed scepticism with his account of Pyrrhonism, and to developing this version of the solution to the problem of beginning, as well as to seeing to what extent the reservations that Hegel expresses concerning this idea might be assuaged. The result of this account, I think, is a version of Hegel's solution to the problem of beginning which he himself would recognise, since it follows the form of the solution that he develops in "With what must the beginning of the science be made?" and builds on a suggestion that he himself makes in the *Encyclopaedia* by means of Hegel's own remarks on Pyrrhonian Scepticism, even if it is not a version of the solution that he himself explicitly endorsed (although I think that perhaps he should have).

5.2.1 Completed Pyrrhonism

The attraction of Pyrrhonian Scepticism in the context of the search for the correct element of mediation in Hegel's solution to the problem of beginning is that it offers itself as a programme for examining the presuppositions of ordinary thought (or natural consciousness) that would have an entirely negative outcome, just as Maker took the *Phenomenology of Spirit* to. Before developing this idea, however, I think it is worth briefly providing some further evidence for the claim that Hegel is thinking of specifically Pyrrhonian Scepticism in *EL* §78.

One of the clearest reasons for thinking that Hegel has Pyrrhonism in mind at this point in the *Encyclopaedia* is that, very shortly afterward, he returns again to the topic of a 'genuine scepticism' which consists in 'the complete despair of everything fixed by the understanding', adding that 'the resulting attitude is undisturbedness'. He continues, 'This is the high, ancient scepticism, namely as we find it presented by Sextus Empiricus' (*EL* §81Z2). It is this explicitly Pyrrhonian Scepticism that Hegel characterises as having a 'merely negative result' on the basis of its 'mere, i.e., abstract negation', and he suggests that this Scepticism has as its result the 'nullity of everything finite' (*EL* §81Z2): precisely what the completed scepticism of *EL* §78A was supposed to achieve.

In fact, Hegel's identification of Pyrrhonism as a possible element of mediation in the beginning recalls aspects even of his earlier engagements with the topic of Scepticism. In "On the Relation of Scepticism to Philosophy", for example, Hegel claimed that:

> [O]rdinary understanding or ordinary consciousness . . . holds fast to the given, the fact, the finite (whether this finite is called "appearance" or "concept") . . . the Sceptical modes show ordinary consciousness the instability of such certainties in a way which is likewise close to that of ordinary consciousness; namely, Scepticism likewise calls upon appearances and finite things for help, and from their diversity and the equal right of all of them to count as valid, from out of the antinomy to be discerned in the finite itself, it discerns their untruth. Scepticism can thus be seen as the first step towards philosophy, for the beginning of philosophy must be the elevation above the truth that ordinary consciousness gives, and the idea of a higher truth'. (*VSP* 332/2:240)

This passage, I think, is clearly on the way to the idea of a Sceptical introduction to speculative philosophy, of the kind being entertained in *EL* §78.

If one accepts, then, that that Hegel's negative science of completed scepticism is to be understood in terms of his engagement with Pyrrhonian Scepticism, as I think that one should, it is important to consider what it would mean for such a project to be "completed", if this were what it would take for it to coincide with the empty thinking of the beginning of Hegel's *Logic*. As I emphasised in Section 1.1.2, Sextus himself strongly gives the impression that he conceives of Sceptical inquiry as something that can be completed.[16] He takes the Sceptics to have investigated *all* of the claims made by the Dogmatists (*PH* I:198, 200), across what he takes to be a 'more complete' account of the various parts of philosophy (*M* VII:16), as well as the various disciplines investigated in *Against the Learned*. He finds that 'every object of inquiry can be referred to' the Agrippan modes (*PH* I:169), to say nothing of the other Sceptical modes which he makes use of, and he takes the conclusion of these exhaustive inquiries to be 'suspension of judgement about everything' (*PH* I:31). That Sceptical inquiry can be completed is thus clearly suggested when Sextus claims that the Sceptics have 'come to hold no beliefs' (*PH* I:12). Significantly, Sextus even suggests that the principles, phrases, and arguments that the Sceptic makes use of in order to carry out their inquiry are ultimately abandoned, 'destroyed by themselves, being cancelled along with what they are applied to, just as purgative drugs do not merely drain the humours from the body but drive themselves out too along with the humours' (*PH* I:206). This thoroughgoing rejection of dogmatic claims and presuppositions, this global suspension of judgement and lack of belief, would thus represent the completion of Sceptical inquiry.

---

16. A recent defence of this view is offer by Smith, who argues that 'from the sceptic's point of view, a complete investigation is possible because it has been carried out in an ordered and systematic manner' (Smith 2022: 79).

As I suggested in Section 1.2.1, Hegel is among those readers of Sextus who takes the idea that Sceptical inquiry might be completed in this fashion seriously.[17] Indeed, as I pointed out, he even takes the scope of the "principle of Scepticism", that 'opposed to every argument there is an equal argument' (*PH* I:12), further than Sextus himself, since, while Sextus takes Sceptical inquiry's completeness to consist in the fact that this principle applies to every dogmatic claim that the Sceptics have yet encountered (on the basis of their investigations), Hegel treats it as a principle that straightforwardly applies to all dogmatic, finite treatments of thought, calling it 'something universal' (*VGP* 469/19:374). Accordingly, Hegel takes Sceptical inquiry to be 'exhaustive against the determinate' thinking of ordinary consciousness (*VGP* 480/19:394) and, like Sextus, takes the Agrippan modes to apply unrestrictedly to dogmatic presuppositions, suggesting that 'there are no more suitable weapons against Dogmatism' and that, used against the dogmatism of ordinary thought, 'they must be victorious' (*VSP* 335/2:245). That Hegel takes seriously the possibility that Sceptical inquiry might be completed is also clear in his characterisations of the conclusion of such an inquiry. As I have already indicated, he takes Pyrrhonism to point out 'the antinomy in *all* the concepts that it found in the sciences' (*WL* 158/5:217, my emphasis), and describes the result of such an exhaustive, negative inquiry in terms of 'the complete quiet of the mind' (*VL* 72/84), as an 'empty abyss', or even as '*pure nothing*' (*PhG* §79/3:74).[18] This "pure nothing", I would suggest, coincides with the "total presuppositionlessness" which Hegel describes as the result of a completed scepticism in *EL* §78A.[19]

Whether Hegel is right to suppose that a Sceptical inquiry that makes use of, among other things perhaps, the Agrippan modes, could really *completely* eliminate all dogmatic presuppositions is a question that cannot satisfactorily be answered here. One suggestion that might be made in Hegel's favour is the following: in Section 1.1.3, I suggested that the Agrippan modes provide the format for various "Agrippan problems", one of which is the epistemic regress problem, which targets the attempt to provide evidence in support of a claim. Being able to do this, arguably, is essential for the justification of any of the claims of dogmatic, ordinary thought.[20] Although I obviously can-

---

17. I suggested Ribeiro (2002) as a good example of someone who disputes the claim that Sceptical inquiry could ever be completed.
18. This characterisation of the result of Pyrrhonian inquiry seems to require that Hegel adopt a more "radical" or "rustic" interpretation of the Sceptic's beliefs or lack thereof. As I noted in Section 1.1.2, however, it is clear that Hegel has such a interpretation, even if it is not clear that it is, in fact, the interpretation that makes the best possible sense of Sextus' text.
19. Compare Franks 2008: 72: 'What does Hegel think is the *upshot* of Agrippan scepticism . . . ? A rigorous answer would be: *nothing at all*'.
20. Hegel, at least, takes ordinary consciousness without exception to be committed to a model of justification which turns on 'ground and consequent' (*VSP* 337/2:247).

not launch into a survey of recent responses to the epistemic regress problem here, I think it is safe to say that it is at least not obvious that any one proposed solution is, in fact, successful. Along such lines Fogelin, a little while ago now, commented that 'recent philosophical writings on justification have made no significant progress . . . Things are now largely as Sextus Empiricus left them almost two thousand years ago' (Fogelin 1994: 11), while more recently, Cling has suggested that there is no good solution to the epistemic regress problem, at least for as long as we insist upon having 'reasons that are nonarbitrary from our own point of view' (Cling 2009: 340). If such commentators are, in fact, right, this speaks in favour of the efficacy of the use of the modes in a Sceptical inquiry that would genuinely result in the "pure nothing" of "suspension of judgement about everything".

At this point, I think it is helpful to recall what is required by the form of Hegel's solution to the problem of beginning. The form of his solution, I suggested in Section 3.3.1, required that the concept of pure being unify determinations of immediacy and mediation: both the empty, presuppositionless thinking of the beginning of the *Logic* and some presupposed inquiry, the result of which both necessitated and coincided with that empty thinking. Maker's account of the *Phenomenology*, the fundamentals of which I set out in Sections 3.3.2 and 4.1, suggested a way in which this could be accomplished: If the trajectory of the *Phenomenology* were a "radically negative" one so that the conclusion of its critical investigation of the presuppositions of natural consciousness were just the total elimination of all such presuppositions, then this result would necessitate and coincide with the presuppositionless immediacy of the beginning of the *Logic*. Although the argumentative trajectory of the *Phenomenology* turned out, I argued, not to support such an account, the idea of a completed Pyrrhonian Scepticism which I have sketched here suggests itself, I think, as a better candidate for the element of mediation in the concept of pure being.[21] Hegel himself has characterised its result explicitly in terms of total presuppositionlessness, or in terms of "pure nothing". But "pure nothing", Hegel will famously go on to argue, is 'the same as what pure *being* is' (*WL* 59/5:83). I think that this suggests a successful version of the solution to the problem of beginning by Hegel's own lights, since it is one that allows him to appeal to the force of the arguments of a completed Pyrrhonian Sceptical inquiry in order to reject the objection that beginning with pure being is indistinguishable from beginning with an arbitrary assertion, while at the same time pointing to

---

21. It is also striking, I think, that Hegel's suggestion, in *EL* §78, that *all* 'presuppositions or prejudices [are] to be given up upon at the entrance to the science, whether they be taken from representation or from thought' echoes Sextus suggestion that the Pyrrhonian Sceptic is concerned to set out oppositions between and suspend judgement concerning 'things which appear and are thought of in any way at all' (*PH* I:8).

the presuppositionlessness of the beginning—its complete lack of a relation to any supporting presuppositions, since even the arguments of the Sceptical inquiry have eliminated themselves like "purgative drugs"—in order to reject the objection that beginning with pure being depends problematically on further reasons, the validity of which themselves must be questioned, and so on.[22]

To further develop this version of Hegel's solution to the problem of beginning, as well as to more closely examine the extent to which it might really be taken as a successful one by Hegel's own lights, I think that it is worth returning to the limitations that Hegel perceived in Pyrrhonian Sceptical inquiry, which I discussed in Sections 1.2.1 and 1.2.2. Seeing how these perceived relations related to the idea of a completed scepticism which could mediate the beginning of logic offers the opportunity to further investigate Hegel's reasons for rejecting the idea, as well as to see whether it might to some extent be defended against Hegel's criticisms and thus be more suitable for playing its role in the solution to the problem of beginning than he realised.

The first of these was that Scepticism operates at the level of the understanding only, rather than exploiting the speculative resources of the kind of thinking Hegel refers to as that of reason. This might amount to a limitation in terms of the philosophical potential of Pyrrhonian Scepticism itself, from Hegel's point of view, but I do not think that it is necessarily a problem for the idea that such a Scepticism could mediate the beginning of logic by eliminating all dogmatic presuppositions. Instead, the fact that Scepticism, in Hegel's opinion, operates merely at the level of the understanding, recommends it, in a certain way, for this purpose, since it lends itself well to the project of the *immanent* criticism of the claims of ordinary, dogmatic thought. Hegel himself seems to recognise this in the passage from "On the Relationship of Scepticism to Philosophy", which I cited earlier in this section, where he suggested that the ancient Sceptics "show ordinary consciousness the instability" of its "certainties", "in a way which is likewise close to that of ordinary consciousness", i.e., by utilising evidence and argumentative standards that one's dogmatic interlocutors already recognise as authoritative, in order to rebut their claims, "by calling on appearances and finite things" and showing "the equal right of all of them to count as valid", thus motivating suspension of judgement. This account coheres with the widely recognised tendency of

---

22. A comparison might be drawn between the radically negative result of a completed Sceptical inquiry and elements of Bowman's (2013: 48–54) treatment of Hegel's logic of negation (Bowman himself is following the account provided in Henrich 1978). The eventual turning of Sceptical argument upon itself, according to Sextus' metaphor of the "purgative drugs", describes a moment where the argumentative negation of dogmatic claims becomes a negation of that argumentative negation itself. It thus resembles the following aspect of Bowman's discussion of "autonomous negation" in particular: 'Since autonomous negation is the negation *of negation*, its immediate result is the vanishing of negation. The absence of negation is affirmation or simple being' (Bowman 2013: 51).

the Pyrrhonian Sceptics to argue "dialectically" in just such a fashion.[23] The restriction of Sceptical inquiry to the thinking of the understanding, then, arguably facilitates the idea of an effective completed scepticism, precisely because it will be more effective when it comes to challenging dogmatic presuppositions than merely holding that such presuppositions can be seen to be illegitimate from the perspective of a speculative reason the validity of which one's interlocutors do not recognise.[24]

The second, related limitation that Hegel saw in Pyrrhonian Scepticism was that it restricted its notion of negation to a merely "abstract negation" in finding the arguments in favour of opposing claims to be equally strong and suspending judgement, rather than recognising the possibilities of "determinate negation"—the kind of negation which Hegel takes to result, for example, from the criticism of various shapes of consciousness in his *Phenomenology*, which I discussed in Section 4.2.2 and which finds that the negation of such material always results in some new content, so that it is at the same time positive and provides some new material to be critically examined in turn. This aspect of the procedure of the *Phenomenology* was what allowed Hegel to characterise it as a "self-completing scepticism", and this tendency of the criticisms developed in that work always to provide the next step of the argument undoubtedly play an important role in Hegel's conception of the scientific nature of its investigation. I will say more about this topic shortly, but here I think that it is worth noting that it is precisely the restriction of Pyrrhonian Scepticism to merely abstract negation that allows its result to be the "pure nothing" that can successfully coincide with the empty thinking of the beginning of the *Logic*. As I argued in the previous chapter, the *Phenomenology*'s use of determinate negation, whatever its other benefits, guaranteed that its conclusion would be a positive, contentful one that was incompatible with the presuppositionlessness of the beginning of the *Logic*.

The third limitation that Hegel sees in Pyrrhonian Sceptical inquiry is expressed in *EL* §78A itself: that Scepticism, not proceeding by way of determinate negation, 'would have to find the finite forms [of thought] only empirically and unscientifically, and to take them up as given'. This seems

---

23. See Machuca 2019a for a good discussion of the Sceptic's dialectical argumentation.
24. See Heidemann 2011: 96–97. Heidemann criticises, as I have already noted, Hegel's tendency to assume the legitimacy of a notion of speculative reasoning which a Sceptic will not automatically accept. But if, as I suggested earlier, a completed Sceptical inquiry involves ultimately turning the negative force of its arguments against themselves (like purgative drugs), and this negation of negation results in the empty thinking of pure being, then it can arguably be seen as a *demonstration*, on the opponent of speculative philosophy's own grounds, of the possibility of speculative reasoning, whereby the negation of a claim can be seen to have a positive result. A completed Sceptical inquiry, in coinciding with the beginning of logic in pure being, would amount to the moment at which the abstract negation of Scepticism would, of its own accord, become the determinately negative or dialectical reasoning of speculative philosophy. I take this again to count in favour of the version of Hegel's solution to the problem of beginning under examination here, as I shall argue in section 5.3.

like the sharpest of Hegel's challenges to a successful, completed Pyrrhonian Scepticism, since Hegel appears to be suggesting that a Pyrrhonist would be in no good position to be assured of the genuine completeness of their inquiry, since it is always possible that there are other ordinary, finite, dogmatic claims and presuppositions which they have not examined and have not been able to sceptically rebut. This is importantly not the case with the argument of his *Phenomenology*,[25] which he takes, as I have indicated, to proceed demonstratively by way of determinate negation through the complete series of shapes of natural consciousness, until it comprehends 'the whole system of consciousness' (*PhG* §89/3:80), the unity and completeness of which is assured by the fact that the investigation forms a circle, its conclusion reaching 'the *certainty of the immediate* . . . the beginning from which we started' (*PhG* §806/3:589–90).[26]

To a certain extent, I think that Hegel's criticism hits its mark here. Sextus, I pointed out earlier, does not take the completion of Sceptical inquiry to have quite the universal scope that Hegel suggests it might, arguing that his use of the "Sceptical principle" means only that '[t]o every argument I have scrutinised which purports to establish something in a dogmatic fashion, there appears to me to be another opposed argument . . . equal to it in convincingness or unconvincingness' (*PH* I:203). A completed Scepticism, for Sextus, then, although it features suspension of judgement about everything and the holding of no beliefs, always involves a kind of watchfulness, since it can never be assured that some new dogmatic conception or argument will not present itself and require further investigation before it can be rebutted. It is thus arguably not quite so "complete" as Hegel takes the investigation of his *Phenomenology* to be.[27]

But despite this limitation, it may be that Pyrrhonian inquiry is not so "empirical and unscientific" in its approach as Hegel takes it to be. Plínio Junqueira Smith, for example, in defending the idea that a completed Pyrrhonian inquiry would involve a genuinely global suspension of judgement against Barnes, who claims that suspension of judgement 'is a particular attitude, essentially directed towards some specific issue' (Barnes 1997: 59), argues that 'the Pyrrhonist can

---

25. Nor, presumably, is it the case with the "sceptical" side of Hegel's logical science itself, but I have already given my reasons above for thinking that it is unsatisfactory for Hegel to appeal to this in order to reject the idea of an introductory negative science of completed scepticism, at least when it comes to solving the problem of beginning.

26. I discussed Hegel's Fichtean insistence on circularity as a criterion of the completeness of a scientific investigation in Section 3.4.1.

27. Even as he complains, however, that Pyrrhonian Scepticism can only 'take up as given' presuppositions to be negated 'in an unscientific manner', Hegel says that the ancient sceptics 'show that *all* these forms [of finite thought] contain a contradiction in themselves' (*EL* §24Z3, my emphasis), which suggests that he does not suppose this problem to rule out the possibility of a completed scepticism, only to make it a difficult one.

and does talk about a suspension of judgement about everything . . . he can and does talk this way because he has a complete (and ordered) conception of philosophical investigation, and he has carried out a complete investigation, producing an *aporia* about everything' (Smith 2022: 83).

The more ordered, systematic elements of Pyrrhonian inquiry that Smith has in mind here are, first of all, those passages where Sextus sounds closest in his approach to Descartes in the First Meditation, passages that Hegel seems to neglect.[28] At the opening of *Against the Physicists*, for example, Sextus claims the Sceptics' 'method of investigation' does not proceed by 'dwelling on particulars', but instead by

> attacking the most important and all-encompassing points, by means of which we shall have the rest put into impasse as well. For just as in sieges those who undermined the foundations of the wall get the towers to come down along with it, so those in philosophical inquiries who have defeated the initial assumptions of a subject have in effect ruled out the entire apprehension of the subject. (*AP* I: 1–2)

Sextus similarly suggests in *Against the Learned*: 'We will take for our refutations not everything said by the people we are refuting (for besides being tough and unmethodical, this may also be impossible) . . . but things that, if they are done away with, make everything done away with too' (*M* I:39–40).[29] This approach of targeting the most foundational claims that the Sceptic can identify, in order to, in one stroke, motivate suspension of judgement concerning a series of more particular claims which depend for their justification on the more foundational ones, suggests that the Pyrrhonists are not as limited to merely "empirically and unscientifically" waiting for dogmatic claims to come their way in order to rebut them as Hegel suggested they were. Instead, the Sceptics seem to have a reasonably clear methodology which transforms their approach from that of endlessly sifting through a vast pile of dogmatic claims into one whereby the goal of suspension of judgement about everything looks quite reachable. In fact, one might expand on this aspect of Sceptical methodology somewhat by pointing out that the Agrippan modes in particular, as Hegel is well aware, operate by asking for the evidence or grounds supporting a dogmatic knowledge claim. If none is given, as I explained in Section 1.1.3, the Sceptic will suspend judgement on grounds of arbitrariness, but if grounds are provided, then the Sceptic will

---

28. Smith (2022: 142–50) also thinks that Sextus is operating with clear methodological commitments concerning the structure and components of the divisions of philosophy which are to be investigated, as well as the order in which specific Sceptical arguments are deployed. I cannot discuss this material here.

29. See also *PH* II:21, where Sextus deploys this approach to Dogmatic discussions of the criterion of truth, so that his investigation will be 'systematic and complete'.

inquire further into the grounds upon which the Dogmatist takes these to be true, and so on. What this amounts to, in effect, is a method for identifying which are the most "foundational" of the Dogmatists' presuppositions, so that the Sceptic's criticisms can then target those, for greatest effect, as Sextus suggested in the extract earlier.[30] It seems to me to be at least *prima facie* plausible that a Sceptic pursuing this course, perhaps by extensive, repeated appeal to the epistemic regress problem, to return to the example I briefly discussed earlier, would eventually begin to hit bedrock among the presuppositions of ordinary thought and, if they suspend judgement there, would run out of dogmatic presuppositions to investigate. They would have ended up in a place where it is not obviously possible to think anything determinate at all.[31] This again sounds like the 'indeterminate immediacy' of pure being, however (*WL* 59/5:82), which should again speak in favour of the success, at least by Hegel's lights, of this version of the solution to the problem of beginning.

The final limitation that Hegel perceived in Pyrrhonian Scepticism was that its criticisms did not gain purchase on speculative philosophical thought but target only all of the dogmatic presuppositions of ordinary thought. This final issue, I take it, is obviously no problem here, since Hegel's idea of a completed scepticism is precisely of a scepticism which would target all of the presuppositions of ordinary thought in order to necessitate the beginning of a project of speculative logic which, Hegel continues to think, will prove immune to Sceptical criticism.

The idea of a completed Pyrrhonian Sceptical inquiry, then, cannot replace all of the features that recommended the *Phenomenology* as the presupposition to the beginning of the *Logic*. It would not proceed by determinate negation and would thus not be a "self-completing scepticism". It therefore might not be said to proceed by strict demonstration, as the argument of the *Phenomenology* did, and requires more in the way of argumentative, sceptical work on the part of the philosopher, rather than just "looking on" as shapes of consciousness undermine themselves. Nor, relatedly, does it offer the same prospects for having demonstrated that its critical treatment of the dogmatic presuppositions of ordinary consciousness has been completed once and for all by exhausting its subject matter by showing that its account has turned in a circle, thereby, according to Hegel, presenting a unified, systematic account. Instead, the Sceptical inquiry would always be, to some small extent, only

---

30. I am not suggesting that Sextus explicitly understands the Agrippan modes to be used to identify foundational claims in this way, merely that such a use is plausible.
31. The term "place" might not even be appropriate here, I suppose. In the context of the idea that the result of a completed Sceptical inquiry is, as Hegel says, *"pure nothing"*, if one were to draw the analogy between the space of reasons and physical space, one might be reminded of old hypotheses about the "Big Crunch" in which all of space (and all of its content) collapses in on itself and implodes.

provisionally completed, and would demand a continuing watchfulness for dogmatic claims and arguments which have not been treated or anticipated in the Sceptical treatment which resulted in the pure being of the beginning of logic. Nevertheless, there appears to be, I have suggested, a meaningful sense in which a Pyrrhonian Sceptical inquiry might be completed, one which Hegel acknowledges, and it is one that appears to lend itself rather better to coinciding with the empty thinking of the beginning of logic than the *Phenomenology* did. What is more, despite the limitations which, according to Hegel, prevented Pyrrhonian Scepticism from amounting to a genuinely systematic, scientific inquiry, I have suggested that it is not nearly so "empirical and unscientific" as he appears to think, and that this speaks strongly in favour of its capacity to conduct the complete critical negation of the presuppositions of ordinary consciousness demanded by a successful solution to the problem of beginning.

I think that this is to have said enough about the idea that a completed Pyrrhonian Scepticism might successfully play the role of the element of mediation in Hegel's solution to the problem of beginning. It seems to me that this version of Hegel's solution to the problem of beginning is a more plausible one that the one that depends on the argument of the *Phenomenology of Spirit*, but before concluding, it is worth returning briefly to that first version of the solution and to the problems I identified for it, to see whether those problems might also beset the version of the solution I have set out earlier.

5.2.2 Comparing the Solutions

In the previous chapter, I focused upon three problems for the compatibility of the conclusion of the *Phenomenology* with the beginning of the *Logic* and, thus, for the version of the solution to the problem of beginning which depended upon the argument of the *Phenomenology* as the element of mediation in pure being. Those problems were:

1. The argument of the *Phenomenology* includes the development of already-scientific content, which renders its conclusion incompatible with the presuppositionless beginning of the *Logic*.
2. The argument of the *Phenomenology* proceeds by way of determinate negation, which guarantees that its conclusion be contentful, which makes it incompatible with the presuppositionless beginning of the *Logic*.
3. The argument of the *Phenomenology* is an attempt to secure the idealist standpoint of Hegel's philosophical science. This involves a significant metaphysical result which is not compatible with the presuppositionless beginning of the *Logic*.

It is only reasonable, I think, to briefly ask here whether the version of the solution which instead depends upon a negative science of completed scepticism in the place of the *Phenomenology* might run into the same problems.

Regarding (1), there is no reason, I think, to suppose that Hegel takes Pyrrhonian Scepticism itself to feature the production of speculative philosophical claims which would render its results incompatible with the presuppositionless beginning of logic.[32] Hegel is aware, as I indicated in Section 1.2.2, that '[t]he ancient Sceptics generally called every philosophy dogmatic to the extent that it set up definite doctrines. In this wider sense, genuinely speculative philosophy also counts as dogmatic for Scepticism' (*EL* §32Z). Here, he clearly opposes Scepticism to the generation of philosophical or "scientific" content.[33]

I have already addressed (2) in the previous section, pointing out that although Hegel sees Scepticism's restriction to the thinking of the understanding and to merely abstract negation as a limitation, it in fact renders it, as an introduction, compatible with the presuppositionless beginning of logic precisely because it ensures that the result of its inquiry has no positive content which would count as a problematically substantive presupposition from the perspective of the logical science. Here, Scepticism's failure, in Hegel's eyes, to recognise the possibilities of proceeding by determinate negation, actually count in its favour.

In the case of (3), I think that it is clear that a completed Pyrrhonian Sceptical inquiry that concludes with the "*pure nothing*" of the total absence of all presuppositions cannot be taken to establish something like the standpoint of Hegel's speculative philosophy, where this involves establishing at least the rudiments of a metaphysical idealism which can then be developed in the *Logic*.[34] This again counts in favour of the viability of the version of the solution to the problem of beginning under consideration here, even though it does appear to have consequences for how one approaches Hegel's claim that logic coincides with metaphysics. I will address this briefly in the concluding section of this chapter. In the meantime, however, it seems to me that the version of Hegel's solution to the problem of beginning which depends upon a negative science of completed scepticism fairs rather better than the version that depended upon the *Phenomenology*, at least as far as the three problems considered here go. This again supports the idea, I think, that this is the version of the solution which Hegel ought to have endorsed.

---

32. Hegel's peculiar attribution of some genuine speculative insight to the Sceptics concerning the nature of space at *VGP* 481/19:396 notwithstanding.

33. And, as Fulda (1975: 36–37) notes, Hegel takes Scepticism to address its material only in an 'unscientific' manner.

34. I take it that this is the case, despite Hegel's tendency to read the Sceptics themselves as endorsing a certain kind of subjective idealism, as I discussed in Sections 1.2.1 and 2.1.

5.3 CONCLUSION

Over the course of the preceding chapters, I have attempted to accomplish three things. I have provided a critical commentary on Hegel's essay "With what must the beginning of the science be made?", which addresses all of the key moments of its argument and relates it to relevant material elsewhere in Hegel's *Logic* and his other works. I have also made a case for the importance of Hegel's engagement with and understanding of Pyrrhonian Scepticism in the context of the arguments of the beginning of his *Science of Logic*. Finally, and perhaps most extensively, I have tried to set out the development and nature of the problem of beginning with which Hegel grapples at the beginning of his treatment of logic, and to explicate and evaluate the solution that he provides to that problem.

The problem of beginning, I have argued, is an Agrippan problem, taking its dilemmatic form from Sextus' presentation of the Two Modes. It thus also shares its form with earlier German Idealist expressions of the problem of legitimising a fundamental principle from which to begin elaborating a systematic, scientific metaphysics, although Hegel, I have argued, separates the problem of beginning from the problem of the fundamental principle, suggesting instead that the fundamental principle can be understood as one of the *results* of his logical science, proved by way of the derivation of logical categories that, as it progresses, "retreats into its ground". This leaves Hegel with his Agrippan problem of beginning as the problem of where one must begin a derivation of fundamental determinations of thought if that project is not to remain vulnerable to a sceptical rebuttal at its outset. The problem, as an Agrippan problem, amounts to a dilemma between two problematically arbitrary alternatives, both of which invite sceptical rebuttals: the straightforward arbitrariness of beginning with something immediate or presuppositionless, and the arbitrariness of beginning with something mediated, whereby the beginning remains problematically dependent upon the questionable presuppositions which mediate it.

Hegel's solution, I have argued, turns on affirming specific versions of both horns of the dilemma at once. If mediation and immediacy can be unified in the beginning, so the suggestion goes, then the problematic arbitrariness of the presuppositionless immediacy of the beginning is avoided, since it is necessitated by what mediates it. At the same time, the arbitrariness of the element of mediation is also avoided if its result coincides with the immediacy of the beginning in such a way that substantive presuppositions which would call into question the validity of the beginning are eliminated. The success of this solution thus requires that Hegel identify elements of mediation and immediacy which can properly coincide without any incompatibility, in order for the two to be properly unified and to allow them to nullify the sceptical objections which threaten any attempt to begin merely with something mediated or merely with something immediate.

In this final chapter, I have attempted to argue that the version of Hegel's solution which he himself discounts, from *EL* §78, represents the strongest version of that solution. If the element of mediation is identified with the idea of a completed Pyrrhonian Sceptical inquiry which suspends judgement concerning *all* the presuppositions of ordinary thought, and if the element of immediacy is identified as the empty, presuppositionless thinking which Hegel describes in the beginning of the *Logic*, I have suggested, then the two horns can indeed coincide and be affirmed together in the concept of pure being. Such an understanding of this first concept of Hegel's logical science—in terms of the unity of *scepticism and presuppositionlessness*—offers itself as a way to begin working through the implications of pure being, through Hegel's science of logic, without remaining vulnerable to the charge either that this concept is a merely arbitrary assertion, or that it depends problematically on further presuppositions, the evaluation of which would threaten to show that it is, again, a merely arbitrary concept with which to begin.

This version of Hegel's solution has another advantage, which I have not fully addressed so far: The solution to the problem of beginning, I have explained, involves rejecting the dogmatic assumption of an exclusive opposition between the elements of mediation and immediacy. This means a move from the type of thinking Hegel characterises as that of the understanding (*Verstand*) to that of reason (*Vernunft*). But of course, the success of the solution cannot turn on a mere *presupposition* in favour of the validity of Hegel's notion of speculative, opposition-encompassing reason, since this is precisely what a sceptical interlocutor will not accept.[35] Arguing that a completed Pyrrhonian Sceptical inquiry coincides with empty thinking, however, is to suggest that an argument which proceeds, as Hegel acknowledges, entirely at the level of the understanding, by way of abstract negation, could conclude in a pure nothing which *turns out* to be identical to empty thinking and which turns out to be describable in positive terms, as the concept of pure being. It is thus an illustration, on the sceptical interlocutor's own, merely *verständig* terms, of the speculative possibility of unifying opposing determinations in a higher concept. Kant memorably suggested that an unrestricted use of reason would result in scepticism (*KRV* B22-23). Here it is exactly the other way around. In suggesting that abstract negation, pushed sufficiently far, might be transformed into determinate negation, or that scepticism, pushed sufficiently far, might transform into dialectical or speculative reasoning, the version of the solution to the problem of beginning under consideration in this chapter can make an additional claim, I think, to address and convince and opponent of the possibility of speculative logic on their own terms.

---

35. Heidemann (2011: 91–97) makes this observation, as I have already noted.

What has been achieved if this version of Hegel's solution to the problem of beginning is indeed a valid one? In a sense, very little: the argument of "With what must the beginning of the science be made?", or a slightly modified version of it, can be taken to show that Hegel is right to begin his logic with the examination of the concept of pure being. The beginning of his logical project is, therefore, secure. The challenge to the scientific status of that project from concerns about the arbitrariness of its beginning has been defeated, but much more would need to be accomplished before the necessity of any of the *results* of Hegel's science of logic could be accepted as having been demonstrated. In Section 0.1, I acknowledged Wolff's suggestion that an adequate investigation of the scientific status of Hegel's treatment of logic would cover the legitimacy of its beginning, the success and rigour of its dialectical or speculative method of demonstration, according to which its derivation of logical categories proceeds, and the manner in which its conclusion guarantees that its treatment of its subject matter is a complete and systematic one. I have suggested here that the first of these three elements might be evaluated positively, that Hegel has a case for beginning a science of logic with the concept of pure being in a manner not vulnerable to sceptical objections which would undermine the scientific status of the inquiry. This leaves open various possibilities which could still prove fatal to Hegel's claim to have developed a science of logic. It might be that any given step in the strict derivation of concept from concept which Hegel undertakes in his *Logic* could, under closer examination, turn out to fail, by simply not giving rise to a further concept and stalling, for example. It might be that the immanent method according to which the science of logic proceeds proves vulnerable to criticism of some kind. It might be that the solution to the problem of beginning's unification of opposing determinations in order to evade sceptical objections turns out not to generalise to wider method of defeating scepticism, so that further results of Hegel's speculative philosophy remain problematically vulnerable in this respect. It might be that the derivation of fundamental determinations of thought which Hegel undertakes turns out, under examination, not to convincingly form a circle and guarantee the systematic unity and completeness of its treatment of its subject matter. It could, instead, for all that has been shown here, simply peter out. Or it could turn out to form a circle far too quickly, so that it becomes clear that crucial, fundamental concepts required for thinking have not been treated in it.[36] All

---

36. These possibilities, if they turned out to be actual, on the basis of a reading of the *Logic*, would suggest that Hegel, in providing a successful solution to the problem of beginning, would be in an analogous situation to the one that Fogelin (1994: 118) suggests many proponents of traditional theories of justification find themselves in: that of isolating some very small number of propositions that, they suppose, are invulnerable to scepticism but of being quite unable to build from those to any of the propositions that one would normally want to have justified. In such a situation, scepticism would really have won the day after all.

of this is simply to say that a careful, rigorous reading of Hegel's *Science of Logic* is still required before any of its results can be accepted, but I hope to have shown here that there is a case to be made for accepting its starting point, at the very least.

There is one last issue raised by the version of the solution to the problem of beginning which I have defended in this chapter, which I shall address briefly in closing. As I acknowledged as early as the opening of this book, in Section 0.1, Hegel is clear that he takes his science of logic also to provide the basics of a science of metaphysics: that the fundamental structure of the determinations of thought which he elaborates there is also to be taken as the fundamental structure of the determinations of reality. A standard way in which this identification of logic with metaphysics is taken to be guaranteed, I think, is by appeal to the argument of the *Phenomenology of Spirit*, which begins, as I have noted, from natural consciousness' assumption that thought and reality are fundamentally separate, and exhaustively criticises all forms of this assumption, until the possibility that reality might differ essentially from the categories of thought has been eliminated and a science of logic can be elaborated on the assumption that it is just as much a science of metaphysics.[37] Thus, as I mentioned in the previous chapter, Hegel claims that 'as the course of the *Phenomenology* showed, it is only in absolute knowing that the separation of the *object* from the *certainty of itself* has been completely resolved' with the result that '*the being which is in and for itself is the known concept, the concept as such is the being which is in and for itself*' (*WL* 29/5:43). This view—that reality itself has a conceptual structure available to pure thinking—is commonly taken to amount to an essential element of Hegel's idealism.[38]

In chapter 4, however, I rejected the version of Hegel's solution to the problem of beginning which assumed the results of the argument of the *Phenomenology of Spirit*, in large part on the grounds that the establishment of metaphysical idealism was incompatible with the presuppositionless beginning of a science of logic.[39] I have also suggested earlier, in this chapter, that

---

37. A notable alternative account of this topic is provided in Houlgate 2006: 124–29. Houlgate claims that Hegel's presuppositionless thought of pure being amounts to an intellectual intuition of being itself, and that this guarantees that the account of the logical categories which Hegel derives from pure being is also an account of the categories of being itself, without needing to rely upon the argument of the *Phenomenology*. I cannot give this suggestion the discussion that it deserves here, but my sympathies are with Stern's (2009: 221–22, n.330) suggestion that a genuinely presuppositionless beginning for logic would be one that suspends judgement concerning the identity or non-identity of logic and metaphysics.

38. See Stern 2009: 67–76, for a widely, albeit not universally, accepted defence of this idea. I take it that the accounts of Hegel's idealism defended by Houlgate (2006), Bowman (2013), Kreines (2015), Giladi (2016), and Knappik (2016) to provide just a few examples, and for all of their substantial differences, are broadly in support of this kind of "conceptual realist" interpretation.

39. I have not, however, rejected the validity of the argument of the *Phenomenology*, or the idea that it could successfully establish a metaphysical idealism. Such conclusions could only be defended on the basis of a close, critical reading of the *Phenomenology* in its entirety.

there is no reason to suppose that a completed Pyrrhonian Sceptical inquiry would conclude by establishing idealism in the manner that the *Phenomenology* is commonly taken to do, since its result is merely a total suspension of judgement concerning all dogmatic presuppositions, including those concerning the question of metaphysical realism and idealism. This means that, in endorsing the version of Hegel's solution to the problem of beginning which I have sketched in this chapter, I have suggested that, if the beginning of the *Logic* is to avoid sceptical objections, then it cannot rely upon at least one of the more notable ways in which Hegel tries to demonstrate that logic coincides with metaphysics. In the absence of other arguments which could establish that coincidence in an unproblematic fashion, this would be to suggest that one might have to at least *begin* to read the *Science of Logic* without the identification of logic with metaphysics in place, or merely as an attempt at an a priori derivation of our fundamental conceptual scheme, without having eliminated the possibility that this scheme might not capture the fundamental structure of reality. Considering how best to respond to this issue is a task I cannot accomplish here, but I note that Hegel, or so it seems to me, has plenty of other resources to which he can appeal in arguing for the identity of logic and metaphysics, none of which have been examined here. Possibilities include the contents of the argument of the *Logic* itself, the relation between logic and *Realphilosophie*, his redeployment of elements of the argument of the *Phenomenology* in his Philosophy of Spirit, or simply the various criticisms he directs towards those of his philosophical forebears and contemporaries who reject the idealism that he endorses. There is still a great deal to say, I think, about the claim that logic coincides with metaphysics, even if this is not the place to say it.

Bibliography

Aikin, S. (2011) *Epistemology and the Regress Problem* (Oxford: Routledge)
Aristotle. (1984) *The Complete Works of Aristotle* (2 Vols) J. Barnes (Ed.) (Princeton, NJ: Princeton University Press)
Barnes, J. (1990) *The Toils of Scepticism* (Cambridge: Cambridge University Press)
Beiser, F. (1987) *The Fate of Reason: German Philosophy from Kant to Fichte* (Cambridge, MA: Harvard University Press)
Bell, J. (2011) 'Nothing Matters: Skepticism, Spinoza, and Contemporary French Thought' *Crisis and Critique* Vol. 8, pp. 52–75
Berger, B. (2019) 'The Idea that *is*: On the Transition from Logic to Nature in Hegel's System' *Pli* Vol. 31, pp. 69–87
Berry, J. (2020) 'Sextan Skepticism and The Rise and Fall of German Idealism' in K. Vogt and J. Vlasits (Eds.) *Epistemology After Sextus Empiricus* (Oxford: Oxford University Press), pp. 154–72
Bett, R. (2018) 'Pyrrho' in E. Zalta (Ed.) *The Stanford Encyclopedia of Philosophy* (Winter 2018 Edition)
Bett, R. (2019) *How to be a Pyrrhonist: The Practice and Significance of Pyrrhonian Scepticism* (Cambridge: Cambridge University Press)
Black, D. (2014) 'How Do We Acquire Concepts? Avicenna on Abstraction and Emanation' in J. Hause (Ed.) *Debates in Medieval Philosophy* (New York, NY: Routledge), pp. 126–45
de Boer, K. (2010) *On Hegel: The Sway of the Negative* (Basingstoke: Palgrave Macmillan)
de Boer, K. (2020) *Kant's Reform of Metaphysics:* The Critique of Pure Reason *Reconsidered* (Cambridge: Cambridge University Press)
de Boer, K. (2021) 'Does the Investigation Kant Carries Out in the *Critique of Pure Reason* Amount to a Science?' in N. Schleich (Ed.) *Philosophie als Wissenschaft: Wissenschaftsbegriffe in den philosophischen Systemen des Deutschen Idealismus* (Hildesheim: Georg Olms Verlag), pp. 31–46

Bondeli, M. (1995) *Das Anfangsproblem bei Karl Leonhard Reinhold: Eine Systematische und Entwicklungsgeschichtliche Untersuchung zur Philosophie Reinholds in der Zeit von 1798 bis 1803* (Frankfurt: Vittorio Klostermann Verlag)
Bowman, B. (2013) *Hegel and the Metaphysics of Absolute Negativity* (Cambridge: Cambridge University Press)
Brandão, E. (2020) 'Skepticism and Negation in the Young Hegel: Schulze, Fichte, and Nihilism' in V. Rosaleny and P. Smith (Eds.) *Sceptical Doubt and Disbelief in Modern European Thought: A New Pan-American Dialogue* (Cham: Springer)
Brandom, R. (2019) *A Spirit of Trust: A Reading of Hegel's* Phenomenology (Cambridge, MA: Harvard University Press)
Breazeale, D. (2013) *Thinking Through the Wissenschaftslehre: Themes from Fichte's Early Philosophy* (Oxford: Oxford University Press)
Breazeale, D. (2016) "Reinhold/Schulze/Fichte: A Re-Examination" in M. Bondeli, J. Chotaš, and K. Vieweg (eds.) *Krankheit des Zeitalters oder heilsame Provokation? Skeptizismus in der nachkantischen Philosophie* (Paderborn: Wilhelm Fink Verlag), pp. 151–79
Brennan, T. and Lee, J. (2014) 'A Relative Improvement' *Phronesis* Vol. 59, pp. 246–71
Bristow, W. (2007) *Hegel and the Transformation of Philosophical Critique* (Oxford: Oxford University Press
Cahoone, L. (2013) *The Orders of Nature* (Albany, NY: SUNY Press)
Cameron, R. (2022) *Chains of Being: Infinite Regress, Circularity, and Metaphysical Explanation* (Oxford: Oxford University Press)
Carlson, D. (2007) *A Commentary to Hegel's Science of Logic* (Basingstoke: Palgrave Macmillan)
Carreiro, J. (2009) *Between Two Worlds: A Reading of Descartes's "Meditations"* (Princeton, NJ: Princeton University Press)
Catapano, M. (2017) 'The Two Modes of Scepticism and the Aporetic Structure of Foundationalism' *Méthexis* Vol. 29, pp. 107–20
Chisholm, R. (1973) *The Problem of the Criterion* (Milwaukee, MI: Marquette University Press)
Cling, A. (2008) 'The Epistemic Regress Problem' *Philosophical Studies* Vol. 140, pp. 401–21
Cling, A. (2009) 'Reasons, Regresses, and Tragedy: The Epistemic Regress Problem and the Problem of the Criterion' *American Philosophical Quarterly* Vol. 46, pp. 333–46
Comay, R. and Ruda, F. (2018) *The Dash—The Other Side of Absolute Knowing* (Cambridge, MA: The MIT Press)
Dancy, J. (1985) *An Introduction to Contemporary Epistemology* (Oxford: Blackwell)
Deleuze, G. (2004) *Difference and Repetition* trans. P. Patton (London: Continuum)
Descartes, R. (1984) *The Philosophical Writings of Descartes* (2 Vols) J. Cottingham, R. Stoothoff, and D. Murdoch (Eds.) (Cambridge: Cambridge University Press)
Diogenes Laërtius. (2018) *Lives of the Eminent Philosophers* trans. P. Mensch (Oxford: Oxford University Press)

Dudley, W. (2003) 'Ancient Skepticism and Systematic Philosophy' in D. Duquette (Ed.) *Hegel's History of Philosophy: New Interpretations* (Albany, NY: SUNY Press), pp. 87–106
Dunphy, R. (2020a) 'On the Incompatibility of Hegel's *Phenomenology* with the Beginning of his *Logic*' *Review of Metaphysics* Vol. 74, pp. 81–119
Dunphy, R. (2020b) 'Agrippan Problems' *Logos and Episteme* Vol. 13, pp. 259–82
Dunphy, R. (2021a) 'Hegel and the Problem of Beginning' *Hegel Bulletin* Vol. 43, pp. 344–67
Dunphy, R. (2021b) 'The Scientific Status of Hegel's *Logic*, its Circular Structure, and the Matter of its Beginning' *Revista Eletrônica Estudos Hegelianos* Vol. 18, pp. 45–66
Dunphy, R. (2022) 'From Proto–Sceptic to Sceptic in Sextus' *Outlines of Pyrrhonism*' *Apeiron* Vol. 55 Issue 3, pp. 455–84
Dunphy, R. (forthcoming) 'Schulze's Scepticism and the Rise and Rise of German Idealism' in R. Dunphy and T. Lovat (Eds.) *Metaphysics as a Science in Classical German Philosophy* (London: Routledge)
Düsing, K. (1973) 'Die Bedeutung des Antiken Skeptizismus für Hegels Kritik der Sinnliche Gewissheit' *Hegel–Studien* Vol. 8, pp. 119–30
Eichorn, R. (2020) 'Sextus Empiricus on Isostheneia and Epochē: A Developmental Model' *Sképsis* Vol. 11, pp. 188–209
Emundts, D. (2014) 'Hegel as a Pragmatist' *British Journal of the History of Philosophy* Vol. 23, pp. 611–31
Ferejohn, M. (2009) 'Empiricism and First Principles in Aristotle' in G. Anagnostopoulos (Ed.) *A Companion to Aristotle* (Chichester: Wiley-Blackwell), pp. 66–80
Ficara, E. (2021) *The Form of Truth: Hegel's Philosophical Logic* (Berlin: De Gruyter)
Fichte, J. G. (2000) "Review of Aenesidemus" trans. G. di Giovanni in G. di Giovanni and H. Harris (Eds.) *Between Kant and Hegel: Texts in the Development of Post-Kantian Idealism* (Indianapolis, IN: Hackett), pp. 136–57
Fichte, J. G. (2021) *Foundations of the Entire* Wissenschaftslehre *and Related Writings (1794–95)* trans. D. Breazeale (Oxford: Oxford University Press)
Fogelin, R. (1994) *Pyrrhonian Reflections on Knowledge and Justification* (Oxford: Oxford University Press)
Forster, M. (1989) *Hegel and Skepticism* (Cambridge, MA: Harvard University Press)
Forster, M. (1998) *Hegel's Idea of a Phenomenology of Spirit* (Chicago, IL: Chicago University Press)
Forster, M. (2008) *Kant and Skepticism* (Princeton, NJ: Princeton University Press)
Förster, E. (2012) *The Twenty-Five Years of Philosophy: A Systematic Reconstruction* trans. B. Bowman (Cambridge, MA: Harvard University Press)
Franks, P. (2005) *All or Nothing: Systematicity, Transcendental Arguments, and Skepticism in German Idealism* (Cambridge, MA: Harvard University Press)
Franks, P. (2008) 'Ancient Skepticism, Modern Naturalism, and Nihilism in Hegel's Early Jena Writings' in F. Beiser (Ed.) *The Cambridge Companion to Hegel and Nineteenth Century Philosophy* (Cambridge: Cambridge University Press, 2008), pp. 52–73

Frketich, E. (2021) 'The First Principle of Philosophy in Fichte's 1794 *Aenesidemus Review*' *Fichte Studien* Vol. 49, pp. 59–76

Fulda, H. (1975) *Das Problem einer Einleitung in Hegels Wissenschaft der Logik* (Frankfurt: Klostermann)

Fulda, H. and Horstmann, R-P. (Eds.) (1996) *Skeptizismus und Spekulatives Denken in der Philosophie Hegels* (Stuttgart: Klett–Cotta)

Gabriel, M. (2009) *Skeptizismus und Idealismus in der Antike* (Frankfurt am Main: Suhrkamp)

Gentry, G. (2021) 'Hegel's Logic of Purposiveness' in G. Gentry (Ed.) *Kantian Legacies in German Idealism* (London: Routledge), pp. 36–70

di Giovanni, G. (2000) 'The Facts of Consciousness' in G. di Giovanni and H. Harris (eds.) *Between Kant and Hegel: Texts in the Development of Post–Kantian Idealism* (Indianapolis, IN: Hackett), pp. 2–50

Giladi, P. (2016) 'Hegel's Metaphysics as Speculative Naturalism' in A. de Laurentiis (Ed.) *Hegel and Metaphysics: On Logic and Ontology in the System* (Boston, MA: De Gruyter), pp. 149–62

Haack, S. (1993) 'Double–Aspect Foundherentism: A New Theory of Empirical Justification' *Philosophy and Phenomenological Research*, Vol. 3, pp. 113–28

Haarparanta, L. and Heikki, J. (Eds.) (2012) *Categories of Being: Essays on Metaphysics and Logic* (Oxford: Oxford University Press)

Hankinson, R. (1995) *The Sceptics* (New York: Routledge)

Hankinson, R. (2010) 'Aenesidemus and the Rebirth of Pyrrhonism' in R. Bett (Ed.) *The Cambridge Companion to Ancient Scepticism* (Cambridge: Cambridge University Press), pp. 105–19

Hanna, R. (2013) 'Kant, Hegel, and the Fate of Non-Conceptual Content' *Hegel Bulletin* Vol. 34, pp. 1–32

Harris, H. (2000) 'Skepticism, Dogmatism, and Speculation in the Critical Journal' in G. di Giovanni and H. Harris (Eds.) *Between Kant and Hegel: Texts in the Development of Post–Kantian Idealism* (Indianapolis, IN: Hackett), pp. 252–71

Heidemann, D. (2007) *Der Begriff des Skeptizismus: Seine systematischen Formen, die pyrrhonische Skeptizismus, und Hegels Herausforderung* (Berlin: Walter de Gruyter)

Heidemann, D. (2011) 'Hegel on the Nature of Scepticism' *Hegel Bulletin* Vol. 32, pp. 80–99

Henrich, D. (1971) *Hegel im Kontext* (Frankfurt am Main: Surhkamp)

Henrich, D. (1978) 'Hegels Logik der Reflexion (neue Fassung)' *Hegel–Studien* Vol. 18, 204–324

Hentrup, M. (2018) 'Self–Completing Scepticism: On Hegel's Sublation of Pyrrhonism' *Epoché: A Journal for the History of Philosophy* Vol. 23, pp. 105–23

Hentrup, M. (2019) 'Hegel's *Logic* as Presuppositionless Science' *Idealistic Studies* Vol. 49, pp. 145–65

Houlgate, S. (2005) *An Introduction to Hegel: Freedom, Truth, and History* (Oxford: Blackwell)

Houlgate, S. (2006) *The Opening of Hegel's Logic: From Being to Infinity* (West Lafayette, IN: Purdue University Press)

Imhoff, S. (2016) 'Maimon Zwischen Schulze und Reinhold' in M. Bondeli, J. Chotaŝ, and K. Vieweg (eds.) *Krankheit des Zeitalters oder heilsame Provokation? Skeptizismus in der nachkantischen Philosophie* (Paderborn: Wilhelm Fink Verlag), pp. 93–109

Jacobi, F. (1994) *The Main Philosophical Writings and the Novel* Allwill trans. G. di Giovanni (Montreal: McGill–Queens University Press)

Janáĉek, K. (2008) *Studien zu Sextus Empiricus, Diogenes Laertius und zur Pyrrhonischen Skeptizismus* (Berlin: de Gruyter)

Kajamies, T. (2009) 'A Quintent, a Quartet, a Trio, a Duo? The Epistemic Regress Problem, Evidential Support, and Skepticism' *Philosophia* Vol. 37, pp. 525–34

Klein, P. (2007) 'Human Knowledge and the Infinite Progress of Reasoning' *Philosophical Studies* Vol. 134, pp. 1–17

Kleingeld, P. and Willaschek, M. (2019) 'Autonomy Without Paradox: Kant, Self-Legislation, and the Moral Law' *Philosopher's Imprint* Vol. 19, pp. 1–19

Knappik, F. (2016) 'Hegel's Essentialism. Natural Kinds and the Metaphysics of Explanation in Hegel's Theory of "the Concept"' *European Journal of Philosophy* Vol. 24, pp. 760–87

Kreines, J. (2015) *Reason in the World: Hegel's Metaphysics and its Philosophical Appeal* (Oxford: Oxford University Press)

Koch, A. (2014) *Die Evolution des Logischen Raumes. Aufsätze zu Hegels Nichtstandard–Metaphysik* (Tübingen: Mohr Siebeck)

Kozatsas, J. Faraklas, G, Vieweg, K., and Synegianni, S. (Eds.) (2017) *Hegel and Scepticism: On Klaus Vieweg's Interpretation* (Berlin: De Gruyter)

Krijnen, C. (2021) 'The Beginning of Thought' in C. Cheng and C. Krijnen (Eds.) *Philosophical Methodology in Classical Chinese and German Philosophy* (Nordhausen: Verlag Traugott Bautz), pp. 41–68

Machuca, D. (2019a) 'Pyrrhonian Argumentation: Therapy, Dialectic, and Inquiry' *Apeiron* Vol. 55, pp. 199–221

Machuca, D. (2019b) 'Sources of Doxastic Disturbance in Sextus Empiricus' *Oxford Studies in Ancient Philosophy* Vol. 56, pp. 193–214

Maker, W. (1994) *Philosophy Without Foundations: Rethinking Hegel* (Albany, NY: SUNY Press)

McGilvary, E. (1897) 'The Presupposition Question in Hegel's Logic' *The Philosophical Review* Vol. 6, pp. 497–520

Messina, J. (2011) 'Answering Aenesidemus: Schulze's Attack on Reinholdian Representationalism and its Importance for Fichte' *Journal of the History of Philosophy* Vol. 49, pp. 339–69

Moore, A. (2012) *The Evolution of Modern Metaphysics: Making Sense of Things* (Cambridge: Cambridge University Press)

Morison, B. (2019) 'Sextus Empiricus' in E. Zalta (Ed.) *The Stanford Encyclopaedia of Philosophy* (Fall 2019 Edition)

Nuzzo, A. (2010) 'Dialectic, Understanding, and Reason: How Does Hegel's Logic Begin?' in N. Limnatis (Ed.) *The Dimensions of Hegel's Dialectic* (London: Continuum), pp. 12–30

Nuzzo, A. (2011) 'Thinking Being: Method in Hegel's Logic of Being' in M. Baur and S. Houlgate (Eds.) *A Companion to Hegel* (Oxford: Blackwell), pp. 111–39

Nuzzo, A. (2018) *Approaching Hegel's Logic, Obliquely: Melville, Moliere, Beckett* (Albany, NY: SUNY Press)

Ogden, S. (2021) 'Avicenna's Emanated Abstraction' *Philosopher's Imprint* Vol. 20, pp. 1–26

Orsini, F. (2021) 'The Problem of Circularity Between the *Phenomenology of Spirit* and the *Science of Logic*' *Studia Hegeliana* Vol. 7, pp. 37–57

Palmer, J. (2000) 'Skeptical Investigation' *Ancient Philosophy* Vol. 20, pp. 351–75

Perin, C. (2010) *The Demands of Reason: An Essay on Pyrrhonian Scepticism* (Oxford: Oxford University Press)

Perin, C. (2015) 'Skepticism, Suspension, and Norms of Belief' *International Journal for the Study of Skepticism* Vol. 5, pp. 107–25

Pinkard, T. (2002) *German Philosophy 1760–1860: The Legacy of Idealism* (Cambridge: Cambridge University Press)

Pippin, R. (1989) *Hegel's Idealism: The Satisfactions of Self-Consciousness* (Cambridge: Cambridge University Press)

Pippin, R. (2019) *Hegel's Realm of Shadows: Logic as Metaphysics in the* Science of Logic (Chicago, IL: University of Chicago Press)

Popkin, R. (2003) *The History of Scepticism: From Savanarola to Bayle* (Oxford: Oxford University Press)

Reinhold, K. (1978) *Über das Fundament des philosophischen Wissens. Über die Möglichkeit der Philosophie als strenge Wissenschaft* (Hamburg: Felix Meiner Verlag)

Reinhold, K. (2003) *Beiträge zur Berichtigung bisheriger Missvertständnisse der Philosophen* (2 Vols) (Hamburg: Felix Meiner Verlag)

Ribeiro, B. (2002) 'Is Pyrrhonism Psychologically Possible?' *Ancient Philosophy* Vol. 22, pp. 319–31

Rosen, M. (1992) *Problems of the Hegelian Dialectic. Dialectic Reconstructed as a Logic of Human Reality* (Boston, MA: Kluwer)

Rosen, S. (2014) *The Idea of Hegel's Science of Logic* (Chicago, IL: University of Chicago Press)

Röttges, H. (1987) *Dialektik und Skeptizismus* (Frankfurt am Main: Athenäum Verlag)

Sanches, F. (1988) *That Nothing is Known* trans. D. Thomson (Cambridge: Cambridge University Press)

Sankey, H. (2011) 'Epistemic Relativism and the Problem of the Criterion' *Studies in History and Philosophy of Science Part A* Vol. 42, pp. 562–70

Scarfe, A. (2003) 'The Role of Skepticism in Hegel's "Doctrine of the Concept"' *The Journal of Speculative Philosophy* Vol. 17, pp. 77–91

Schafer, K. (forthcoming) 'Kant on Method' in A. Stephenson and A. Gomes (Eds.) *The Oxford Handbook of Kant* (Oxford: Oxford University Press)

Schmid, S. (2021) 'Spinoza Against the Skeptics' in Y. Melamed (Ed.) *The Blackwell Companion to Spinoza* (Hoboken, NJ: Wiley), pp. 276–85

Schnell, A. (2021) 'Why is the First Principle of the *Grundlage der gesamten Wissenschaftslehre* Foundational for Fichte's *Entire Wissenschaftslehre*?' *Fichte–Studien* Vol. 49, pp. 79–93

Schulze, G. (1996) *Aenesidemus oder über Fundamente der von dem Herrn Professor Reinhold in Jena gelieferten Elementar-Philosophie* (Hamburg: Felix Meiner Verlag)

Sedgwick, S. (2012) *Hegel's Critique of Kant: From Dichotomy to Identity* (Oxford: Oxford University Press)

Sienkiewicz, S. (2019) *Five Modes of Scepticism: Sextus Empiricus and the Agrippan Modes* (Oxford: Oxford University Press)

Simons, P. (2013) 'Metaphysics in Analytic Philosophy' in M. Beaney (Ed.) *The Oxford Handbook of the History of Analytic Philosophy* (Oxford: Oxford University Press), pp. 709–28

Schaffer, J. (2009) 'On What Grounds What' in D. Chalmers, D. Manly, and R. Wasserman (Eds.) *Metametaphysics: New Essays on the Foundations of Ontology* (Oxford: Oxford University Press), pp. 347–83

Smith, P. (2022) *Sextus Empiricus' Neo-Pyrrhonism: Skepticism as a Rationally Ordered Experience* (Cham: Springer)

Staehler, T. (2017) *Hegel, Husserl, and the Phenomenology of Historical Worlds* (London: Rowman and Littlefield)

Stang, N. (2021) 'With What Must Transcendental Philosophy Begin? Kant and Hegel on Nothingness and Indeterminacy' in G. Gentry (Ed.) *Kantian Legacies in German Idealism* (London: Routledge), pp. 102–35

Stekeler-Weithofer, P. (2019) *Hegels Wissenschaft der Logik, ein dialogischer Kommentar: Band 1* (Hamburg: Felix Meiner Verlag)

Stern, R. (2009) *Hegelian Metaphysics* (Oxford: Oxford University Press)

Stewart, J. (2000) *The Unity of Hegel's Phenomenology of Spirit: A Systematic Interpretation* (Evanston, IL: Northwestern University Press)

Tahko, T. (2013) 'Metaphysics as the First Philosophy' in E. Feser (Ed) *Aristotle on Method and Metaphysics* (Basingstoke: Palgrave Macmillan), pp. 49–67

Testa, I. (2013) 'Scepsis and Scepticism' in A. de Laurentiis and J. Edwards (Eds.) *The Bloomsbury Companion to Hegel* (London: Bloomsbury), pp. 71–102

Trisokkas, I. (2012) *Pyrrhonian Scepticism and Hegel's Theory of Judgement: A Treatise on the Possibility of Scientific Inquiry* (Leiden: Brill)

Vieweg, K. (1999) *Philosophie des Remis: Der junge Hegel und das ‚Gespenst des Skeptizismus'* (München: Wilhelm Fink Verlag)

Vieweg, K. (2007) *Skepsis und Freiheit: Hegel über den Skeptizismus zwischen Philosophie und Lieteratur* (München: Wilhelm Fink Verlag)

Vieweg, K. (2020) *The Idealism of Freedom: For a Hegelian Turn in Philosophy* (Leiden: Brill)

Vogt, K. (2011) "The Aims of Skeptical Investigation" in D. Machuca (Ed.) *Pyrrhonism in Ancient, Modern, and Contemporary Philosophy* (Dordrecht: Springer), pp. 33–49

Westphal, K. (1988) 'Hegel's Solution to the Dilemma of the Criterion' *History of Philosophy Quarterly* Vol. 5, pp. 173–88

Westphal, K. (1989) *Hegel's Epistemological Realism: A Study of the Aim and Method of Hegel's* Phenomenology of Spirit (Dordrecht: Kluwer Academic Publishers)

Westphal, K. (2017) *Grounds of Pragmatic Realism: Hegel's Internal Critique and Reconstruction of Kant's Critical Philosophy* (Leiden: Brill)

Westphal, K. (2020) 'Aphorisms on the Absolute: Editorial Introduction' *The Owl of Minerva* Vol. 51, pp. 1–10

Willett, C. (1990) 'The Shadow of Hegel's *Science of Logic*' in G. di Giovanni (Ed.) *Essays on Hegel's Logic* (Albany, NY: SUNY Press), pp. 85–92

Williams, M. (1999) *Groundless Belief: An Essay on the Possibility of Epistemology* (Princeton, NJ: Princeton University Press)

Williams, M. (2010) "Descartes' Transformation of the Sceptical Tradition" in R. Bett (ed.) *The Cambridge Companion to Ancient Scepticism* (Cambridge: Cambridge University Press), pp. 288–313

Winfield, R. (2011) 'Is Phenomenology Necessary as an Introduction to Philosophy?' *The Review of Metaphysics,* Vol. 65, pp. 380–81

Winfield, R. (2013) *Hegel's Phenomenology of Spirit: A Critical Rethinking in Seventeen Lectures* (Lanham, MD: Rowman & Littlefield)

Wolff, C. (2019) *Über den Unterschied zwischen einem systematischen und einem nicht–systematischen Verstand* trans. M. Albrecht (Hamburg: Meiner)

Wolff, M. (1996) 'Die 'Momente' des Logischen und der 'Anfang' der Logik in Hegels philosophischer Wissenschaft' in H. Fulda and R-P. Horstmann (Eds.) *Skeptizismus und Spekulatives Denken in der Philosophie Hegels* (Stuttgart: Klett–Cotta), pp. 226–45

Wolff, M. (2013) 'Science of Logic' in A. de Laurentiis and J. Edwards (Eds.) *The Bloomsbury Companion to Hegel* (London: Bloomsbury), pp. 71–102

Wolff, M. (2014) 'Hegels Dialektik—eine Methode? Zu Hegels Ansichten von der Form einer philosophischen Wissenschaft' in A. Koch, F. Schick, K. Vieweg, and C. Wirsing (Eds.) *Hegel—200 Jahre Wissenschaft der Logik* (Hamburg: Felix Meiner), pp. 71–86

Woodruff, P. (2010) 'The Pyrrhonian Modes' in R. Bett (Ed.) *The Cambridge Companion to Ancient Scepticism* (Cambridge: Cambridge University Press), pp. 208–31

Xiong, Z. (2022) Alternativelessness: On the Beginning Problem of Hegel's *Logic*' *Idealistic Studies* Vol. 52, pp. 92–106

Zuppolini, B. (2016) 'Aristotle's Foundationalism' *Dissertatio* Vol. 44, pp. 187–211

Index

absolute knowing, 150–152, 155–56, 163–164, 169–172, 199
Agrippan dilemma, 13, 24, 36, 45–49, 54–55, 108–109, 116–117, 134–137, 160n.18, 178n.2, 181, 196
Agrippan problems, 13–14, 35–49, 108–109, 112–119
Agrippan trilemma, 13n.29, 39–43, 45–46
Aikin, Scott, 39n.30, 46n.48, 48n.52
a posteriori, 96
a priori, 1, 3, 8, 16, 20, 73n.15, 75, 80, 84–86, 125, 128, 135n.34, 143, 149, 200
arbitrariness, 1, 10–11, 17–18, 36–47, 92–97, 105–109, 113–149, 154–157, 196–198
Aristotle, 5, 14, 38, 69, 72–73, 74n.19, 75n.21, 85

Barnes, Jonathan, 36n.21–22, 38n.27, 39, 40n.34, 41, 191
being, 5, 10, 15, 70, 81–83, 101–104, 172–173, 199; pure, 2, 9–11, 15–16, 19–25, 110–111, 117–147, 174–178, 180–182, 188–190, 193–194, 197–199
Beiser, Frederick, 12n.21, 88n.51

de Boer, Karin, 4, 86n.41, 91n.55, 105n.85
Bondeli, Martin, 21n.33, 88n.49
Bowman, Brady, 4n.9, 9n.18, 105n.85, 105n.88, 189n.22, 199n.38

Carlson, David Gray, 2n.3, 140–144
categories, 3–8, 54–64, 71–72, 105–111, 128, 179–181, 198–199. *See also* thought determinations
circle, 5, 23, 98, 138–144, 191, 193, 198. *See also* reciprocity
Cling, Andrew, 39n.30, 42n.39, 46–48, 188
cognition, 5, 80–81, 85–86, 126–127, 152–154, 164–165, 177–178, 183
Concept, the, 4–5, 56–58, 104–107, 179
concepts, 3–7, 14–16, 53–60, 142–147, 179–180, 198. *See also* categories
criticism: immanent, 50, 128, 152, 153n.6, 155, 156n.11, 162, 164, 166, 168, 184, 189; Kantian, 3–4, 6, 80, 84–91, 102n.79, 114n.5; Objective Logic as, 4, 55–57, 60, 119n.15, 179–182; Sceptical, 28, 55–57, 60, 62, 72, 74, 77, 104, 119n.15, 127, 137, 146, 179–182, 193

Deleuze, Gilles, 118n.12
demonstration, 8–10, 80–81, 91–92, 110–114, 124–127, 131–133, 137–139, 141–144
Descartes, René, 8, 69n.75, 68–69, 70n.7, 72, 75–76, 78–80, 82–84, 86, 97n.70, 98n.71, 161, 183, 184n.12, 192
dialectic, 7, 9–10, 56–60, 63n.83, 158–159, 178–181, 197–198
Doctrine of Being, 3, 15, 115n.8, 123, 126, 136n.36, 144
Doctrine of the Concept, 4, 9, 13, 105, 116n.11
Doctrine of Essence, 3, 120n.16
dogmatic, 61–62, 78–79, 114–115, 130–132, 136–139, 146–147, 151–152, 176–182, 186–195
Dogmatism, 29, 32, 34–35, 38, 40, 42–43, 45, 58, 60, 192n.29, 193

empirical, 20, 60, 73–78, 125, 128, 190–192
empiricism, 19n.32, 72, 74–75
empty thinking, 123–132, 145–157, 160, 175–176, 182, 184, 186, 188, 190, 194, 197
epistemic regress problem, 36, 39, 42, 44–46, 48, 93–100, 104–108, 117, 187–188, 193
experience, 60, 73–78, 85–87, 89, 93, 96, 98–100, 135, 182

Fichte, Johann Gottlieb, 8, 10, 18, 21–22, 68, 70, 72n.12, 77n.26, 83, 88, 91–92, 95n.63, 96–104, 106, 108, 116–117, 140, 142, 143n.49, 191n.26
finite thinking, 4, 50, 52–53, 57, 60–64, 105n.88, 122, 147, 177n.1, 184–191
finitude, 4, 53, 56, 105n.87
Förster, Eckart, 84n.36, 88n.51, 91n.56, 94n.60, 97n.67, 103, 151n.1, 161n.21
Forster, Michael, 11–12, 35n.17, 50n.53, 52n.55, 55n.64, 58n.73, 62n.79, 84n.34, 103n.82, 115n.10, 153, 159–160, 178n.2
foundationalism, 8, 23, 42, 44–45, 74, 78–79, 82, 93, 98–100, 144n.52, 155, 192–193; metaphysical, 7n.15, 47, 68–69, 71, 89–91, 100, 104–106, 110–111, 117
Franks, Paul, 12n.22, 40n.33, 47n.49, 88n.51, 94n.60, 95n.63, 105n.85, 106n.90, 187n.19
freedom, 5, 50–51
Fulda, Hans-Friedrich, 13n.27, 127, 180n.6, 183n.10, 195n.33
fundamental principle, 4, 8–10, 18–19, 68–72, 75–77, 79–85, 87–108, 116–117, 142

ground, 18–19, 70–73, 77–80, 88–90, 99–101, 104–106, 110–111, 117, 138, 196

Hankinson, Richard, 36n.21, 37n.25, 42n.38, 44n.42, 53n.60
Heidemann, Dietmar, 12n.23, 13n.27, 38n.27, 58n.71, 61, 63n.82, 178n.3, 190n.24, 197n.35
Henrich, Dieter, 2n.3, 189n.22
Hentrup, Miles, 3n.4, 12n.23, 13n.29, 59n.76, 112n.23, 116n.11, 119n.15, 137–144
Houlgate, Stephen, 2n.3, 5n.11, 78n.29, 82n.32, 115n.9, 118n.12, 123n.20, 124n.21, 130, 131n.29, 136–137, 154n.10, 160–161, 170–171, 178n.2, 199n.37
Hume, David, 70n.7, 71–72, 74, 78–79
hypothesis, 21–23, 140–141, 182; mode of, 38, 40–45, 48n.51, 54n.63, 62, 76, 78n.28, 95, 100, 115, 116n.11

I, 18, 21–22, 70, 82, 97–101, 103n.83, 104, 140
idea, 5, 23, 57, 62n.81, 64n.85, 69, 138, 140, 143n.50, 144n.52, 180n.7

idealism, 6–8, 13n.28, 61–64, 78–91, 100–106, 153–156, 169–174, 194–195, 199–200
immediacy, 5, 10, 16–20, 109–147, 149–152, 156–157, 175, 177–181, 188, 191, 193, 196–197
infinite, the, 4, 53, 56, 105n.87
infinite regress, 13, 37–38, 40–45, 46n.47, 48, 54, 62, 74n.18, 86, 96, 114n.7, 116n.11
intellectual intuition, 75, 82–84, 94, 97–99, 102n.80, 103, 106n.90, 199n.37

Jacobi, Friedrich, 19n.32, 82n.31, 93–94
Janáček, Karel, 36n.22, 41n.36, 45
justification, 18, 38–49, 79–80, 93–94, 100–103, 110–113, 123–124, 150–161, 165–166, 169–173, 187–188, 192

Kajamies, Timo, 39n.30, 45n.44
Kant, Immanuel, 3–6, 8, 12, 19n.32, 47, 68, 70, 72, 80, 82–91, 93, 94n.60, 97, 98n.71, 100, 101n.78, 102n.79, 105, 142n.47, 143, 197
Kreines, James, 47n.49, 86, 140n.43, 199n.38
Krijnen, Christian, 3n.4, 67n.1, 77n.25, 78n.27

Locke, John, 70n.7, 71n.10, 78
logic: and metaphysics, 5–9, 17–18, 55–58, 61–64, 79–85, 100–108, 171, 199–200; objective, 55–57, 60, 71, 106, 179–181

Machuca, Diego, 30n.8, 190n.23
Maker, William, 3n.4, 24, 129–131, 135, 151, 154–157, 160–163, 170, 175, 177, 185, 188
McGilvary, Evander, 135, 137n.40, 169n.31

mediation, 16–17, 19–20, 109–147, 149–157, 173–185, 188–189, 196–197
metaphysics, 5–9, 17–18, 25, 53–64, 68–92, 96–108, 168–174, 195–196, 199–200
modes: five, 35n.18, 36–42, 54, 186–188, 192; ten, 35n.18, 74; two, 13–14, 24, 36–37, 40–46, 48n.51, 54, 60, 62, 64, 109, 114–116, 137, 147, 196

natural consciousness. See ordinary consciousness
nature, 3n.7, 5, 47, 84n.37, 101, 102n.79, 103n.83
necessity, 8–10, 60, 80, 96–98, 107, 111–114, 124–125, 133, 151, 174–177
negation: abstract, 59–60, 161–163, 183–185, 190, 195; determinate, 9, 59–60, 153, 161–163
nothing, 59, 162–163, 183, 187–190, 197
Nuzzo, Angelica, 2n.3, 55n.65, 143n.51

ordinary consciousness, 20, 52, 122–123, 125, 128–132, 135, 150–173, 182–194

Perin, Casey, 31n.9, 33n.14
phenomenology, 20–21, 63n.84, 99n.73, 125–133, 149–174
Pinkard, Terry, 88n.51, 93n.51
Pippin, Robert, 2n.3, 5n.11, 7n.15, 111n.1, 152n.3, 172n.32
presuppositionlessness, 20, 114–115, 120–133, 135–137, 146, 148, 158, 171, 177, 187–190, 197
principle: of non-contradiction, 53n.58, 95n.65, 183; of scepticism, 49, 51, 53–55, 60, 187
problem of the criterion, 12, 36, 41–46, 74, 158, 164–172

pure knowing, 113, 122–129, 139, 147, 152–154, 164

rationalism, 8–10, 78n.29, 84, 86n.41, 87
reality, 50, 54n.61, 61–64, 85, 103, 172, 199–200. *See also* being
Realphilosophie, 5, 143n.48, 152n.3, 200
reason, 52, 55–57, 61–64, 180, 189–190, 197
reciprocity, 38, 40–45, 48n.51, 114n.7, 165
Reinhold, Karl Leonhard, 8, 12, 18, 21n.33, 68, 88–97, 98n.71, 100, 104, 106, 108, 141n.44
Ribeiro, Brian, 35n.17, 58n.72, 187n.17
Rosen, Menahem, 114n.6, 140n.3
Rosen, Stanley, 2n.3, 3n.4, 67n.1, 69n.6, 72n.13, 113n.4, 114n.6
Röttges, Heinz, 11n.20, 13n.28, 51n.54, 54n.62, 63n.82, 116n.11

Schelling, Friedrich Wilhelm Joseph, 18, 47n.49, 64n.85, 68n.2, 72n.12, 88, 101–104
Schulze, Gottlob Ernst, 11–12, 63n.84, 90n.54, 95–97
science, 1–11, 15, 56, 73, 75–76, 78–81, 110–113, 117–119, 196–199; negative, 20, 24, 58, 126–128, 133, 147, 175–186, 191n.21, 195
sensuous certainty, 158n.14, 167–168
Sienkiewicz, Stefan, 37n.25, 38n.27, 40n.34, 41n.37, 42n.38, 44n.42
Smith, Plínio Junqueira, 35n.16, 186n.16, 191–192
Spinoza, Baruch, 8, 69, 71, 76, 83n.33, 96, 101, 103, 105

spirit, 3, 5, 28, 50, 102n.79, 131, 154, 160, 163–164, 170–171, 200
Staehler, Tanja, 12n.25, 184n.15
standard, *see* problem of the criterion
Stekeler-Weithofer, Pirmin, 2n.3, 3n.4, 13n.29, 67n.1, 69–70
Stern, Robert, 78n.29, 199n.37
sublation, 56, 59, 120n.17, 122–124, 152, 156, 159–160
suspension of judgement, 29–39, 44–45, 49, 53n.58, 57–60, 74n.17, 95, 118, 162, 179, 184–193

thought, 1, 3–5, 8, 10, 15–17, 23, 102–104, 110–111, 128, 169, 179–181, 199
thought determinations, 3, 8, 52, 55n.64, 56, 97, 107, 109, 114n.7. *See also* concepts
Trisokkas, Ioannis, 12–13, 54n.62, 62n.80, 116n.11, 163n.25, 172n.34

understanding, 55–61, 119n.15, 120n.17, 189–190, 195, 197
unity of opposites, 59, 61–63, 123n.20, 132, 146, 152, 162, 177, 179, 181, 197

Vieweg, Klaus, 3n.4, 12, 114n.7, 120n.16, 121n.18, 183n.10

Westphal, Kenneth, 12, 63n.84, 128n.27, 166–169, 172n.34
Williams, Michael, 33n.13, 39n.31
Winfield, Richard, 131n.29, 163n.22
Wolff, Michael, 3n.4, 7–8, 10n.19, 112n.3, 114n.6, 121n.18, 133n.31, 198

Zhong, Xhili, 99n.74, 116n.11, 140n.42

About the Author

Robb Dunphy is Alexander von Humboldt postdoctoral research fellow at the Albert Ludwigs University of Freiburg. He previously held research fellowships at the Goethe University Frankfurt, University College Dublin, and the University of Hamburg. He has taught philosophy at Northeastern University London, the University of Winchester, and the University of Sussex. His primary research interests are in the theoretical philosophy of Kant and the German Idealists, as well as the history of scepticism. He is the co-editor of *Metaphysics as a Science in Classical German Philosophy* and has published research articles in journals including *Apeiron*, *The Review of Metaphysics*, the *Hegel Bulletin*, and *Logos and Episteme*.

www.ingramcontent.com/pod-product-compliance
Lightning Source LLC
Chambersburg PA
CBHW021354300426
44114CB00012B/1218